Rock and Roll Tourist

Graham Forbes

Northumbria University Press
Newcastle

Published by Northumbria University Press
Trinity Building, Newcastle upon Tyne NE1 8ST
www.northumbriauniversitypress.co.uk

First published in Great Britain 2009

A Catalogue Record for this book is available from the British
Library.

ISBN 9781904794356
Typeset in Enigma Regular
Designed by Glynn McGee

Printed in Great Britain by Bookmarque, Croydon

Thanks

This is where I get to thank all the people who have helped. In many books, these lists are like telephone directories and extremely boring for anyone else to read. I suspect they are designed that way to make the book seem far more important than it really is.

So I'll just give a quick but very grateful editorial nod to Alan Forbes, David Fletcher, Andrew Peden Smith, Alice Stoakley, Ryan Praefke and Tom Lamb.

Cover photo by Lorraine Dingwall.

A wee biography

At the beginning of books there's always a wee biography of the author. They are presented in a way that gives the impression someone else has written it. In fact they are usually always written by the authors, and they sieze the opportunity to say wonderful things about themselves that no one else would. So I won't try to kid anyone that I didn't write the following myself . . .

When I was young I dreamed of playing football for Partick Thistle. But I was hopeless. Fortunately when I was 13 I heard the Stones, bought an electric guitar for £7 and have been playing in bands ever since. I will play with anyone, any time, anywhere, from a bus shelter to a festival. Except jazz (far too many weird chords), or 1980's music – I hate all that popping, pinging, slapping, arty-farty bass nonsense. Or let's say hypothetically, if it involves travelling to friggin' Bogota with a famous punk rock band to play three gigs because the singer's young boyfriend just happens to live there and I'd have had to pay the hotel myself because he had booked the band into a backstreet brothel to save money. But that aside, I love touring and being on stage, especially if there are plenty of people and there's free food afterwards . . .

When I'm not off somewhere, I live some of the time in Glasgow, where everyone drives faster than me, and some of the time in Florida, where everyone drives slower. Although not attaining the academic qualifications necessary to attend classes, I have been an active member of Glasgow University gym for many years, but have inexplicably not yet been awarded an honorary degree. I hope that Northumbria University Press, who have published the fine work of literature you are holding in your hands, will soon remedy this sad oversight.

Introduction

Having just finished that young whippersnapper Alex James's excellent memoir *A Bit of a Blur*, Graham Forbes's *Rock and Roll Tourist* seemed to me less ... well, cheesy.

Former Blur bassist Alex James, like Graham, has given up mood-enhancing substances and, largely, the rock and roll lifestyle, in favour of becoming a tweedy poster boy for the bucolic Cotswold landed gentry. Alex has his own farm and he makes his own cheese, which is allegedly very good indeed.

Graham, on the other hand, is older than Alex and has not, as Mr James has, reputedly spent £1m on cocaine and ancillary stimulants. He has, however, spent quite a lot of time obtaining prescriptions for dubious pills which, thankfully, he has now flushed down the toilet of experience. He's a better skier and rock climber than Alex, lives in Glasgow and the USA, still plays bass, and manages his son's band Darkwater.

A host of weird and wonderful characters pop up here, the true wild men of rock, like the Irish show band member who was an obsessive masturbator, by no means all musicians or camp followers. There is some wonderful descriptive writing, and a great piece about, of all things, rock and roll transportation, in the form of the legendary Edwin Shirley Trucking company.

And I mustn't forget such insights as the influence of Scottish pipe band drumming on modern funk, the way that Clive Palmer (of the Incredible String Band) smells, and Very Bad Things That Can Happen in Mallorca.

This is a very funny, occasionally disturbing, sometimes moving book. It's a middle-aged man's meditation on what rock means for him, and in the end, on what it's like to pass the baton on to the next generation. I heartily recommend it.

Tom Morton, BBC Scotland

For Alan and Graham.
My Boys

Contents

1

TAMPA

Kiss and Aerosmith

I BLAME Kiss for what happened. Nobody should play as loud as they do. Anyone who has seen a heavy metal band knows Kiss; masters of excess, just look at bass player Gene Simmons with his monstrous lashing tongue. I mean where did he get that? From the first moment he saw it in the mirror he must have known there could only be one path, he had been placed on Planet Earth to be a rock star. It's like it was ripped from a horny bull and transplanted straight into his gob. When he wiggles it at the girls, it drips and dangles and sways below his chin in a way that gets them panting, or at least he seems to think so. He leers as he flicks the tip up and down. . . it's a long, long way from the days when cuddly, grinning pop groups used to dress up in smart matching suits and shampoo their hair before every gig so that it was nice and soft and bouncy and the most daring thing they did was wink or shout '*ooo*' into the mikes.

Then there's the circus make-up plastered all over their faces, their stage clothes like Batman and Robin on acid, their huge clumping high-heeled boots, and just in case their zillion watts of amplification haven't bludgeoned us into quivering submission, they end every show with massive explosions and pyrotechnics designed to deafen us completely. If you like rock music just slightly quieter than an Apollo launch, then Gene's your man. It's brilliant.

I had recently sold my business, nothing glamorous, just a removal and storage company, and after the 25-year slog it had taken to get to the Thank God cheque I was finally taking a long vacation in Florida, on a beautiful island called Longboat Key. It was great relaxing after all the stress of running a company in Glasgow, constantly fighting off gangsters and extortionists – the Inland Revenue in Scotland doesn't fanny about – but sometimes it's good to drag yourself away from the beach to make sure your heart is still pumping.

So I went to Tampa to see Kiss.

The morning of the gig, I woke with a sore neck. I'd had bother with it before, but put this down to playing too many pub gigs with the weight of a heavy bass guitar hanging from my shoulders. I had been doing a lot of rock climbing, which didn't exactly help either, but I loved clambering up jagged cliffs in the Scottish Highlands. And I loved to ski whenever I could, even when a deranged, inbred little turd of a drag-lift operator amused himself by running it too fast over a lethal bump he had built, drooling and chortling as he watched bones cracking when everyone hurtled into the air then crashed onto the concrete-hard Aberdeenshire ice.

When I woke that day with the golden Florida sunshine streaming into my room, I was puzzled because I hadn't been doing anything more strenuous than snoozing by the pool or walking on the beach watching for little groups of dolphins splashing in the calm water of the Gulf of Mexico. But my neck really hurt. Although I was due to fly back to Scotland in a few days, I decided to go to a local doctor; something was definitely wrong. I thought they'd send me for an X-ray or something, but the woman who saw me briefly touched my back then cheerily diagnosed a muscle spasm. She told me a few pills would have me right as rain in no time and gave me a prescription. Oh, and she had a sample of something that was good; I could have that free. Take one of these last thing at night and the next thing I'd know would be the birds singing at dawn. That sounded just the job. She was very nice and I felt much better. You see, I told myself, nothing wrong at all.

I'd promised to go with my son, Graham, to the Kiss gig and we drove up to the hotel we'd booked so we wouldn't have to join the freeway crawl after the show. They were sharing the bill with Aerosmith at the St Pete's Times Forum, an oval, glass and steel stadium as tall as a 15-storey skyscraper, gleaming in the sun at the edge of Tampa Bay. It's quite a sight.

American rock concerts are great, especially in Florida. As you walk to the gig, the air is warm and balmy, everyone seems in a good mood, there's always a friendly carnival atmosphere. The local rock radio station was broadcasting live, with the Sunshine Coast's most beautiful girls throwing tee shirts, stickers and CDs to the crowd. At the side of the broad plaza in front of the entrance, a Led Zep tribute band was playing 'Whole Lotta Love' and 'Stairway'. At big gigs in Glasgow, you often have to wade through staggering armies of shell-suited yobs pissing in the street and swilling from Buckfast bottles – you don't want to mess with Daniel O'Donnell's fans – but here everyone was relaxed and smiling.

Inside, the Forum was buzzing, 20,000 people, like a huge rowdy party with an endless supply of fast food. I followed Graham to our seats, glancing into the corporate suites at lanky Orlando Magic basketball players wearing gold chains and chunky Rolexes, and wee fat politicians wallowing in champagne and giggling blonde cheerleaders.

The warm-up band were on stage, a Lousiana-based bottleneck-guitar group playing thick, gutsy blues songs about waking in the morning and picking cotton, the old black P90 guitar pickups on their beat-up Gibsons growling and wailing in the hot arena. People wandered around, found their seats, sat down for a few minutes then rushed to the concession stands to gather buckets of popcorn, gallons of beer, pails of fizzing cola, juicy burgers, peanuts, pretzels and plump hot dogs smothered with mustard and ketchup.

After a short break and microphone tests by skinny, hollow-eyed roadies with braided, waist-long hair, 1 – 2, *CHECK!* 1 – 2, there was a massive burst of white lights and the explosion of glitter, make-up, platform boots and lashing tongues that we know and love as Kiss charged on stage. *Bloody hell, they're deafening!* I couldn't understand why the people way down in the front rows weren't keeling over; the flesh on their faces was pinned back as if they were staring into a Stealth bomber's jets. Each pounding riff seemed to unleash more pain in my neck until I began to think Gene Simmons had a vendetta against me. I closed my eyes as his thundering bass sent shuddering low-frequency shock waves though the building. The metal seats were vibrating so much I felt like I was strapped to a clattering roller coaster hurtling over vertical drops. Then the band punched out their signature hit, '*I wanna rock and roll all night, and par-tay ev-ery day*', amid a blitzkrieg of flares, fireworks, sparks and more noise than I have ever heard before in an enclosed space.

Normally I would have loved Aerosmith. The first time I saw them was in Central Park when they were young, wild and just hitting the big time. They've grown up now and are super-slick, but it was good to see Steve Tyler still pouting and mincing around in his skin-tight pants, waving his silk scarves, Boston's version of Mick Jagger. Joe Perry was at his side, playing the familiar riffs and solos – some guitar players have a natural stage presence that seems to reach out and fill a hall, and the crowd can feel it. They were great, but the pain in my neck was getting worse. I swallowed another pill. It didn't work. I kept shuffling around, standing up, sitting down, folding my arms, holding up my chin; nothing made any difference.

After almost five hours, the gig ended like an indoor Pompeii with more eruptions of fireworks. *Great, temporary blindness too.* Outside, the streets were packed with people making their way to nearby bars and car parks. We couldn't find a taxi and it took us almost an hour to walk back to the Holiday Inn. My neck felt like it was in a clamp. I didn't want to tell Graham how much I was hurting and he gave me puzzled looks when I kept stopping for a rest and looking in shop windows. I'd never shown any interest before in mops, buckets and drain cleaners. As soon as we reached our room I took the knock-out pill I'd been given, lay on my bed and . . . *Ah . . . that's better.*

The next day Graham drove me back to Longboat Key, the first time he'd driven in America. It's much easier than in Scotland; the roads are wider and the traffic coasts along rather than charging like an invading army. We waited until late morning when the freeway was quiet and then drove to the Sunshine Skyway, a five-mile bridge that spans Tampa Bay. I sat back, rubbing my neck, trying to relax and enjoy looking at the sparkling water as the radio played 'Sweet Home Alabama', AC/DC and Zeppelin. FM radio in America always seems clearer than in the UK; I don't know why, but I always seem to hear more stuff going on in these songs.

When we got back to the house I took another pill and fell asleep. I woke around two in the morning, like most men my age.

My mouth felt like sandpaper so I reached out and picked up a glass of water from the nightstand. It fell out of my hand; I often drop things, so I didn't think much about it. A pee, another pill and I was warm and snug again in Valium Valley.

Next morning the pain was worse. I lay on the floor for a long time, the only way I could get comfortable, and stared mindlessly at Judge Judy and fat rednecks fighting on the Jerry Springer Show. When I wandered to the kitchen to make coffee, I vaguely noticed that I couldn't lift the kettle with my left hand. Then I put my arm in the air and it fell back down. I couldn't hold it up. *That's odd.* Sometimes I'm a bit slow on the uptake, but I realised that this might not be a good thing and decided to go back to the local surgery. When I told the assistant what was happening she quickly called the doctor.

He looked at me, frowned, and said that it was either a stroke or a herniated disc. Not good. I needed an MRI scan right away. The local hospital could do it. He checked his watch. Frowned. *It's after six. This is Friday night so the unit might be closed.* He said I should go to the casualty department and let them know what was happening, they might manage something. Graham drove me to the Memorial Hospital, a sparkling new building that looks like a posh hotel, just a little down Highway 41 opposite the Pizza Hut and Blockbuster video store that we often used.

Many wealthy people have retired to Sarasota and the investment in health care has been exceptional; the hospital has one of the best neurosurgical units in America. Within 20 minutes I was on my back, being pushed head first into the narrow tunnel of an MRI machine. Like most people, I hated the thought of being stuck in a narrow metal tube but I knew I better not whinge, I was very lucky that they were seeing me so quickly. I told myself to relax: *it's just like lying on a sun bed.* I had to lie still;

if I moved they would have to start again. After about 30 minutes, the loud humming noise of the scanner fell silent, the bright light switched off and I was pulled back out.

Soon afterwards a young, very helpful neurosurgeon arrived. *Ah, you're Scottish, I have grandparents who are Scotch.* He showed me the MRI pictures. He pointed to my spine. A disc in my neck had popped out and was cutting in to my spinal cord. *I'm afraid you need immediate surgery.* If I was not operated on right away my left arm would be permanently paralysed – it was halfway there already. At worst, I might have to spend the rest of my life in a wheelchair, unable to move anything but my head.

Well, there's a thing.

He was very reassuring. He told me he'd do a bone graft and bolt two vertebrae together – *yes, these ones there* – with a metal plate and five screws. I asked how long it would be before I could climb and ski again. He smiled sympathetically. That might take a while. Maybe next year I'd be able to ski, although I'd have to be careful. No jumping off cliffs or anything. That sounded hopeful, I've never wanted to jump off cliffs anyway, although I've fallen off a few. *Don't worry – the operation has a good chance of a successful outcome.* What does that mean? A *good* chance? He told me that they would get at my spine from the front by making as small a cut in my throat as possible. *Eh, excuse me, but when you're using the words scalpel and throat there's no such thing as small.*

I glanced at Graham and could see nervousness in his eyes. He looked at me, nodded, then told the surgeon to go ahead, it had to be done. I was wheeled to a bed in a private room, which was very nice of them, pumped full of morphine, which was even nicer, and settled into that half-asleep, dream-like state, where you have a dumb smile and wish there was some Rolling Stones music to listen to.

Graham went back to our house and spent the night trawling the Internet to make sure there was no alternative to surgery. In Britain we have the idea that American hospitals are only interested in money but I can't remember being asked if I could pay the bill, which they said they would send to me eventually. They were very relaxed; didn't ask for a credit card, or to see my passport. I could have taken the surgery and run ... well, sort of. They just smiled and told me they'd get me fixed up real quick: *Hey, don't worry about it.*

I won't twitter on about the operation, I'll save that for the day when I'm propped up in a chair in the residents' lounge of a home for the bewildered and I've run out of farts. When I got out of hospital the next week, I had to stay in Florida on my back and watching more daytime TV before I could travel. Those two weeks just flew by.

Back in Glasgow, I found a good physiotherapist, a large German lady. Apart from the usual muscle pounding she gave me lots of acupuncture, although the sharp little needles made my legs jerk like a fairground puppet. Every day, I took a stroll up the small hill in the grounds of Jordanhill College, which gave a good view towards the Highlands. I could see snow on the mountains and longed to get back out skiing or climbing – I had been very fit and wasn't used to sitting around. As soon as I could, I began going to Glasgow University gym; gentle cycling on the exercise bikes while wearing my surgical collar, then swimming 10, 15 and finally building up to 20 lengths of the pool.

One day I noticed that I was really happy when two o'clock came round, then six was another highlight, but I felt sure that was because I'd eat something nice. And ten o'clock just couldn't roll along fast enough. I gathered up the bottles of pills I'd brought back from America, read the labels and decided to have a look on the Internet and see what it was I was taking.

It was a drug called Oxycontin and there was plenty of information on the websites. It is a powerful painkiller, an opiate that is more addictive than heroin. All sorts of people are hooked on it, from Hollywood stars to trailer-park rednecks, who call it hillbilly heroin. It's one of the favourite prescription drugs that New York stockbrokers swallow at night to chill out after a hard day frantically running around waving bits of paper. Apparently the street price can be as high as $85 a pill. The time for doe-eyed addiction could be as little as 10 days and at most three weeks.

I had been swallowing them for almost three months.

The scary thing about Oxycontin is that it makes you feel so content; it doesn't leave you wallowing about feeling stoned, you have a warm sense of well-being and calm. It might cross your mind that you were becoming a wee bit too fond of them, but you feel so good it doesn't worry you.

If I wanted to work I could concentrate on one thing at a time, a new sensation for me. So I wrote my first book. If I wanted to sit around listening to music I became totally lost in it – even jazz sounded great. I never felt out of control – I could drive my car, pick up a movie and a mouth-watering pizza. When I met friends, I seemed to crack an endless stream of jokes and clever remarks – they'd never seen me glow like this. One of them looked at me with a concerned expression. 'Be careful. The drug companies haven't spent all those billions of dollars on research for nothing.' I had become like an evangelist. I told anyone who would listen how wonderful 'perkies' made me feel.

I knew I had to quit, but my neck still hurt like hell. I'd also been give diazepam, to stop muscle spasms, and needed to get rid of them too – so I had some fun days ahead of me. I visited my GP and asked for a weaker painkiller, oxycodone, which she gave me reluctantly because it also is addictive, and I weaned myself off Oxycontin using that, then switched to co-codamol and finally to Solpadeine, a UK non-prescription painkiller containing codeine, which apparently some people get hooked on, presumably why it is sold in crate-size value packs.

It wasn't easy, a lot like stopping smoking, but more dramatic. I'd wake up in the middle of the night, tingling, soaked in sweat, hallucinating, gibbering, all that stuff. I'd get up, take a pill and play about on the Internet, firing emails off to friends, arranging to meet them next day, then completely forget to go. I'd manage a couple of nights without taking anything, then, feeling lousy through lack of sleep, would take a Oxycontin or a diazepam, then feel guilty and doped-up all next day.

I hated not being able to go on skiing and climbing trips, I even missed the fun of getting there. I enjoy finding my way around airports, trying to sneak into the VIP lounges, stretching back in an extra-legroom seat, looking out the window as the plane takes off and soars above the city, watching countries slip away, entering different time zones, that feeling of freedom of simply going somewhere else.

Then I had an idea. Musicians travel more miles than airline pilots, they're always on the move. I've been a musician all my life and loved touring, especially when I was young and playing with the Incredible String Band. I love the humour of musicians; I love the stories, the tales of being on the road, the things that happen in any working band. But most of all, it's the people you meet, the characters. In a surge of enthusiasm I realised that people fly all over the world to wander around dusty museums, eat fancy food or flop on beaches; why not travel to interesting places to see some really good bands?

2

BARCELONA

Incredible String Band

L ED Zeppelin knew how to have a good time. When they went on tour they piled into a sumptuous private jet that had plenty of room for wild and merry parties. That way of avoiding check-in queues at airports all over America did not excuse them from breaking the unblinking law that could have ended the careers of so many rock bands – transporting enthusiastic teenage girls across a state line. It just made it easier. When the Incredible String Band toured Spain in May 2005, the airline they used was the less glamorous, but vastly cheaper Ryanair. You'd really be going some to have a bacchanalian orgy on one of those flights.

I was feeling a lot better and my first book was about to be published – *yes!* I was looking forward to that, but was in the mood for a wee jaunt so I called Mike Heron to see what he was up to. I had played with Mike in the Incredible String Band until the group split up in New York in 1974. Mike had recently relaunched the band and they were heading to Spain to do a few acoustic gigs. Their manager, Mark Astey, emailed me details of the flights and hotels so that I would find myself in more or less the same time and space continuum, not something to be readily assumed in the case of the Incredible String Band. And so I diligently sat down with a supply of strong coffee for a long session on the Internet.

I know it's fashionable to make sarcastic remarks about the irritations of online booking – the demands for more *information*; the *mandatory* fields that *must* be completed; those red, angry asterisks like boils on the screen, *unexpected log-outs*; *illegal operations* and all that guff – but it's great to be able to book a flight at two in the morning, even if you log on in the middle of the night in the hope that the website somehow becomes less pernickety, a sure sign of losing the plot.

At last I found myself with the booking references that would allow me to link up with the band. No tickets to lose, it's all done by numbers these days, which suits me very well since I can write them on my arm and, unless I am very unlucky, I won't leave that in the taxi to the airport.

After a quick flight from Glasgow, I arrived at East Midlands airport bright and early and headed straight for the coffee shop where I met up with Mark and the four band members: Mike, Clive Palmer, who helped form the band 40 years ago in Edinburgh; long-time session musician Lawson Dando from Wales; and Fluff, as she is known, a classically trained multi-instrumentalist who is, at 29, younger than some of the clothes the rest of the group were wearing.

Touring bands usually attract stares in airports and the Incredible String Band, as you might expect, draw more than most. Dando, as everyone calls him, was dressed in his usual black robes, an embroidered maroon and gold Tibetan waistcoat with the sweet scent of patchouli, and a purple fez perched on his head. With tiny glasses balanced on his nose, and his long, greying hair in a ponytail, he looks like a kindly antiquarian bookseller.

Mike was wearing his favourite blue denim shirt, jeans, soft leather shoes and a sleeveless fleece jacket, a proven safe bet: cool when unzipped, but snug in cold climates, such as when the band had played in Iceland, a country that loves esoteric music. Sticking out of his pocket was a well-worn notebook full of photographs of anything he might need: a taxi, an airport, a telephone, a concerned and attentive-looking doctor, a pharmacy, the welcoming smile of a Chinese waiter, an Indian restaurant, and appetizing pictures of his favourite food – steak, chips, ham, eggs.

Mark was wearing sandals and, with his flowing white hair, is often called Gandalf, while Dando is happy to be known as the Hobbit. They are a merry bunch, and crack a constant stream of jokes. As soon as we finished our coffee, Mark hurried everyone to the check-in. Low-cost airlines, as they like to be known, are merciless to anyone late or with a packet of crisps more than their meagre baggage allowance. The Incredible String Band carries a lot of extra weight: guitars, keyboards, aluminium cases filled with cables, plugs, hand drums, and a few Eastern instruments, all vital to the show. Mark had to fill in a long form for each item and write out a large cheque. The reams of paperwork finally attended to, we wheeled the teetering pile to the excess baggage counter at the other side of the airport and watched it disappear on the conveyor belt. Then we joined the long line of passengers stripping off their clothes and shoes as they waited to be searched, groped and X-rayed for explosive devices.

It is puzzling to look in the glass cases showing prohibited items. Razors and nail files, obviously. Swiss Army knives and other sharp items need to be confiscated, especially from anyone with wild, darting eyes, sweating profusely and muttering prayers to their ancestors. But I can't imagine that any pilot would hand over the plane to a kid waving a Jedi Light Sabre or Star Trek pistol not even the ones with realistic bleeping noises.

As we approached the metal detectors, Mike held up the old canvas bag he was carrying and whispered, 'Shit, I've got some dodgy stuff in here. Are they searching everyone?'

I felt my scalp tingle. What the hell did he have? Surely he hadn't brought mood-mellowing substances on an international flight? I have a pal who plays in a world-famous band that always carries a stash of hash in their amplifiers. They reckon the risk of getting caught is far less than that of being robbed by gun-toting drug dealers in some of the countries they play.

I glanced at Mike. Whatever he had, there was still time to get rid of it. 'What have you got in there?'

'Oh, nothing serious, just wire cutters, a file, a knife. I need them for changing strings.'

'Mike, they don't even let you take a cup of coffee through. Look at them; they're even paranoid about plastic fucking forks. When they open your bag they'll evacuate the airport.'

'You think so? Oh well, we'll see.'

Two minutes later, the security staff were gathered round, rubbing their hands, keeping an alert eye on Mike as they poured the contents of his bag onto a metal table, and spread out the various lethal edges he'd packed. They stared at him as if he might be carrying a bandolier of grenades. The rest of us decided to attract as little attention to ourselves as possible and scarpered to the café.

When we reached the self-service counter, Fluff shook her head in exasperation. She always carries a roll of gaffer tape so that she can seal the locks of the guitar cases before they clatter away on the conveyor belt. She turned to Mark. 'They've confiscated my bloody tape!'

'Why?' asked Clive. 'What can you possibly do with that?'

'Oh, you can tape people up with it,' she said cheerfully. The band grinned. *Yes, we see*. . . Her cheeks turned red. 'Oh shit . . . I don't believe I just said that.'

As we waited for the outcome of Mike's interrogation, secretly hoping they would bend him over and delve deep, we collected plates of food, carried them to a table and elbowed off the debris left by previous diners. Time for a trough. Clive set down his English breakfast platter – bacon, eggs, fried mushrooms, tomato, and a smiling sausage floating in a sea of beans and ketchup. He rolled up his sleeves, sighed contentedly, and got stuck in.

He is an odd character, and very likeable. He looks like a scarecrow; his hair is grey, long and straggly, it hasn't been touched by a hairdresser in 20 years. When the mood takes him, he hacks a few inches off. His jeans looked like Oxfam specials, the waist was hanging over his belt, and they were rolled up at his ankles. He was wearing an old woollen jacket, bought in a Kathmandu street market, that had a strong, not unpleasant, aroma of wood smoke. I couldn't help staring at his glasses – the lenses didn't fit the frames; there were gaps between the glass and the rims. He took them off and showed me them. 'The proper frames broke but I managed to wedge the lenses in these reading glasses I got in Woolworth's for a quid. There's gaps but I can see fine.'

On his upper gum he has one remaining tooth that shines like a fang, especially when he's laughing, which is a lot, his eyes crinkling warmly. As he attacked the heaped plate of fried food, he caught me looking at his molar and grinned. 'Yeah, I've only a few left now. When I get toothache I just bombard the fucker with paracetamol until I can work it loose enough to pull out. Saves going to the dentist. Dentists are expensive. Don't need 'em.'

As a child he contracted polio, which left him with a bad limp. When he walks his body almost topples over, and he seems very frail, but he has a firm handshake, the strength of a farmer or builder. He lives in Brittany where he was able to buy an old crumbling cottage and repair it himself. For years before that he lived in one with a dirt floor, no water or electricity. He enjoys being self-sufficient and survived for years by busking in the nearby village and making musical instruments.

When bands are on the road they love telling tales about tours they have done. Clive is a great storyteller, he has a rich, mellow voice that soars and falls, drawing you in. A relieved Mike had been released by the bemused security staff, and he joined us with a lighter bag, and a large plate of double egg and chips. Clive was entertaining us with a story from the American tour the band had done the previous year, and the people at nearby tables were listening and smiling.

'And our driver – don't ask me about our fucking driver! As usual we had to do the whole fucking tour as cheap as possible, there was just no money to pay a proper driver. We had to sack the first guy the agency sent. He was nice enough but he didn't know how to drive. The dozy pillock hadn't a clue. He picked us up when we landed at Newark and it was supposed to be a five minute drive to the hotel. We were staying at the Holiday Inn, right beside the fucking airport, and he got lost. Took him two fucking hours to find it. Right beside the airport!' Clive laughs, then pauses while he cuts a large piece of bacon into one-tooth bites.

'Then he crashed three times in the first two days. Three fucking times! Said he'd never driven a van before. Don't think he'd driven anything before. I know he was cheap but for fuck's sake. He smashed the mirror on a police car on 42nd Street. He did a runner, lucky he didn't get us all shot. Then he hit a parked truck. How could he not see a parked truck? The third time was at a freeway off-ramp. Bumped a car. There was no damage done, but the driver was a lawyer's wife – she took one look at us and called in the state police. Took us two hours to sort that lot out. Nearly missed a radio show. We had to sack the stupid bastard. Useless.'

The people at the tables next to us were listening and smiling. Even though Clive swears with the speed of a sub-machine gun nobody seemed to notice; there's gentle warmth in his voice. He sounds like a cockney version of Billy Connolly, who gave him an expensive banjo when Clive's old one fell apart.

'The next guy the agency sent was even worse. He was a fucking maniac. He thought he was going to be driving a young English rock band. He couldn't wait to get at all the groupies. When he saw us his fucking face fell. Any groupies we get will be old-age pensioners!'

He forked in a mouthful of food and swallowed a large slurp of tea. 'He was dangerous. Fucking insane. We'd be driving along the freeway and he'd suddenly shoot right across six lanes to get off. Right in front of huge trucks, buses, everything. I think he was half blind, he always waited until the last second. Once he left it too late and reversed all the way back up the grass verge. I finally had enough in Utah. We were driving along the side of a cliff at two in the morning and he's doing seventy miles an hour. You couldn't see anything, just this huge black drop below us. I put my hands round his fucking throat and told him, "*You're a stupid reckless bastard! Cut the speed or I'll fucking throttle you!*" But of course he's American and they don't like you criticising them. So he says, "*Sir, you can't speak to me like that.*" I wouldn't take my hands off his fucking throat until he slowed right down.'

Clive pauses, builds a roll-up, and looks around for somewhere he can light up. There's a smoking area at the other end of the departure lounge but he decides it's too far to walk and contents himself by sucking on it.

Our flight is called and we endure the usual budget airline mêlée of passengers elbowing each other out of the way in the rush to get on the plane. The seats don't tilt back and the pockets in the seat backs have been removed so that you can't leave any litter. It feels like a flying youth hostel, as though you are expected to endure a little hardship and do a chore to show your gratitude for the cheap fare.

As we wait for the plane to move, Clive loudly explains to Dando how it gets off the ground. Several passengers are beginning to look worried.

'You see, the pilot has to tilt the wings at exactly the correct angle as it roars down the runaway. A degree or two out and the fucking thing will crash and we'll all be incinerated. There would be no escape. It's very clever how they do it.'

We settle back for the flight to Barcelona. Mike checks over his songs in a large leather-bound book and decides what to play tonight, while Clive tells a story about rural France and a lethal mixture of home-brewed wine and magic mushrooms that the farmers enjoy at autumn picnics. Then he switches to sport, his voice booming through the cabin, laughing loudly as he names a Wimbledon champion who had to give up the game because of 'chronic fucking haemorrhoids'. A group of schoolchildren stare at him and giggle. The two-hour flight passes in a flash.

When we land at Gerona airport, Ramon, the local concert promoter, is waiting to meet the band, smiling and shaking hands. They are relieved that he has a proper driver with him and happily pile into the minibus for the drive along the tree-lined road to Barcelona. It's good to be back in Spain, even the motorway has a nice smell, a sort of warm, heady mixture of wild lavender and, I don't know what it is, herbs and flowery things. It's very pleasant; you know you are in Spain the minute you smell it, it's like a welcoming handshake. As we coast along the autopista it's nice to look at the shining limestone mountains – I've enjoyed some great rock-climbing trips there with demented pals from Glasgow. On the outskirts of Barcelona we see a massive warehouse.

'What's that called?' asks Clive, squinting through his glasses as he reads the name. *"Ikea"*. 'What do they sell – computers?'

We explain the concept of Ikea to him and how thousands of people congregate there at weekends.

'I've never bought any furniture. The folk in the village where I live give me stuff. I did buy my bed. Got it in a jumble sale. Cost fifteen quid. It's very old but it's a good'un. It's got proper springs. I can never get to sleep in hotel beds – can't settle down into them. They're too level, too flat.'

We check into the hotel, a time-consuming palaver involving the photocopying of passports. The gig is down a side street just a short distance away, in a beautiful old church that was converted to an arts centre many years ago. It's easy to imagine the ghosts of flamenco dancers and gypsy guitarists playing songs of revolution to fiery-eyed crowds. Judging by the people relaxing in the café inside, I'm guessing that a lot of wacky baccy gets smoked too.

There's a bar with nice coffee made by smiling girls wearing lip rings, Indian nose studs, belly-button piercings, colourful tattoos, tiny denim skirts, and embroidered silk tops. Ramon, Clive and Dando chain-smoke and we all drink cups of strong, creamy espresso until our bones are jangling. The guy who runs the place has been an Incredible String Band fan since he was a teenager and he asks me to sign one of the albums that I played on all those years ago. I love it.

He has laid on a special meal and Ramon shows us how to eat a Catalan favourite: grind a tomato into a chunk of bread then cover it with olive oil, or perhaps it's the other way round. Anyway, it tastes good until I notice that half of my tomato has rotted and been chewed by insects. I suppose organic food has its downside. Clive is telling us about his travelling days many years ago when he went off for a long wander around 'Persia'. He talks animatedly about the massive ancient Buddhist statues, the Bamian, that the Taliban destroyed when they seized Afghanistan.

Then we were off again, carried along on one of his favourite tales, his dead dog story, about when he was dossing on a boat on the Ganges. *Filthy fucking place that.* A terrible smell had kept him awake all night. The corpse of a dog had swollen up like a beach ball and stuck to the side of the boat. Clive was on his feet, showing us how he'd tried to shift the thing with a pole but it kept swirling back.

Mike and Dando were doubled over because Clive had told the story to them in a New York radio station just moments before they played a live show being broadcast all over America. They couldn't stop laughing. Then, while Mike was being interviewed, Clive had amused himself by absent-mindedly rubbing sandpaper over a wooden flute he was making, unaware that the sound was being picked up by the studio's microphones. The engineers were in a panic, unable to locate the source of what sounded like white noise, and cut to an unscheduled commercial break while they investigated.

At about half past ten the band are on stage, in front of a big crowd that is wildly enthusiastic, as if welcoming old friends. The band sit in a semicircle, playing songs from their early records. In 'Spirit Beautiful', Mike becomes animated, as the pounding rhythm builds to a percussion-driven climax. The crowd nod their heads and pat their knees, and some clap in time to the music which sounds like a mixture of a Native American chant and a raga from ancient India. It is a strange moment, and a long way from the hot, packed streets outside where fashion-conscious clubbers are heading for the bars, beginning their typical Barcelona weekend.

Then Clive is singing alone under the stark white spotlight, a lonely figure hunched over his banjo, smoke and dust slowly curling up to the rafters. It is a slow song and the chords rattle as his voice fills the old hall; only the band know who he is singing about.

> *Since you went away, I hope and pray*
> *You come back some day.*
> *You went and I can't sleep at night*
> *Without you, it's not the same.*

3

PALMA

Incredible String Band

I HAD forgotten about this part of touring: getting back to the hotel at 2am, waking the yawning night porter, waiting in the street until he unlocks the door, leaning on the old wooden reception counter, worn shiny by thousands of elbows, while he finds our keys on the old-fashioned numbered hooks, creeping upstairs and somehow managing to grab some sleep – not always easy when the sound of the gig is still ringing in your ears. Mike, Fluff and Ramon decide to head off to a nearby bar for a few drinks. I have learned better; it's an early start in the morning – Mike's stamina is impressive.

In my touring days even the best hotels required you to adhere to their timetables. It was always well after midnight when we got back from whatever gig we had played; we were tired and hungry but the kitchens were always locked, all that was on offer was a few stale ham sandwiches and a packet of crisps. Breakfast was served only between 7.30 and 8.30 – PROMPT, as the menus stated in unambiguous bold type. We needed to sleep, but had to have a decent feed in the morning before the long drive to the next town. I always enjoyed watching the waiters' faces when the entire band and road crew, grinning, dishevelled and, if we were lucky, with a few extra female guests, rushed in at exactly 8.29 and they had to reset a dozen places for us.

One thing we couldn't mess about with was the departure time from the hotel. Bands employ or are assigned tour managers by their management companies to ensure that everyone ends up at the same place at the correct time, a thankless and often difficult task. I have a pal who was the tour manager for one of the most famous pop stars in the world and travelled everywhere by private jet and limousine, but he gave it all up because he was becoming a gibbering wreck trying to pander to increasingly insane demands.

Some tour managers are officious, bad-tempered buggers, others are diplomatic but efficient; all of them are harassed and use a variety of tactics to ensure the band gathers on time to make the next flight or road journey. Some gently cajole the musicians, others fine them $10 for every minute they are late. I knew a guy who worked for the Stones who abandoned one of the road crew in Budapest to teach everyone the importance of punctuality. The Incredible String Band once had a very good tour manager who quietly noted any band member who didn't have the concept of time figured out – usually the drummer – and gave him meeting times half an hour earlier than everyone else. It was always funny to see him rush down to reception, thinking he was late and about to get chewed out, when in fact he was five minutes early. Mark has 20 years' experience, is easy-going and pleasant and told us all to be ready and waiting at the front of the hotel no later than 8.15am. We had a flight to catch to Mallorca and he was worried how long the check-in would take with all the excess baggage.

In the morning, Dando and I were surprised to find ourselves alone in the breakfast room, where we helped ourselves to coffee, croissants, yoghurt, cheese and slices of those cold meats they always have in Continental hotels. There was so much nice food on offer that we forgot to check our watches as he told me about his early days on the road. After years of trudging round clubs and pubs he and a pal were signed by a big-shot manager who whisked them off to America to record an album. They were in the studio for weeks and rarely saw daylight. One night they arrived and were told their manager had disappeared owing the studio thousands of dollars. The owner locked up their guitars and threatened them with jail, and they had to beg relatives for plane tickets home. It was a familiar story.

We went downstairs at 8.30 and found Mark twitching at the reception desk, and dialling Mike's room on the hotel phone. Fluff mentioned something about getting back from the bar around 3am, but that was the last sighting. Mike eventually shuffled down just after nine. Mark greeted him with a cheery 'good morning' and told him that he would have to pay for new tickets for everyone if we missed the flight. Mike shrugged and grinned, bags under his eyes like a jogger's bollocks, and we shifted over in the minibus as he squeezed in. Everyone was happy.

As we drove to the airport through quiet streets glowing in brilliant sunshine, Fluff excitedly pointed out one of those Gothic cathedral things that Barcelona is famous for, and we caught a glimpse of a couple of squiggly spires designed by some famous architect. It would be nice to visit it, but not today. Most touring bands see very little, there's rarely time. The only place where I can remember doing any sightseeing is Rome. After the gig we hired a cab to drive us around the deserted streets because Rome is pretty nifty, even at two in the morning.

We soon reached Barcelona airport and Mark ushered the band and its five trolleys of instruments into the busy check-in queue. Clutching our boarding cards, we nipped past a group of dithering tourists who were trying to work out how much alcohol their remaining euros would buy, and grabbed a quick coffee. Mike gulped two espressos, then stretched and smiled; we'd made it on time.

It was very nice to have pre-assigned seats and we settled back to enjoy the short flight. The plane took off, soared above the Mediterranean, then started descending almost immediately. I like Mallorca very much. Even though it is dusty and arid, with scrawny, thorny bushes, and tough old olive trees, it's a pretty island with jagged mountains, hidden valleys, and a dramatic coastline with loads of little coves and sparkling limestone cliffs overlooking the turquoise sea.

When we landed, Ramon drove us to a modern hotel on a hill above Palma bay. Bright, American-style rooms with clean, comfortable beds, beech furniture, polished wood floors instead of the usual easy-to-mop imitation marble, Sky TV if anyone wanted the news, and large private balconies looking onto a gleaming pool around which gloriously tanned women were basking topless in the hot sunshine. Mike and Mark immediately dumped their bags and sprinted downstairs for a quick dip.

The image of Mallorca is tinted by Magaluf, or Shagaluf to use its English name. The teenage boffing capital of Europe is a short distance along the coast from the tranquil flowers and restful gardens of Palma. The day after he left school, my youngest son went there with his pals for a big celebration. They checked into their modest hotel, then headed straight to a club advertising a high-octane alcohol and foam party. Next morning, one of his friends woke on a spectacularly stained bed in a strange, dingy apartment, his clothes, credit card and money all gone. He had nothing but his underpants. His head was pounding; couldn't remember a thing. He glanced nervously in the cracked mirror. Neatly written in large black letters across his forehead was one word: CUNT. He had to walk barefoot to his hotel through crowds of laughing holidaymakers. The boys agreed it was the best holiday ever.

We spent the rest of the afternoon lazing around while Mark talked and texted on his mobile phone, setting up gigs and interviews, then everyone gathered in the lobby at more or less the agreed time and we piled into the minibus with Ramon. Local councils in Spain, fed up with complaints from residents about noise, have been forcing clubs to move out of town. We drove to a deserted industrial estate outside Palma. As soon as we walked into the converted warehouse, we could see it was the wrong place for a String Band gig. The tables were painted with Red Bull logos and the walls plastered with adverts for mind-frazzling caffeine drinks mixed with lethal amounts of vodka. Most people who go to String Band concerts prefer gentler products, such as camomile tea, or the powerful marijuana that grows well in secret places on the island.

Mike grimaced as he glanced at a poster of forthcoming bands: thick gothic print screamed names like *Anthrax*, *Hardcore Death Wish* and *Heavy Metal Maniacs*. He sighed. The gentle folkie/world music of the Incredible String Band is not what the tattooed, pierced-tongued, nipple-ringed, scrotally chained regulars would want to listen to on a Saturday night. The stage was far too high and had a metal barrier to stop frenzied head-bangers clambering up on it; Mike likes to be close to the people he is playing to. He shrugged. *Oh well, better get on with the soundcheck.*

Soundchecks are the most boring part of a musician's life. Charlie Watts said he'd spent 25 years with the Stones of which only five had been playing, the other 20 had been hanging around. He was talking about soundchecks. These take a long time, especially when using the 'house' PA system that most venues have nowadays, because the sound engineers are usually unfamiliar with the band's music, but it's far cheaper than dragging around truckloads of equipment.

There are two sound men: one at a full-size mixing desk near the back of the hall who controls what the audience hear, and the other at a smaller desk at the side of the stage. His job is to sort out what the band want fed through the wedge-shaped monitor speakers pointing up at them. The difficulty is that each musician needs different things. One wants more guitar, others want less. Vocals are always tricky. If the singer can't hear his voice in his monitor he might sing out of tune. If he hears someone else's voice too loudly he may start singing a harmony instead of the main vocal, which always sounds amusing. Or he might just sing himself hoarse. It takes a lot of fiddling with the controls to get the right balance.

Fluff loosens her fingers by rattling off a zippy selection from Vivaldi, and then methodically works with the sound engineers until everyone is happy. She is very patient; she doesn't speak Spanish and they don't speak English. I help by tuning all the guitars, something that used to be a nightmare before the days of electronic tuners. Nowadays you can buy one for a tenner in any music shop. If you listen to old live recordings of bands, the tuning is usually miles out. Now musicians often change guitars for every song and a roadie retunes them– they don't even need to be able to hear what they are doing, just plug in the guitar and line up the little lights. It makes life much easier.

The promoter has rustled up a tasty meal, which we eat outside, enjoying the sunset and the warm evening air. Mike sits quietly, watching the road, hoping that a couple of busloads of fans will appear and he can relax a little. There is nothing worse than playing to an empty hall. The signs are not good; leather clad bikers swigging fast whisky and slow beers slouch against the bar as they eye the door for strangers. The menacing clack of pool balls echoes above the wail of heavy metal guitar solos. Two wiry-looking guys, amphetamine-thin but muscular in their sleeveless denim jackets, begin shoving each other like bulls in an arena, one gripping a San Miguel bottle, the other a thick cue. *If the boys wanna fight, you better let 'em.* Mike had been looking forward to this gig, he loves Mallorca and the way Spanish fans dance and sing at String Band gigs; this is not what he'd expected.

Mike played to huge audiences with the Incredible String Band, the biggest being Woodstock. It looks like this gig is going to be almost empty; he hates the thought that any promoter would lose money putting on his band. It's time to go on stage. He peers into the echoing darkness of the steel and concrete warehouse. Only 20 people. *Shit. Give it another half hour, see if it fills up a little.* He drinks some red wine and a cold bottle of beer, trying to cheer himself up. The people who have come deserve his best shot, he knows that, but sometimes it's hard to play to the people in front of you and not be depressed by the large empty space of the people who aren't.

The band go on to an enthusiastic cheer, but the hollow sound of missing voices is difficult to ignore. Mike grins, welcomes them and starts playing, the same running order of songs as last night. A few people behind the barrier in front of the stage begin swaying. They have long white hair with straggly beards and look a little bewildered. One guy is dancing wildly, out of his mind on something that instantly converts brain matter to explosions of neurons.

In a quiet corner there's a young guy with his girlfriend, both beautiful in that braided-hair, brown-skinned, flowing white cotton look. They're holding each other close, smiling at one another, their teeth gleaming against their perfect tans. They seem to know these songs well, even though Mike wrote them before they were born.

A lot of 1960s' music was about shagging; blues songs stating the growling desire to be 'your backdoor man', or, as John Lee Hooker plainly and ominously threatened, 'shoot you right down, get you into ma bed, make love to you'. In 'Hoochie Coochie Man', Muddy Waters left the gentle womenfolk of Chicago in no doubt that he would call on the dark powers of voodoo if that's what it took. Some songs, in retrospect, such as the seemingly innocent 'Shout' by the Isley Brothers, are actually quite worrying.

In the 1960's, the cherubic 17-year-olds who were the brilliant Small Faces sang cheerfully about 'picking her up on a Friday night', making it clear they would settle for 'all or nothing'. Paul Rogers, the singer with Free, didn't waste time; if he saw a girl he wanted, he'd take her 'home to his place, watching every move on her face'. The stars of the day sang from the groin. By comparison, Mike wrote songs with thoughtful lyrics full of poetic optimism, dreams and visions reminiscent of Keats and Blake.

Mike grew up in Edinburgh, trained for a while in accountancy, but soon left to hang out with other intellectuals, many of whom played a big part in shaping the British music industry. It was a good time to be young, the last days of the beatniks, and he puffed countless joints on the wooden floors of semi-derelict apartments with the original members of the band, Robin Williamson and Clive. There were always interesting people around: guitar-masters Bert Jansch, Davie Graham and John Martyn, who are still working musicians, and Bruce Findlay, who started a chain of record shops and eventually managed Simple Minds and other groups. Those were gentle days filled with music, poetry, Eastern religion, mind-expanding drugs, books by Jack Kerouac, and all-night discussions. The depth of Mike's knowledge is in his songs; it's hard to think of any other songwriter who manages to quote Thomas Traherne, a 17th-Century mystic:

> You'll never enjoy the world aright
> 'til the sea itself floweth in your veins
> 'til you are clothed with the heavns
> and crowned with the stars.

When he sings of the darkness of cold, wet Edinburgh streets, it is with the same dream-like vision he had almost 40 years earlier:

My Friday evening footsteps plodding dully through this black town,
Are far away now from the world that I'm in.

Or the song he closes his gigs with, his message of goodwill:

May the long time sun shine upon you, all love surround you.
And the pure light within you guide you all the way on.

The small crowd knows these words; music from early Incredible String Band albums is folk music's equivalent of The Beatles' *Sergeant Pepper*.

After almost an hour, the band play the final song of the first half, 'Spirit Beautiful', and then, drenched in sweat from the hot, airless stage, they file quietly into the dressing room. Mike grabs a beer and drinks it silently in the corner. Then another glass of wine. There's a tension in the dressing room that I've seen before, many times, many places. Musicians take their craft very seriously, and when gigs go wrong they feel a crushing pain that might be difficult to comprehend for anyone who hasn't placed their soul on the firing line. There's something going on between Mark and Mike, something only they know about, and I know it's going to flare at any moment. Whatever it is, it only needs the smallest spark, only needs the catalyst of a hot, edgy venue like this to ignite it.

I don't want to see this, and I'm aware my presence in the room is not helping. When bands argue, they usually keep it amongst themselves, they don't want to betray their emotions to outsiders. I decide to leave the room; I'm intruding. When I come back, it's over. I don't know what has been said but I can tell by the way Fluff and Dando are staring at the floor that harsh words have been exchanged, cuts that won't ever heal. Even Clive looks pensive, as he sits in a corner, slowly turning a beer bottle in his hands, gazing at it. Mike is staring coldly at Mark. As the band goes on for the second half, Mark sits alone in a dark corner and stares at the stage. He and Mike will never work together again.

Next morning the band heads home: Fluff to Crewe, Dando to Wales, Mike to Edinburgh, Clive to Britanny and Mark to Chesterfield. My flight to Glasgow isn't until later so I wander off to catch the Palma to Soller train, one of the most beautiful railway journeys in the world. It's almost a century old and the carriages are gleaming wood and black iron, with those overhead luggage racks a child could sleep on, and there's even a first-class cabin with deep leather sofas and armchairs; no extra charge. It's cheap; the return journey costs next to nothing.

The train chugs along the city streets with a lovely clackety-clack sound, picking up speed as it pulls out of Palma into the countryside, past sunny orange groves and cornfields swaying gently beside the track. After a while it passes the sleepy town of Bunyola and the Tolkien-like gorge of Sa Gubia, before clattering through a five-mile tunnel to the coastal town of Soller. There's just time to sit on the beach with an ice cream before the train begins the journey back. One of the carriages is full of excited children on a school trip and their Spanish songs fill the warm air.

It belongs to another time. But the spirit is still strong and the music beautiful.

4

GLASGOW

U2

I TURNED up at Palma airport nice and early. The Spanish girls behind the check-in desks were busy varnishing their fingernails; the Glasgow flight was delayed. I'd arrived just ahead of a couple of packed coaches and patiently stood at the front of the restless queue for an hour until I finally got my boarding pass. I looked up at the departures board: six hours to kill.

The airport was a heaving mass of holidaymakers in green and white Celtic shirts, blue Rangers tops, flip-flops, droopy sombreros and bikini bras exposing large rolls of sun-seared flesh and wobbling pink bellies. The smoke-filled bars were packed, reverberating with the thump of Robbie Williams: *Let me ent-ur-taain yoo*. Swaying people spilling onto the concourse, sprawling on the floor, slouching against the walls, swilling down whisky and lager – well-pished. Packs of kids kicking plastic balls, lunging across the slippery floor in leg-breaking tackles. Judging by the panicked faces of the shop assistants, the annual East End Shoplifters Convention was in full swing too. Everyone was enjoying themselves, had saved a fortune on the price of their holidays by taking the kids out of school for a couple of weeks, and they were having a final fling before going back to the rainy streets of Scotland. As long as the bevvy was flowing, nobody was caring about flight delays.

The burger and pizza stands were mobbed, but on the top floor of the airport, out of sight of the main shopping area, there is a little café that serves freshly made coffee and pastries, the cute kind that would be a big hit at a Kelvinside book group. It's always quiet; I've never seen more than one or two people in it, usually airline staff slowly leafing through *El Pais* and chatting over an espresso. I walked upstairs, bought two cups of strong coffee because it was about to close and, anyway, I like caffeine. I carried them to a glass-roofed atrium that is usually deserted and lay on a plastic lounger, looking at the stars, sipping my coffee, grateful to the genius who invented the iPod.

In summer, the sun rises bright and early over Scotland, so it was already daylight when the plane coasted over the River Clyde and bumped along Glasgow airport's high-friction runway, the bleary-eyed passengers jerking awake, cheering and clapping as it trundled to a stop. Home again. Twenty minutes later I flopped into bed, glad to feel my comfortable old mattress. Just as I was drifting to sleep, the shipyard horn blew, as it has done for countless years. If you live anywhere near the Clyde you will know its wheezy sound, like a train whistle from a Hank Williams song. It's nice to hear it when you are warm in bed, *stinking in your pit*, as my father used to say in that gentle way of his. Mind you, I bet the financial advisers, personal-injury lawyers and pre-owned vehicle consultants who live in the new, hundred-grand-a-room apartments overlooking the river probably don't feel quite the same way at dawn's first blast. Heh heh.

When I was a schoolboy in the west end of Glasgow, you could clearly hear the yards even though they were miles away, the clatter of hot rivets and clang of steel. When I was trying to make the big time and short of the next payment on my guitar, I often got jobs in offices or factories, although I was usually sacked for staggering in hours late after playing a gig the night before. I managed to stick at some jobs for long enough to clear a few weeks' overdue rent, but I never worked in a shipyard. My father had spent most of his working life in the docks; I reckon he would have broken my legs first.

A lot of clever men worked in the yards, wee guys who had to leave school at 13 but quickly learned how to build the finest ships in the world. I once played guitar for a cabaret singer who had served his time as an electrician in the yards. He had done a bit of moneylending when he worked there, and managed to raise enough money to open a music shop. He wasn't a hard man and it was dangerous territory, but he never failed to collect a debt. He had one simple rule. The dockers could borrow whatever they needed provided they paid back everything they owed, plus interest, when they collected their wages on Friday morning. They could have a fresh loan in the afternoon but they had to have paid everything back first.

Every Friday at four o'clock there would be an impatient queue of men waiting for loans from him or they would be short in the pay packet they took home to their Govan wives. If anyone had not repaid him, he would tell the men he wouldn't be lending any money today because Joe down the paint shop hadn't cleared his debt. He'd promise them that as soon as Joe paid what he owed, everyone could borrow again. He rarely had to wait more than a few minutes.

Glasgow has always had a grim reputation for violence but it can be the friendliest place in the world. If you ask directions from almost anyone, they'll often go out of their way to take you there. It has more parks than any other European city – Glasgow

Green is the oldest in the world. The parks have glorious flower displays and I've never seen one vandalised, although many of them seem to be fertilised with dog turds. The old ornate bandstands have long since fallen apart, but after the war, summer concerts by brass bands used to attract hundreds of people. It was a good way for homecoming soldiers to be part of a large crowd again without throwing themselves to the ground whenever a passing car backfired.

Glasgow used to be a great place for football. Celtic won the European Cup with a team of players who had all been born within 30 miles of their stadium. That will never happen again. Rangers won the European Cup Winners Cup with eleven Scots. Now both teams spend millions on foreign internationals, but usually don't get past the opening rounds.

When I was a kid, football grounds were full every Saturday and Hampden Park packed in massive crowds. In the intense atmosphere there was often trouble. I remember my father taking me to a midweek match against Austria one warm night in 1963. To the delight of 97,000 supporters, Scotland were winning 4 – 1. With only 10 minutes to go the referee had to abandon the game because the players were kicking the shit out of each other even though there was nothing at stake. The game was a friendly.

When the evangelist Billy Graham held a rally at Hampden, he recruited thousands of followers from 100,000 people who packed into the stadium to hear him preach the gospel. Yet when Rangers played Celtic, there was mayhem. It didn't matter who won; even a draw could end with a riot. Long before kick-off, the frenzied crowd would start taunting each other with Ulster and IRA battle songs they had learned as children in their Protestant or Catholic school playgrounds. There were fights, stabbings, pitch invasions, slashed faces, and hundreds of arrests; guys born as neighbours had grown up to become enemies in different football shirts.

In those days, the crowd stood for hours, jammed together on dusty terracing, drinking screw top bottles of beer and peeing at their feet; even if you managed to squeeze through to the toilets at the back of the stadium you'd never get back to your pals and, anyway, no one wanted to miss a moment of the game. Every so often there would be a startled shout and a brief space would open up while someone spectacularly puked up a steamy mixture of cheap wine and greasy pie, but the football was terrific. Dennis Law, Jimmy Johnstone, Jim Baxter, Willie Henderson . . . so many brilliant players. I was so lucky to see these guys stroking the ball around, leaving dazzled defenders sprawled in the mud. Nowadays everyone reclines in comfortable seats but the football is heartbreaking.

It's a good place for a gig, though.

U2 were playing, and I had a ticket. I hadn't heard them before but met them once when I was playing at a posh country club beside Loch Lomond. I had just set up my gear when I noticed Bono and the Edge having a quiet drink in the corner. I went over and had a wee chat with them; they were very friendly. I didn't have any dreams that Bono would recruit me for U2's next world tour, but if he had been looking for a bass player, I don't think busking along on 'Moon River' would have swung it for me.

Hampden has a vast car park – politicians, businessmen and SFA hangers-on need plenty of space when Scotland are playing – and tonight it's packed with rows of dusty articulated trucks and double-decker tour buses filled with bunk beds for U2's road crew; it looks like an army camp. Inside the stadium, the hallowed turf is protected by hundreds of sheets of plywood taped together. The band will be playing on a circular stage that reaches right out into the crowd. At either side, black PA speakers tower as high as the roof. I should be able to hear them just fine – I suspect that people as far away as Gretna might catch a few notes too.

In the 1960's and 1970's, music papers took rock musicians very seriously, and interviewers asked them weighty questions about politics and the meaning of life, although they would probably have got equally articulate answers from any Millwall footballer or heavyweight boxer. Ever since, musicians like Bono have been regarded as opinion leaders on world problems, but unlike many of his predecessors, he seems to genuinely care about poverty.

U2 are the biggest band in the world and suddenly they are here, on stage and playing. There have been hundreds of four-piece groups: a singer, a guitarist, a bass player and a drummer, it's the simplest of all rock line-ups, but U2 are unique. Bono's voice is terrific. All top singers have one thing in common: their own distinct sound. It doesn't matter what the song is, when you hear any of them sing, you immediately know who it is. Some people don't like Bob Dylan's singing, or Rod Stewart's. But they all have something unique, they don't sound like anyone else, their voices have recognisable personality and so people immediately feel a connection with them, it's as if they are friends.

Guitarist Edge is at Bono's side. He's one of the top guitarists in the world because as soon as he plays, you know it's him. Most guitarists sound alike, only a few have their own sound. It's great to hear him playing his jangling arpeggios laced with echo, soaring above the old stadium into the hot June night.

Drummer Larry Mullen, looking like a 1950s' biker, and white-haired bass player Adam Clayton are the solid foundation of the band. They keep it simple, don't draw attention to themselves. It would be easy to think that there are many other musicians who could do their job, but if they had not been part of U2 the spirit of the group would have been different and it might never have evolved from playing in Dublin pubs. The chemistry of any successful band is a unique and mystical thing.

If you want respect in a working-class town like Glasgow, you have to do your job well, especially if you are charging £60 a skull for a ticket. From the first song, 'Vertigo', to the last, an encore of the same song, 40,000 Glaswegians are standing, singing together in a way that only used to be heard when Scotland beat England. It's great to watch, to feel part of it. You know how you can walk into a room containing one angry person and feel the tension? This is the opposite. It's like pure energy, a feeling of joy rising from the packed pitch.

Photographs of the gentle Burmese martyr Aung San Suu Kyi are flashed on the band's huge video screens and it would be nice to imagine that while she is under house arrest by the military dictators of her country, she will somehow feel the support towards her tonight. In cities all over the world there will be similar scenes as the mighty U2 touring machine rolls on. Every audience agrees: there must be an end to war, poverty and oppression.

When Bono stands and reads the International Declaration of Human Rights, everyone nods in agreement, even here in a city that still demands religious apartheid in its schools. The stadium that has seen so much bigotry and hatred is now packed with people from all religions as they join together in the music. So what I can't understand is this. When one wee Irishman and his rock band can generate so much goodwill among millions of people, how is that a tiny number of evil people can cause so much suffering on this small planet?

5
LJUBLJANA
Bootleg Beatles

When I was a teenager, delighted students flocked to university to study things that gave them qualifications in useless subjects, at least as far as practical skills were concerned, musings like classical Greek, poetry of the Renaissance and stuff like that. They spent three years lurching happily from the beer bar to all-night parties before emerging with a degree in some esoteric fantasy. Yet within hours they were snapped up by major international corporations, desperate to pay them huge salaries augmented by gleaming company cars, pension plans and lavish expense accounts. Nowadays, students sweat diligently over subjects that are rigidly practical, things like mechanical engineering, business management or applied electronics, then find themselves flipping burgers in McDonald's or stacking supermarket shelves and facing years of repaying student loans. It doesn't seem fair.

In the 1970's, before rock became part of the establishment, it cost bands money to play. Record companies regarded touring as a loss leader. The cost of hauling tons of sound and lighting equipment and accommodating musicians, hangers-on and ever-hungry road crews in Holiday Inns was huge compared to the revenue from ticket sales, but it was the only way to sell records. When Led Zeppelin played at the Albert Hall in 1969, tickets were

75 pence, less than half the cost of their records, and about the same as a couple of packs of cigarettes.

As soon as captains of industry and world leaders were seen shaking their asses at Springsteen and U2 gigs, the devil's music became respectable and corporate sponsorship of rock tours arrived – *Budweiser proudly presents* . . .Suddenly bands realised they could make big bucks on the road. As the cost of CDs fell, and free or cheap downloads of MP3's soared, ticket prices rocketed and are now mind-bogglingly expensive – the Stones are not embarrassed about asking £100 for a balcony seat. In America, even a binocular-view of the stage can set you back as much as a month's groceries.

Most bands still need to have a new record on sale to help make their roadshows viable, but the Bootleg Beatles are an exception. They've managed to tour the world since 1980 without recording a single tune. In some ways they could be called the ultimate touring band; their only product is live performances. They're not doing it to shift their Greatest Hits album, because they have none.

Almost every well-known group has imitators, but most are tedious, in the same way as a visit to Madame Tussaud's is usually a fairly brisk experience. No matter how good they are or how close to the original they play, for some reason most tribute bands begin to sound boring after the first few songs. Even worse are the glorified karaoke singers that use backing tracks.

The Bootleg Beatles are completely different. I suppose calling them a tribute group is accurate, but only in the same way that the London Symphony Orchestra could be called a Mozart Tribute Group. The Bootlegs tour the UK regularly, but, hey, why go to Cleethorpes to see them? The show they were doing in Slovenia sounded like a much more interesting trip. I had seen

Ljubljana in a travel show where the presenter was twittering about the *wonderful* dried fish and *joyfully delightful* wine. Aye, right. I was happy to go just to see the band. But first, how to get there?

First, a flight to Stansted then a connection to Ljub-what's it called? In that endearing way of cut-price airlines there's always some hoop you have to jump through and candidate for Haemorrhoid of the Year Award is that easyJet do not consider their flights linked so I couldn't check in for both flights at Glasgow. I had reached Stansted and was trudging to the Slovenia check-in queue before it suddenly occurred to me in the dyslexic way I have with place names that the gig might be in Slovakia and that I had booked a flight to the wrong country. Sometimes I get mixed up, probably because of the substances I took when the original Beatles were still together. It might be Slovakia – the Bootlegs have played almost everywhere, even India and Japan, where they filled the Budokan. They were among the first Western rock bands to play in Russia, although they suspected *Pravda* had misunderstood the press release – thousands of hysterically screaming fans all over the USSR clearly believed they were watching the original Fab Four.

I had arranged to meet band members Graham Preskett and Annette Brown at the departure gate, so I called Annette to make sure I hadn't got my cities confused. She was stuck in a traffic jam, but she needn't worry, the check-in looked as if it would take a long time. Thankfully it was Slovenia we were headed for, something we had in common with a couple of triathlon teams who were going there to take part in one of those testosterone-fuelled iron-man challenge things. They were causing chaos by checking in truckloads of mountain bikes, tents the size of circus marquees, bulging rucksacks full of abseil ropes, and boxes packed with the latest *technical* clothing. They were even dragging canoes up to the desk, and one of them was driving everyone crazy by demanding that he should be allowed to take his favourite paddle on as hand luggage. His dimly lit, carb-loaded, protein-numbed brain seemed incapable of realising that a heavily wrapped canoe paddle looks exactly like a fucking rifle, and the mood of the queue behind him was growing dangerously unsympathetic.

The teams posed and strutted, looking strong and slender with tanned, sinewy arms, a couple of the older guys wearing that smug, self-important, up-their-own bahooky look of mountain athletes, as some like to call themselves. Their sponsors were picking up the tab for all their baggage; climbers never pay a penny for anything if they can avoid it. I've been on trips with pals who clambered onto planes laden down with clanking hardware around their waists rather than paying a few quid for the excess weight. I've seen exhausted climbers, gaunt, unshaven, unwashed – totally bowfing – having abseiled from the top of some craggy mountain then staggering straight onto their flight still wearing their down-filled anoraks, sweat-saturated fleeces and heavy plastic climbing boots. They take the damn things off as soon as they sit down and spend the flight snoring in the steam from their thick socks. OK . . . I've done it too.

The check-in line was backed up all the way to the car park while one of the teams painstakingly checked in their gear. There was another lot in front of me, but I managed to skip ahead of them when they were posing for photographs. As soon as I had my boarding pass, I hurried to the international departure hall and plonked myself down for a strong coffee. Behind the counter were three lovely Filipino girls, as delicate as jasmine and with heart-melting smiles, although a little short of fluency in English, as I am too. I slowed down my Scottish accent as much as I could, and asked for a cappuccino without chocolate but was presented with a hot chocolate without cappuccino. The girl was so lovely, I smiled and drank it.

I met Annette and Graham just before the easyJet staff commanded everyone to stand to attention and form orderly queues for boarding. We managed to find seats within shouting distance of each other and dutifully stared at the flight attendant as she demonstrated how to use the little plastic whistle in the event we found ourselves floating helplessly in a raging sea amid orange-coloured wreckage and burning aircraft fuel.

As soon as the drinks trolley appeared, Graham and Annette ordered gins and tonic, or, as Graham pointed out, the correct wording, gin and tonics. He jokes a lot, is a natural entertainer, he'd be great on a television chat-show. He's a highly experienced music arranger – I found out later that he has kept string sections on their toes backing Tom Jones, Van Morrison and a long list of others.

The Bootlegs hire Graham, Annette and other classical musicians to play the string parts on 'Penny Lane', 'Yesterday' and other Beatles' songs. When he joined the Bootlegs 20 years ago, there were no written scores of these parts. Graham patiently sat beside his stereo, turning the balance to the left and right, and figured them out by ear, something that few classically trained musicians could do. I once played in a wedding band with a pianist who burst into tears when she was asked to play 'Happy Birthday' without sheet music.

Graham and Annette can write down music as they hear it, just like reporters scribbling shorthand. Graham has also scored film music and laughs loudly when he tells me about working on *Thelma and Louise*. The director turned to him: *Hey – I need a fucking harmonica solo. You're a musician, you play the fucking harmonica, right?* Graham had never touched one before, there's not much call for wailing blues solos in the LSO, but such details are lost on big-budget movie directors. He hurried to the nearest music shop, bought one, and after sucking and blowing on it all night was able to play the required part for the soundtrack.

He looks a little tired, he's been working all night composing advertising jingles, and he finds that alcohol is pretty much the best way to keep going. He's toured the world many times, and his body has learned to put up with lack of sleep and a surplus of gin. As he finishes his drink he looks for the flight attendant. One of the older sportsmen is waving a camomile tea bag in the air and instructing her to bring hot water. Graham stares at him with a bemused expression, and asks her for another two gins, please.

Annette and Graham love playing with the Bootlegs, it's different from their usual routine of jazz bands and orchestras. 'It can be tricky,' says Annette. 'I play piccolo trumpet on "Penny Lane" and hitting the high F sharp in the solo is, to use the musical term, a real bastard. Joe Public knows how it's supposed to sound, so if you fuck it up there's nowhere to hide.'

We've safely crossed the Channel, so it looks like we won't need the plastic whistles this flight. As the plane soars over the Alps, Graham and Annette pour their fourth set of miniatures into plastic cups and tell me that they have now spent more than they will earn from playing the gig. But they're happy; they're not doing this for the money.

The flight attendant announces we're about to begin our final descent. The plane is packed – apart from the triathlon teams, many of the passengers are wearing heavy leather walking boots and studying maps. When I looked out of the window, I realised why. Slovenia seems lovely, beautiful grassy meadows with trails and cycle tracks meandering beside gurgling streams and sighing forests. Tranquil, alpine-style wooden chalets with restful balconies gaze over peaceful valleys, and there are spectacular mountains, higher than anything in Britain, but not requiring the assistance of sherpas to hike up them. Apparently, there are 7,000 km of mountain paths, which is quite something bearing in mind how small the country is. There are thousands of caves, although only 25 are open to the public, but I guess cavers just nip down the ones that aren't when nobody is looking. There is a small, unspoiled beach area and even a couple of blue-sky ski resorts, with groomed pistes and glorious views. What a nice place to come for a gig.

The descent is going fine until suddenly we are surrounded by thick, dark clouds and strobe-like flashes of lightning. The cabin falls silent. Muttered prayers and promises never to worry about anything again if only we can land safely. Camomile tea-man is gripping the arm rest, staring straight ahead, his face pale. Even the cabin staff look queasy when we finally bump onto the tarmac. Sighs of relief mingle with a couple of pent-up farts.

The promoter's daughter is waiting for us at the arrivals gate. A welcoming smile, beautiful teeth. Tumbling blonde hair. Clear skin, sparkling eyes. She shakes our hands. *Hi, I'm Eva.* She says it's short for a Slavic name none of us could pronounce. She grins. She's lovely.

She gives us an umbrella and we huddle under it as we hurry from the terminal building through torrential rain to a gleaming silver Mercedes. We quickly pile in. *My boyfriend will drive you to the hall. It won't take long.* She tells us he's a pilot in the Slovenian air force acrobatic team, which I don't suppose is the sort of work you usually see offered at the local job centre. She is in her final year at university, she's going to be a doctor. They live in a village near here, they'd like to buy a flat in the city, but even small apartments are so expensive. I hate to think what will happen to property prices once the Essex estate agents find their way here.

Her boyfriend drives fast, very fast, and quickly introduces us to the concept of the 90-degree turn. Approaching a road junction, he hurtles towards it, then spins the car sideways, brakes screaming, throwing us from one side of the car to the other, his foot jammed on the accelerator. Presumably it's tame stuff compared to Mach 2 somersaults, and I hope I don't let the side down by honking up my easyJet sandwich.

Eva speaks fluent English in a lovely lilting accent, and Graham asks her to teach him some Slovenian words. As the wet streets flash by, he repeats various expressions, mainly requests for exotic cocktails. There's no time to do any sightseeing but a glance at the map of Ljubljana is interesting. It appears to be not so much a city as a group of five parks with a town tastefully set out within them. As we drive into the centre it looks very pretty; trees, flowers, pathways and greenery everywhere.

The gig is at the national basketball arena in the Tivoli Gardens, a pleasant, tree-filled park that seems to spread for miles. There are tennis courts, friendly little coffee stalls, hardly a scrap of litter, and not a steaming turd to be seen anywhere, animal or human. Cyclists meander along, stop for a leisurely coffee or a beer and park their bikes against trees without bothering with heavy chains and padlocks. It's perfect; I'm going to come back some day with my bike.

Inside the large hall, the Bootlegs are in the middle of their soundcheck. Technicians are busy at each side of the stage erecting huge video screens, and setting up camera angles and lights. The band is playing through old Vox amplifiers, the same kind as the Beatles used. Drummer Hugo Degenhardt and guitarist Andre Barreau are session musicians who have worked with Robbie Williams. Neil Harrison, who looks like John Lennon, is a successful composer, and has written songs for Lulu. Bass player Dave Catlin-Birch, artistic and almost fragile, toured the world for 10 years with a great band called World Party.

Old valve amplifiers have a great sound, especially ancient Vox AC 30s. Like all electronic equipment, amplifiers have changed a lot in the last 40 years, but the Bootlegs know that it is impossible to get that warm, mellow sound out of cold microchips and transistors. They also use the same guitars as The Beatles – original 1960s' Gretsch and Rickenbackers, and a Hoffner Violin Bass. Dave uses old-fashioned, tape-wound strings, which are much heavier than modern strings. Hugo spent ages tracking down 40-year-old cymbals before finding a set in Los Angeles. They cost about the same as a car but he shrugs and tells me they're worth it, they have a special ring; modern cymbals sound harsh.

The soundcheck lasts nearly two hours then everyone goes backstage for some burgers, courtesy of the promoter. In the dressing room, Graham runs through the set with a cellist and violinist, Tamara and Spela, two local girls who attended a school for musically gifted children in Serbia, then graduated from the Academy of Music in Ljubljana. They read Graham's scores perfectly and are excited to be playing with the band.

I decide to keep out of the way for a while, bands usually like a bit of privacy before they go on, and I go for a wander around the park, which is busy with locals strolling to the gig. The storm has moved off, the sun is shining, and there is a relaxed, summer evening atmosphere.

By half past eight, 2,000 people are crammed into the hall. The lights are dimmed, then the spots flood the stage as the band run on. It's weird; as soon as they begin 'I Wanna Hold Your Hand', hundreds of teenage girls start screaming, shouting for Paul and John. Listening to records made back then only hints at what so many groups sounded like; the old reel-to-reel tape recorders in even the best studios never really captured the warmth and pulsating beat of the 1960's. At the time, most record companies reckoned that beat groups would be a rapidly passing novelty; George once said that in a few years they'd probably be back in Liverpool, working as electricians or decorators.

The Bootlegs' sound engineer, Mark Langley, has been in the business almost 40 years. I first met him in New York when I played there with the Incredible String Band and he mixed the sound for us on a couple of gigs. He'd taught me a nifty blues guitar tune on an old beat-up Gibson he'd bought cheap in Greenwich Village, but he has no memory of being there. 'I've been doing this for so long, it all becomes a blur. I can't remember half the bands I've toured with. Every so often I'll be somewhere or hear something and a slight memory will filter through, but mostly it's gone.'

Unlike many of today's young sound men, he is an electronic engineer; if you gave him a crate of transistors, control knobs, wire and a soldering iron he could build a sound desk from scratch. At one time – he thinks it might have been 1969 – he toured Italy with a heavy rock band whose gigs usually ended in riots. 'Sometimes we had to completely rebuild their equipment overnight. The guys doing sound nowadays wouldn't know where to start, they'd just call the record company and tell them to FedEx new gear out to them.'

He wears a head torch, the little halogen beam shining at the controls on his sound desk. His fingers are always moving, making tiny adjustments. At the start of the gig he mixes as close as possible to how it would have sounded in the 1960's. 'You have to remember The Beatles didn't have anything like the sort of PA equipment we have now, so that means I have to keep some frequencies very flat. But the kids nowadays would find that too bland after a while because they are so used to having low-end frequencies pounding them.'

I told Mark I'd seen U2 the night before and the bass seemed to hit me full in the chest even though I was a long way from the stage. And I could remember only too well how Gene Simmons' bass felt.

'Yes, it will do that. These are frequencies below eighty kilohertz. They can actually make you feel sick. The technology for these subsonic speakers was developed by the military as a weapon – the idea was to blast them at the enemy and make them too nauseous to fight. But audiences now are so used to ultra-low bass frequencies that music doesn't sound right without it, it sounds thin. By the time the group is playing the "Sergeant Pepper" stuff I have to bring all that up in the mix. I do it gradually because there are older people who want the sound exactly as it would have been and they would notice.'

The gig is going great. The Bootlegs finish the first half with 'All You Need is Love.' I can't help wondering what it must have been like to be living here when Slobodan Milosevic was on the rampage. Everyone joins in, singing every word. It must mean far more to them than it does to anyone who has never heard the rattle of machine guns at the end of their street, or had relatives just a few miles away slaughtered in their homes.

In the second half Dave sings 'Yesterday', playing acoustic guitar, backed by the string section. It's such a short song, only two minutes and seven seconds, but it says as much as a thousand-page book. It's amazing that Lennon and McCartney composed so much music, most of it as near perfection as you could hope for, when they were so young.

When Neil sits at the piano and plays the first notes of 'Imagine', the crowd cheers and sings with him; for a few moments there is an almost religious atmosphere in the high-domed hall. 'I've been doing these shows for twenty-six years,' Neil tells me later. 'Sometimes it's difficult to be always performing other artistes' material, especially when you are exhausted with all the travelling. This is hard work. We have to get into character, we have to be The Beatles. But whenever I play "Imagine", I always feel very close to John Lennon.'

The band finish with 'Revolution' and 'Hey Jude', and as everyone in the crowd sings, a guy rushes towards the stage and starts to clamber up on it. In Britain or America you might expect to see several hulking bouncers pounce and the guy being hurled out of the hall. I wince, waiting to see teeth fly, but a muscular security man simply places a hand on the guy's arm, smiles at him, and gently ushers him back into the crowd.

After the gig, I travel with the band back to the hotel, a luxury casino/leisure complex outside the city. It's late, but they've kept the restaurant open and we all sit at a long table with built-in hot plates. Trays of meat and vegetables are brought to us and we throw them on to sizzle. I have always enjoyed after-gig dinners; musicians are usually great company. Graham grins and waves to a waiter. 'Bring me far too much to drink right away!' Dave treats us to word-perfect renditions of the Goon Shows, complete with all the voices.

Hugo, once he's had a few drinks, earnestly discusses songwriters who have influenced him and some that haven't. 'Its dead easy to write something critical, any whining bastard can do that. The real skill is to create something positive. Something that inspires. I've no time for pseudo-intellectuals spraying cynicism around or creating vortexes of in-jokes. Music should elevate people.'

When no one is looking, dawn creeps up; the night porter is yawning and glancing at his watch. Just as we are about to head for our rooms, Graham leans over and speaks quietly. 'The thing people don't realise is that The Beatles never performed most of their songs live, and certainly none of the music with the string and brass arrangements. We are the only way that people will ever hear this music played live by contemporaries of the band. I think it's very important musically that someone is doing this.'

6

AMSTERDAM

Jerry Lee Lewis

AMSTERDAM is an ancient and wonderful place. Its winding streets are full of beautiful old buildings, churches, tranquil squares, and more canals, we learn, than Venice. There are art galleries packed with Van Gogh and other painter guys, endless rows of flowering flowers and plant life. Flying over Holland on the approach to Schipol is a treat as you look down on neatly arranged farms, dainty little homes and gleaming office buildings. Everything appears orderly and used for something clean and worthwhile; no mountains of rusting metal or derelict factories. Everywhere looks freshly washed; perhaps because they have so little land they value it and make the best use of it. I wish I could keep my house looking like Holland.

I had always wanted to revisit a club called the Paradiso, where I played with the Incredible String Band way back in 1974. I had enjoyed it very much but had never been since then. I was amusing myself on the Internet one night when I noticed that Jerry Lee Lewis was doing a gig there a couple of days later; I figured this might be the last tour he would do so I should see him while I could. A few more clumping strokes on the keyboard and I had found a cheap flight. I was on my way.

Amsterdam is famous for its red-light district, which has

been attending to travellers in need of entertainment for 800 years. When I visited the live sex shows in 1974 with a couple of the guys in the Incredible String Band, the area was not proudly highlighted on tourist maps as it is now. We had knocked back a large amount of saki in a Japanese restaurant, were in a lively mood, and I vaguely recall that we had to hire a cab with a knowing driver to take us there. It was hidden and furtive and we ducked quickly inside the dark entrance of a back-street club, but, I swear, the girls and guys getting down to it were far more attractive than nowadays. The urban myth was that they were all young students doing for money what they would have been doing anyway but in front of a paying audience, and after six months they would have earned enough to buy their first house.

Now it is all very open, but somehow much seedier. The best-known live-sex theatre has a giant tadger outside its brightly lit doors and a proud display of glossy photographs of rutting couples, leaving you in no doubt what your modest admission fee buys.

For those short of money but eager to see love's gentle embrace, there are little booths in amusement arcades where you can pay a few euros and a curtain lifts revealing some old gal and geezer cavorting in the buff. If you watch for a few minutes you might see gasping and wailing as she pretends to reach the glory thrust. A crowd of laughing teenagers from Liverpool was crammed into one of the cubicles, taunting them: *Go on, pal, give it 'er in the walnut.*

Anyone deprived of the tender touch of a loving partner can join the crowds strolling down the Voorburgwal and, without obvious embarrassment, chose an attentive new friend for the next 10 minutes or so. Most of the shop windows have heavy, red velvet curtains open to reveal bikini-clad girls – some of whom seemed worryingly young – posing and pouting in front of sumptuous beds, enthusiastically gesturing to the passers-by, offering a 'suck and a fuck', as a tourist magazine plainly put it, with the warning that it 'might not be the most romantic experience you've ever had'.

Some years ago I stayed at the Amsterdam Marriott with a group of people from the removal industry. We were in Holland to cycle the Nordzee Route, a pleasant pathway running down the coast from the Hook of Holland to Calais. It was a great weekend. We were transported by luxury coach to the start of each day's cycling and we had hot baths, good food and comfortable beds waiting for us at night. After drinking a large amount of wine and chilled Amstel, one of the guys – there were 50 of us, so I'm not giving any secrets away – staggered to the red-light district where he sampled the delights offered by an Eastern European prostitute. He was a typical removal man, good with diesel engines, and although he'd left school qualified only to weld two bits of metal together, had built a good business through years of sweat and toil. He had enjoyed himself: *She were bloody lovely.* It had only cost 30 euros for a *Bill Clinton*, as they say in polite company. After he'd enjoyed her ministrations for the few moments it took, he left with a satisfied smile and was almost back at the hotel when he realised he'd left his expensive Nikon on the floor of her room. His face ashen, he rushed back, expecting her to tell him to fuck off or she'd call a knuckle-cracking minder, but she smiled and told him that she'd kept his camera safe for him. *I am a religious girl. If I stole it, tomorrow God would punish me.*

As probably most grannies know, there is also a great deal of dope in Amsterdam, and many tourists get utterly wasted in the coffee shops where it is sold. It is, I am reliably informed, extremely strong, far more so than the weaker weed available in the UK. Magic mushrooms are also popular, although a pal told me that after he'd taken more than the generally recommended amount he spent the night in a hallucinogenic paranoia, convinced that he'd crapped himself and sidling up to strangers, dropping his pants and asking them to check.

Amsterdam's streets are as busy as New York's. The flow of cars, mopeds, clanking trams and bikes is relentless. If the locals were stoked up on ganja the streets would be awash with human carnage, bodies and limbs flying everywhere. Cyclists seem to hurtle at you from all directions; I was constantly jumping out of the way of their little bells. They are very polite and friendly, even when I continually walked in front of them – it's the cycle lanes in the middle of the pavements I find tricky.

Holland encourages cyclists, all the train stations have convenient lock-ups so people can park their bikes and get around on foot or by tramcar. In Glasgow, it would be great to have well-maintained urban cycle paths kept clear of broken Buckfast bottles and *jakeys*, as we call connoisseurs of cheap wine. There's plenty to eat in Amsterdam and I tried one of the Indonesian restaurants that seem to be down every side street. I have to be careful these days, can no longer eat spicy food – I shouldn't have had so many breakfasts of vindaloo and Tennent's lager when I was young – but I thought I should risk intestinal retribution just this once. I settled into a chair at a nice window table in a quiet eatery where, for 30 euros, I was served 18 courses – all of them, I hate to say, pretty rank. I suppose the chef's enthusiasm has been blunted by large groups of stoned and pissed-witless lads looking for any old scran to soak up the beer.

Alternatively, there's always the Hard Rock Café, the

Amsterdam branch being near lively Leidseplein Square, which is like Edinburgh during the Fringe, buzzing with street performers, buskers and wiry acrobats swinging from lampposts. When the first Hard Rock Café opened in London all those years ago, it was a great place to hang out, and often we did. The girls were the hottest in town, each and every one of them walking wet dreams with tumbling hair, slender legs, dazzling smiles and gentle voices. A few were even from Texas, for Christ sake.

The music was great – look, let's just lay our cards face up; in those days there was absolutely no place in the Hard Rock Café for any tune by the Monkeys, David Cassidy or the Osmonds, OK? The sounds were riff-heavy, the place had a warm, inviting ketchup-and-fries aroma, every table had overflowing relish trays full of tasty green, red and yellow gooey stuff, and there were always hungry bands and swarms of starving roadies who'd raced straight from the Dover ferry at the end of a European tour, or were stopping off for a last good feed before the start of a British one.

You didn't need a map to find the Hard Rock Café, and it didn't need a sign outside. All you had to do was spot the dusty rented trucks strewn as near the door as possible so that the tour managers could keep watch on the fat padlocks locking down the mud-splattered, roller-shutter doors, all that stood between the street and thousands of pounds worth of Marshall stacks, black Les Pauls, dot-neck Gibson 335s and old sunburst Stratocasters. Inside, most of the tables were crowded; noisy road crews with waist-long hair, grasping double-sized burgers in their broken-nailed hands, licking their lips as they swapped wild tales of strong drugs and insatiable women while their truck windscreens gathered a fresh batch of parking tickets that Avis would send on to the record company a month later. Some hope.

The residents of the posh apartments overlooking Hyde Park were not amused: *You just can't find a spot for the Bentley since that bloody restaurant opened.* When the boys were back in town the Hard Rock Café was jumping. It was the only place in London you could get decent American-style food, the kind that so many musicians and roadies had got hooked on when they had toured the US and ate the proper burgers and shakes every diner served in those days. And . . . oh yeah . . . those takeaway boxes stuffed with desserts that would be devoured later with a joint backstage at the Rainbow Theatre, Dingwalls or the Roundhouse. Thirty years later, my tongue gets a hard-on just thinking about the strawberry cheesecake.

None of us in our wildest dreams imagined what the Hard Rock Café would become. Mind you, my sons love it and would eat every meal there or at Pizza Hut. I'm secretly proud – none of that Covent Garden nonsense, they enjoy scoffing the tasty stuff that young people can eat; forget that low-carb, low-cal, low-fat straw-like food for neurotics. I recently read an article in a glossy mag about lunch with one of those boy-band boys; how much fun would that be? He talks like he is royalty but we can all see he's just another wee nyaff. This is what the poncy git had chosen: raki crisp *pleasure*, an *entrée* of *dorsal* lamb slices (whatever the hell those are) flavoured with cumin and accompanied with a *panache* of vegetables and roasted apricot stuffed with cream, followed by the chef's *medley* of summer fruit *drizzled* with . . . I don't know . . . some sort of red shit. He is all of 19 or something. Give me a fucking break.

But this is not why we came to Amsterdam.

There are clubs in every city of the world but few better liked by musicians than the Paradiso in Weteringschans Strasse. The Hard Rock Café built its Amsterdam branch next door to it – not,

I suspect, by chance. Yeah, there's the legendary Marquee, or at least it used to be before they moved it away from Wardour Street. In Greenwich Village there's the Bottom Line Club, where the Incredible String Band did its last gig, and CBGB's where years ago I met the New York Dolls – that was some night – although I heard it's about to be relocated from the *noveau-riche* Bowery to Vegas, or any place with an affordable rent.

There's the steamy Troubadour in LA, and the wild Barrowland Ballroom in Glasgow, where your feet stick to the floor and you'll do fine just so long as you don't even glance at the bouncers. The first time I was in a club was as a wide-eyed schoolboy drooling as I watched a beat group who wore leather waistcoats, black, Cuban-heeled boots and blue checked shirts with tab-collars, in the fab cellar that was the Cavern in Liverpool. They are all great, but the Paradiso is the best.

It is so different to any other club. Since it opened in 1969, it's been run by a non-profit foundation, and there is a pleasant absence of burly bouncers with shaved heads, black jerkins and little earpieces. The club's booking manager, Jan Werner, explains it very simply. 'It is partly the responsibility of the people in the club to create a good atmosphere. If you have security staff all over the place that creates tension, and once you have created that level of tension it is very hard to reduce it.'

Sitting at the edge of a shimmering canal, the beautiful brick and timber, 19th-century building was originally a church. Jan can list hundreds of major-league bands that have performed in it, but the club, he says, is not a museum. He likes helping new acts take the first step to the big-time. Once it was the Rolling Stones, then Pink Floyd; after that came U2 and most recently Franz Ferdinand, who were so impressed by the resident sound engineer they spirited her away with them on their world tour.

Even superheroes like to fit in a gig there just for the fun of it. Jan remembers the night Prince pranced in straight from finishing a huge stadium gig and played a brilliant set, using only a few small amplifiers. It's some place.

I wandered into the club in the afternoon to watch the soundcheck, but discovered there wouldn't be one; Jerry Lee's not in the mood. I had correctly guessed which hotel the band would be staying at and got a room there and so it was that I met Jerry's long-time guitarist, Buck Hutchieson. He is a polite, softly spoken Tennessean, who remembers the days he and the original members of the Memphis Beats toured with Jerry Lee when, as he says, 'The gravy was *really* thin. We were gettin' thirty-five dollars a night and had to pay our own motels and eats.' Dorsal lamb slices were not on the menu.

We talk for a long time and he asks me to send him a copy of my book. Oh, and an old Fender Stratocaster I have at home; he'd like that too if I can spare it. He laughs, shaking my hand. I leave him chatting happily to Dutch fans and wander the short distance to the Paradiso. Inside it's packed, hot and sweaty. I'm looking forward to this.

After a while Buck wanders onto the stage, wearing a black dinner suit and shining cowboy boots. He takes his white Fender Strat out of its case and tunes up, smiling at the yelling crowd who are excitedly waiting for the show to start. The rest of the four-piece band amble on, check their tuning, then the drummer calls out a count-in and they swing into a laid-back, country-style version of 'Johnny B Goode'. Each member sings a song and then the great man, Jerry Lee, marches on to ecstatic roars. He shouts. *Hello. Well, hello!* The Paradiso is bouncing.

Halfway through the first number, Jerry Lee looks angry and suddenly crashes down the lid of the grand piano and hollers at the sound crew, *Turn it down by half!* He glares into the spotlight, picks up the song, plays another chorus then slams the piano lid again. *That's it, Ah'm done, Ah'm leavin' NOW!* Silence. Does he mean it? Surely not. He stands up, turns, then pauses and yells at the soundman. *Lower the damn volume. Ah'm getting blown away by the monitors.* There is frantic rushing about the stage as the sound guys try to pacify him. Someone does something right and he seems happier because he grins, then rolls smoothly into 'What Made Milwaukee Famous' and, Jesus, it's great.

Jerry's band has that warm country sound, that rich, thick combination of treble-bright Fender amps and Stratocasters switched to the bass pickups. One of the things about country music, and probably one of the reasons why musicians living under the hot sun of Nashville play it so well, is that sometimes you have to be able to hold back a little. You have to use the natural feel of the song to give it dynamics and not let volume or playing too fast carry it away. It's all about restraint, something that, ironically, so many country stars have spectacularly lacked when they were in the same room as whisky or drugs.

The gig roars on; there is no set list. I don't know of any other top band that goes on stage without deciding in the dressing room what songs they will play, but Buck says that no one knows what Jerry will do except Jerry; he plays whatever he feels like playing. He even plays 'Johnny B Goode', although the band did it earlier. He's 69 now, looks frail, with thinning arms and a shaky walk, but he's still the *Killer*. As soon as he finishes 'Great Balls of Fire', he lashes out his left foot with a kick like a bad-tempered mule that sends the piano stool crashing across the stage. That's it, the gig is over. Jerry Lee is outta there. The crowd chants for more, but Jerry has locked his hotel room door long before the cheers have finished.

In other venues the crowd might have become rowdy but they eventually accept he's not coming back on and quietly settle down with a drink in one of the club's bars. Some spark up a joint. The Paradiso stays open long after the main act leaves the stage. Although it holds as many as a medium-sized concert hall it doesn't herd everyone outside as soon as the hall lights go on. As Jan says, people like to relax with their friends after a show.

The next morning I hired a bike and cycled through the Vondelpark, near the Paradiso. It's a beautiful place, to the locals what Central Park is to New Yorkers. If you live in a tiny apartment it's nice to have a big park nearby. The sun was shining, the park bustling, folk relaxing, strolling along the paths, pushing prams, speaking Dutch in that sing-song accent. *Hello, how are you?* Hugs and kisses on both cheeks. Every dog kept under control by their smiling owners. The most popular bikes in Amsterdam are the old-fashioned types with the high, inward facing handlebars and the one I hired was great. I was able to cycle for hours without my creaky neck aching, as it does on a mountain bike.

I stayed for another night and went back to the Paradiso to see the legendary and ominous Dr John. Wearing a white suit and hat, he slowly limps on stage, leaning heavily on a walking cane with a silver handle. He sits at the same grand piano thrashed by Jerry Lee last night. On the top, staring at the audience, is a bleached human skull. He plays a flawless set with his band, four N'orlains swamp musicians who have in their veins voodoo forces, or juju or whatever they call it down there.

Sometimes Jan Werner gives new bands the opening spot, even when one occasionally steals his sound engineer. 'In recent years the best was Franz Ferdinand. They were excellent, like the original Rolling Stones, because each member fits and plays perfectly together. You couldn't replace any of them.'

Tonight the warm-up band is a Dutch group called T99. They play a strange mixture of Muddy Waters, Howling Wolf and surfing-style music. They know they will never headline packed stadium gigs, but they belt it out anyway. The drummer wallops his snare with a maraca, and with their screaming slide guitar on full reverb, and pounding double bass they sound like they have come from the Mississippi via Malibu beach. They are fresh, perfect for the Paradiso. The crowd enjoys hearing them and the band love being there.

Me too.

7
GLASGOW

Chuck Berry

I REALLY wanted to see the great man, even if he is rumoured to be a cantankerous old sod. When it came time for him to grace the stage of the packed Royal Concert Hall – a magnificent auditorium, and I'm not just saying that because my son worked there – I couldn't help recalling the words of the late Matt McGinn, a much-missed Glasgow folk singer. His announcement at a gig many years ago would have been equally apt tonight.

'And now, ladies and gentleman, a man who needs no introduction . . . because the bastard hasn't turned up.'

'Cos he didn't.

8

STIRLING

Wet Wet Wet

STIRLING Castle stands proudly on the sheer rock of an old volcano, overlooking one of the coolest things in the world: the Highland Boundary Fault. This is Scotland's San Andreas Fault, the line that cuts Scotland in half, the place where major tectonic plates collided 400 million years ago. The land on the north is full of soaring rocky mountains much loved by mad mountaineers, ice-skiers and gnarly rock climbers, while south of the line there are nice pleasant places to cycle or take the dog for a walk.

There can be few better places than the Castle to play an open-air gig in midsummer, when the Scottish sky seems to stay light forever. I stood on the old, worn cobblestones, staring at Dumyat, a nearby hill, remembering many times I had climbed it with my sons when they were young. We used to love it – Dumyat is one of so many ancient and mysterious Scottish mountains, it would be great to extract the stories embedded in their DNA. Still visible on it are the remains of a hill fort belonging to a warrior tribe known as the Maeatae, and the boys used to keep a wary but excited look out for any head-decapitators that might still be around. In the same way that the English Premier League keep out Rangers and Celtic, the Romans built the Antonine Wall across Scotland to make sure the Maeatae stayed very firmly on the other side.

Wet Wet Wet, one of Clydebank's last great exports, had pulled a big crowd tonight, although nothing like the 100,000 that turned up in 1869 for the opening of the nearby tower of the Wallace Monument. But that was way before *EastEnders* and *Big Brother*.

A cheer brought me out of my daydream – Wet Wet Wet had walked on stage in front of the packed crowd on the castle concourse. They were playing a reunion tour, childhood friends who had fallen out soon after having one of the biggest-selling records of all time, hurt silence for years, heroin, money and the usual stuff bands always seem to end up squabbling about.

They played until the sun dropped behind the hills and couldn't have asked for a more beautiful night – even a shooting star obligingly flashed across the sky just as they finished their set. They are a great band. Drummer Tommy Cunningham and bass player Graeme Clark are excellent, they don't overplay, keep it strong and simple. Graeme Duffin, the Wet who usually appeared at the edge of band photographs, is a virtuoso guitarist with great stage presence, like a Scottish Joe Perry. I first met him when he was 17, and even then he could play dazzling jazz solos, and all those great rhythmic chords used by the Average White Band, Meteors and James Brown.

The castle, of course, has seen troubled days with plenty of bloodshed – the most famous battle being on 11 September 1297, when William Wallace slaughtered the English army under the less than tactically aware Earl of Surrey, who overslept on the morning of the battle. He must have been on drugs – how else could he have slept knowing that he'd be fighting Wallace, a towering 6' 7" with the muscles of a WWF wrestler, considerably bigger than he was portrayed by little Mel Gibson in *Braveheart*? If

13th-century doorways, beds and suits of armour are anything to go by, in those days the average guy wouldn't have reached Wallace's chest, so the big man must have been a fearsome sight.

Wallace liked to lop off English heads with swipes of his huge sword almost as much as he enjoyed shagging any fair maiden who glanced kindly at him. He was also a lot smarter than the Earl, and watched in delight as the Englishman, rather than walk two miles along the riverbank, rashly sent his soldiers across the narrow Stirling Bridge to sort out the tiresome Scots. Wallace waited until half of them were over, blocked the bridge and cut them all to strips of kebab. There are ghosts at the castle still wondering what the fuck happened to them.

When the Wets had finished their second encore I wandered to the guest area and showed the glowering security guys my pass. They were not allowing anyone through, passes or not. I explained that I'd promised Tommy I would give him photographs that he'd asked me to bring backstage after the show. The grim-faced hulks were uninterested. Then, for no apparent reason, they began herding everyone away, including the parents of one of the band members. I couldn't help thinking about what Jan Werner had said about tension creating more tension.

I blame William Wallace.

9

GALWAY

Amos Garrett

MANY years ago I played guitar in an Irish showband. It was a lot of fun and a good way to pay your dues. The idea was simple: you played anything and everything that heavy-booted farm labourers could fling themselves around to in the village halls of the Emerald Isle, or Irish clubs in Scotland. The band leader had moved to Glasgow to keep a low profile when a not-insignificant amount of money had gone missing after some gigs in Ireland. He was a softly-spoken gentleman when sober but when he got his big, meaty hands on a bottle of whisky it was a countdown to mayhem. You quickly learned not to stand within punching distance or leave your Stratocaster unguarded if there was a pawnshop nearby. Eventually he disappeared to Liverpool or somewhere, trying to stay one town ahead of heavyset debt collectors. He was an excellent musician but had become, as one of the band used to say in his thick Belfast accent, *too fond of the drink*.

The drummer was either a wild extrovert or just a lunatic, I don't know which, and once played an entire gig stark naked, for reasons known only to himself. We also had a talented but strange trumpet player. He liked to personally attend to the desires of his flesh. A lot. Eventually his wife noticed that he rarely seemed to want what she called his *conjugular rights*. The tossing had to stop. One day he complained that he could no longer go to the bathroom without her following him. She would stand outside, stare grimly at her watch for precisely 120 seconds, then bang on the door. It was no longer a sanctuary where he could pass a peaceful five minutes with a lively magazine; if he wanted to read any of his filth it had better be where she could see his hands.

This lot was my first professional band.

A typical weekend would have us playing a pub job on Friday night until closing time at ten, then heaving all the equipment into our battered Transit van, amps still steaming, drum kit still set up. We'd pile in as much alcohol as we could steal, then race to an after-hours Irish club in the Gorbals. As soon as we got there we rushed up five flights of stairs carrying all the equipment; we had to start no later than eleven or the club boss would cut our money. He wasn't a man to argue with. I am sure that he had hijacked a derelict hall – part of the building had gaping holes in the roof and pigeons often flew over our heads. There was no heating – the stage felt as cold as a ledge on the north face of the Eiger. In winter we had to wear coats. We had to play for the next five hours without stopping or ferocious fighting would break out. It was brilliant.

One night as we hurtled to the club there was a smell of burning in the van and before our sozzled brains could register what was happening, flames were leaping around our feet. Some drunk, careless idiot – me – had dropped a lighted match onto the brown paper bags that held the precious bevvy. The trumpet player began frantically stamping on them as the bass player yelled *save the fooking whuskey fur fook's sake.*

The Irish club paid well, but there was some kind of hierarchy in the band where the older members seized more of the gig money than the 19-year-old drummer and me, but I still pocketed £35 for a weekend's work. In those days, most professional musicians in Scotland also registered as unemployed and signed on at the local buroo, not only to pick up extra cash but also to avoid the attention of the taxman. My dole money, by comparison, was £9 a week.

When the bass player was himself and not on the rampage wrecking everything and anyone in his path, there was a great atmosphere in the band and we used to play a bouncy little tune called 'Galway Bay'. It wasn't supposed to be bouncy, it was a hopelessly sentimental song apparently written for navvies swinging their pickaxes on building sites far from the *ould countray*. It summoned images of the moonrise over Claddagh, the women in the meadows making hay while the menfolk sat beside turf fires watching barefoot goosoons at their play, whatever they might be. We played the song at breakneck speed because there was less head-butting during fast dances.

I'd never been to Galway; I had known people who had but they were either Irish folk living in Glasgow who were making their annual pilgrimage to see relatives, or kids with parents who liked posh holiday destinations. When I was a boy, most Glaswegians, if they were lucky enough to afford a holiday, went to Rothesay or Millport – Millopuerto – on the Costa Clyde or, as my family sometimes did, rented a holiday hut in a muddy Ayrshire field.

It looked just like a POW camp. The highlight of the week was when the horse-drawn jobby cart slowly meandered up and down the rows of cabins to collect the contents of the toilet bucket belonging to each hut. The happy campers would watch, laughing as rosy-cheeked farm lads emptied the pails into the cart. The children loved it. But in school there would always be some rich kid whose parents would take them youth hostelling in the Highlands, or cycling in Galway and, because it was across the sea, it sounded like the most exotic place in the world.

I decided to go when I had the opportunity to see guitar master Amos Garrett play the annual arts festival and managed to get a very cheap flight – about £25 including taxes – with British Airways. It felt like being on a private jet, there were only four other passengers and it was good of BA not to cancel the flight; it must have cost them a fortune. They even served us a light but satisfying lunch followed by a choice of tea or coffee.

By comparison with neat and tidy Holland, when flying over Ireland I couldn't help noticing that the fields look a shambles, all sorts of shapes and sizes scattered everywhere, like massive ink-blot tests. I suppose they look that way because they have been bought and sold through centuries of complicated land sales, and losing hands at drunken games of cards.

At Galway airport there is large sign: *Failte Chuig Aerophart Na Gaillmhe*. Or something similar. The Gaelic is an ancient tongue; some say that it was carried here from biblical lands. So it's safe to assume that those travellers in long-gone times didn't get here in a Boeing 747. Perhaps the people who make up these pseudo-Gaelic words think that *Aerophart* gives the language a nice modern feel.

Eire is a member of the European Union and no country has milked that cash cow more successfully. The Irish are crafty when it comes to picking up regional development grants and stuff – it is good to see how well they have done out of it. One of the little impositions of Brussels is that the currency is now the euro, something that has caused many dear old rural-dwelling Irish grannies no end of confusion. Outside the arrivals hall – actually at Galway airport there's really only one hall that pretty much does everything including, I suspect, holding ceilidhs at the weekend – I asked a smiling, rosy-cheeked, pleasantly plump cab driver how much it would cost to go to the Warwick Hotel in which Amos and the band would be playing that night.

'That would be twenty-three euros,' said he.

'Sorry, I've only got twenty on me,' said I.

'Aye well then, that will be enough,' grinned he.

I liked him.

On the way, I asked about the Gaelic road signs we were passing every few moments and he sighed. 'It's a load of fooking nonsense. No one knows what the fook they mean. Aye – and oi've lived here all me fooking days. Who the fook are these signs for?'

As we drove, I noticed all the usual names – PC World, Mercedes, Kentucky Fried Chicken, McDonald's – and wondered if I was 20 years too late to see the Galway Bay of the song, but what the hell, the Irish are entitled to a bit of prosperity. The cost of homes has rocketed; as we drove into the picturesque town centre, the taxi driver pointed to a tall, narrow little house that had gone for... he spluttered... *over a million fooking euros, for fook's sake. It's fooking madness, it is.*

Like almost everywhere, Galway has become a worryingly expensive place to live. Homes and rents cost as much as in UK cities and this is wiping out traditional jobs. I remember seeing a TV programme about generations of locals who used to earn a modest living by collecting lavender. This is impossible now. I mean just how many of those wee scented bags would you need to sell to pay an £800 a month mortgage, for Christ sake?

The view over the bay to the gently rolling hills of County Claire is endearing. The way they rise out of a soft mist brushes a chord in your heart and you can't imagine anything but a peaceful life far from the troubles of the world. I asked the cab driver about marching bands and violence. *Ah now, they have nothing to do with us here in Galway.*

It was a beautiful day, the sun hot above the bay, sky a satisfying blue, the sea sparkling, so clean you could see white sand and rocks deep below the surface.

He sighed. 'Aye, we do get a fair drop of rain here, but today's lovely.'

We soon reached the Warwick. The cab driver gave me a card with his phone number and I promised I'd call him next morning for a ride back to the airport.

The Warwick has been a well-known gig for 25 years and has seen some wild nights. Gold discs awarded to Robbie Williams hang on the wall but I'm not sure if he'd played there or the manager had just bought them on eBay.

I wanted to see Amos Garrett because he has played on over 200 records; I guess almost everyone over the age of 30 will have heard something by him, such as his playing on Maria Muldaur's 'Midnight at the Oasis', a piece of string-bending brilliance that Stevie Wonder described as the best guitar solo ever recorded. He was also part of the musicians' and artists' community that lived at Woodstock – John Sebastian, Bob Dylan and the Band, all these guys – before he moved to LA to play with the Paul Butterfield Blues Band. There was nothing that a few penicillin tabs couldn't cure in those days – it was a wonderful time to be young and playing in a Californian band.

He now lives in Canada and when he is not gigging, he spends his time in the vast wilderness, training dogs, hunting and fishing – a life he says is summed up by his favourite quote from an old explorer: *I love to ride a good horse into new country.* For this tour he had teamed up with his old pal Jim Condie, a great slide-guitarist who has played on many records and television soundtracks and is often described as Britain's Ry Cooder. He's a quiet, modest guy, somehow managing to pick up a living doing gigs here and there, including a spell with Van Morrison, and occasionally teaching guitar in his Glasgow flat near Hampden Park. I first met him years ago when he was playing in a 12-piece blues/soul band in Edinburgh that people used to travel from all over the country to hear, one of the best bands in the UK at the time.

Amos had recruited one of the most highly travelled drummers in the UK, Ted McKenna, who has played with Rory Gallagher, Michael Shechter, Gary Moore, and the Sensational Alex Harvey Band, who were, when I saw them in 1975 at the Hammersmith Odeon, the loudest group I have ever heard. *MY MY MY, DELILAH!!!* My ears have never been the same since.

The bass player is Alan Thompson, one of the finest in the world, on a par with Kenny Gradney of Little Feat. Yeah, there's tons of flash-meisters, jazzers and thumb-slappers, and very talented they are too, but playing with subtlety and rhythm is a whole different thing. Alan has been playing since he was a teenager in a little band in Glasgow. One day a guy poked his head into the garage they were rehearsing in and told them he needed a bass player immediately for a British tour. It was John Martyn; Alan has been touring the world with him ever since. He has also played with Rick Wakeman, Andy Summers and Pentangle, and wrote the B-side of Robert Palmer's 'Addicted to Love'. So I was going to see four top-notch players tonight. I was looking forward to it.

But first a stroll round town.

I met up with the band and we headed off for a bite to eat. Despite their undoubtedly vast knowledge of cosmopolitan cuisine, their choice of restaurant was the local chip shop. It would be nice to say that the cod, chips and mushy peas were a tribute to Irish culinary skills, but it would be a lie. You might have enjoyed it had you been at the end of a 14-pint Guinness session, or shivering after a wet day ploughing fields, but I wasn't and it was horrible. Soggy chips floating in vinegar, watered down brown sauce, enough grease to lubricate a tractor.

I suppose the thing about fast food is that it has to be that. When you think of the number of people in any big town clamouring to be fed, all at the same moment, there isn't time for fancy cooking, but God knows what those poor wee fishes did to deserve a fate like that. Working musicians, on top of their wages, are usually paid a small daily allowance – food money – and most pride themselves on eating within that budget so they don't feel they are having to use their own money to do the tour, even if it means occasionally eating stuff that tastes like toxic waste.

Galway is a merry place and loves festivals; it held 24 between April and October. Many of them are the usual things: art, music and literature extravaganzas, rural things like horse racing and pony shows. It also hosted the National Ploughing Championships, a three-day spectacular of . . . eh . . . ploughing fields. It drew a crowd of 66,000 enraptured spectators on a wet Tuesday, followed by a staggering 67,000 on the Wednesday, but a comparatively paltry 45,000 on the final spellbinding day. The *Irish Examiner* reported this, perhaps slightly optimistically, as a total of 180,000 people. Even so, these numbers are far more than the crowd at most Premier League football matches, and Bono might be a tad dismayed that more people turned up to watch tractors churning up muddy fields than his gig at Dublin.

The arts week was in full swing with the usual array of

buskers, acrobats, gypsies selling Celtic jewellery made out of bits of leather and shells, and – my favourite – a grinning middle-aged buffoon prancing around with a cardboard banjo on which he'd written *PLINK PLONK*. A lifetime of Guinness and cheap fish suppers will do that to you.

I went for a wander to keep out of the way while the band did their soundcheck. There seemed to be a huge number of Polish girls, with lovely accents but not the soft, lilting *craic* I thought I'd hear, serving in bars, working in hotels and coffee shops, or just rattling collection cans for some obscure charity; someone must be making a nice living by hiring out Eastern European workers.

When Amos and the band went on, it was in front of far too small a crowd, which was a pity. I thought a lot of people would be interested to hear such good players in a small gig. They have that warm, twangy American guitar sound, and Amos does the big string bends for which he is famous, locking his finger onto the third string and pushing it way across the fretboard, making it sound like a pedal-steel guitar on a Hawaiian beach. Gradually more people arrived and stayed, staring open-mouthed, but it was a shame that the place wasn't packed. Amos is such a top quality player; he may be getting on in years, but he plays his old customised Telecaster better than ever.

If you are a professional footballer you hit a peak at around 28, then it's an ever-steepening downhill road to the pub and being bought pints by strangers who want you to tell them all about your glory days. If you are a good musician your playing gets better every year, but if you haven't cracked it by the age of 28 the chances are, at least as far as world fame is concerned, for you it's over. There are a few exceptions, like the guy in Franz Ferdinand who was about 30 when he hit the big time, but not many. That's not to say you'll spend the rest of your days pulling pints or selling double glazing; if you know the right people you will always be able to find a gig, even haul down some reasonable money if you are lucky enough to land the right tour. But no matter how good you are, when your youthful looks have faded, the chances are that you have got as far as you are ever going to get and that's that.

After the gig, Ted talked about the terrible 1980's when some awful music dominated the charts; all that computer-keyboard shit and smarmy singers with voices like snake-oil salesmen. Musicians who had been used to basking in the sunshine of ovations from massive crowds in Madison Square Gardens suddenly couldn't find anything but pub and wedding gigs. Unknown to many happy couples, the band the agency sent to play at their receptions often had some ex-big-name muzos, unrecognisable in smart beards, short hair and dinner suits, guys that only a few years before had played at Earls Court and packed festivals but were now grateful to pick up £100 for grinding out 'Lady in Red', the 'Birdie Song' and the 'Slosh'.

Next morning, the hotel manager told me the taxi fare should only be twelve euros so I didn't call the guy from yesterday and took the cab the hotel arranged. The driver was equally entertaining and informative and he also told me about the *fooking million fooking euros that some lunatic* had paid for the little house in town.

As we passed the harbour, I asked him if Galway is a thriving port and he groaned. 'Aye, well now, it should be. But they made a *shoite* of it. They decided to build a container terminal, got this huge fooking crane built, then couldn't find anyone to drive the fooker. Then they finally got someone who could and along comes the first boatload of fooking containers. And the fooker couldn't get in the harbour. Some fooking *genius* had forgotten to measure the gap at the fooking entrance. It would have been too big a job to rebuild the fooking harbour so they just closed the thing down. They made a roight scuttur of it. Aye – they kept fooking quiet about the money *that* cost.'

The fare was €23. Oh well. Back at the airport I wandered into the café and the first person I saw was the cab driver from yesterday. He greeted me like an old pal and I apologised for not calling him. He smiled and told me not to think of it, he'd got another hire to bring out here anyway.

What a great fooking place.

10

OXFORD

Anthrax

NOW this is going to take a bit of explaining. Where do I start? Maybe if I take it easy, put the words together nice and slow, but there's so many of them bursting at once in my head that it's like holding back the blast from an explosion.

I've just seen Anthrax for the first time.

It's crazy, ludicrous. Here I was – am – a middle-aged fart who thought he knew a thing or two and I see Anthrax and suddenly my smug world has changed and I don't know whether to feel glad or not. Wait. I need to try to sleep properly for the first time in three days and in the morning, maybe. . .

As their name suggests, Anthrax are not a cute boy-band. It was an accident that had led me to them. The Daily Mail had done a feature on my first book, which was a great buzz, and they had sent along a photographer, Andy Buchanan, to take my pic. We got along well and he mentioned that he worked for Anthrax, travelling with them on tour and shooting live pics for their website. When I mentioned I was writing a book about touring bands it seemed a lucky coincidence and he put me in touch with them.

After a few emails I arranged to meet them at a gig in Oxford and they very kindly agreed to let me travel with them on their tour bus to their next scene of controlled chaos, a big outdoor festival they were headlining in Belgium. I was looking forward to it; sounded like a lot of fun. There was a cheap flight from Galway to Luton with an Irish airline so all I had to do was figure out a way of getting from there to Oxford. I studied the numerous baffling websites linked to Luton airport, but you can only spend so much of your life tapping away at the computer. Besides, it hurts my bloody neck. I decided to see what happened when I landed. Transport links from a London airport should be easy. Right? Yeah . . . right.

At Luton, surly and smirking cab drivers muttered prices from £70 to £130. No thanks. Various bus companies were peddling their wares from stands inside the airport so I decided to try my luck at one of them. After a worrying queue behind unfortunate foreign travellers who were reaching varying states of agitation trying to understand how the hell they could get from one place to another, the sales lady asked me where I was going.

'Oxford? You want to go *where?*' She looked at me as if I was out of my mind and laughed with a throaty, phlegm-rich guffaw, rocking back and forth in her chair, then turned to some cleaners who were leaning on brushes nearby.

'Oi, this ignorant Scottish git, this porage-eating, haggis-munching jock wants to go to bleedin' Oxford. *Oxford!*' Or words to that effect.

She wiped a tear from her eye and glanced at me as if she was about to pee herself, then grunted in a rasping baritone voice, 'You need to go into London first and change there.' She held out her bony hand. 'That'll be thirty-two pounds.'

'And how long will it take?'

She swivelled her eyes as though this was the sort of thing only a dumb Scot from the peat bogs of the far north would ask. There might be many things in the world she gave a shit about but this clearly wasn't one of them.

'About six hours.' She looked beyond me to the next person in line. 'Maybe more...'

Bloody hell. Anthrax would have finished playing by then. I'd miss the gig and their tour bus. I decided to take a cab, knowing with a sinking feeling that whatever I was told it would cost I'd end up in yet another street brawl over the final fare with the driver, usually some chunky-ringed, medallion-laden spiv in a rattling old Ford Escort.

As a last hope I asked a very helpful guy at the lastminute.com desk.

'Oxford? No problem, sir. You take the Virgin bus to Milton Keynes and change there. You'll be in Oxford in under two hours. I can issue you with tickets but I'd have to charge you a booking fee. You'd be cheaper just paying on the bus.' He smiled and pointed to where it would be waiting outside.

I've often navigated through impenetrable darkness, blizzards and murky mist on dangerous and remote mountains, but trying to find a bloody great bus with a huge number on it, parked on a bright, sunny concourse fills me with panic. I get wound up no matter how often I do it; I am the same with all travel connections. My sons find this entertaining, like the time I was hopping from one foot to the other, constantly glancing at my watch and staring up the track as we waited for a train from Ghent to Brussels. I panicked as usual and threw our cases onto the first one that arrived even though it was clearly going in the wrong direction. I just get agitated, OK?

I managed to spot the correct bus with its welcoming driver, smiling as he helped passengers with their cases. He spoke with a lilting Punjabi accent. 'There's about a ten-minute wait at Milton Keynes, then you'll get your connection to Oxford. Rather than buy a ticket for each journey you'd be cheaper with a day pass. It's only six pounds.'

I could have hugged him.

I have to fess up to it, as the current expression has it, when I first planned to include Anthrax in this book it was for a cheap laugh. I wanted a heavy metal outfit in here; there's so many of those bands playing all that devil's riff stuff. Wait a minute; maybe I should explain that.

In the Middle Ages, the Catholic Church took music pretty damn seriously. Go to a piano and play a C followed by an F sharp. Hear that? The church reckoned that interval was demonic and banned it from all music. They called it the devil's interval or devil's notes – believed it could conjure up demons and all that happy crap. No kidding. When it came to eternal damnation, purgatory, Satan, Beelzebub, wee imps, demons with lashing tails, the bloodshot eyes of the undead and that stuff, they had absolutely no sense of humour.

Walk one trembling step further into the haunted realm of darkness. Play a C, then the same note an octave higher, then F sharp. If you had done that in public 800 years ago the chances are you would have found yourself trussed up, piled on top of a bonfire, pissing in your pants as the priests dropped flaming torches at your feet. I bullshit thee not.

Heavy metal bands play this sequence of notes over and over again in a deafening wall of sound. And as if the volume they play it isn't overwhelming enough, the bass players detune their bottom strings to produce even lower-frequency notes that don't half make the metal plate in my neck vibrate.

I'd never taken heavy metal seriously, always reckoned it was just old Led Zep and Black Sabbath riffs played louder and faster, a combination of bam and glam, by guys dressed in outfits straight from comic books. What kind of music needed the guitarists to wear leather masks and chains and all sorts of crap before anyone would listen to them? How could anyone take all that stuff seriously? The whole thing seemed a joke, easy meat for a writer to take the piss.

But that was before I heard Anthrax.

I climbed on the bus and after a pleasant journey along leafy country roads it pulled into Oxford. I hunted for a Borders bookshop where I could get strong coffee and see if they had my book in stock. I worked for years in sales and once a hustler always a hustler. The assistant quickly led me to a shelf where there were three copies, which I proudly autographed, grinning when he put *Signed by the Author* stickers on them. God, that felt good! I had a triple-shot cappuccino, easy on the milk, don't drown it, then wandered over to Waterstone's. They had my book listed on their computer and I eagerly clicked my pen, but someone must have nicked all their copies because they couldn't find any. Oh well.

I'd been passing an hour or so while I waited for a call from Scott Ian, guitarist and founder of Anthrax. My phone rang. They were at the Eagle and Child, a pub that features somewhere in Tolkien's books. Scott loves *Lord of the Rings* and wanted a quiet pint in the bar. He likes Harry Potter too – not something I associated with the waves of destruction of heavy metal. Perhaps JK's next book should be *Harry Bites the Head off a Fucking Bat*.

I wandered along the bustling street in glorious sunshine and met Scott, drummer Charlie Benante and bass player Frank Bello as they were leaving the bar. They look like typical American rock musicians but, except for the occasional fan asking for their autographs or to shake hands, they didn't attract the stares they might have done years ago. When the first Jimi Hendrix photograph appeared in the UK, some people took one look at his frizzy hair and ranted about him as if he was the antichrist; compared with rock musicians today he looked like an accountant.

Scott has a shaved head and a long, thick goatee beard; he is wearing shorts and a vest and has tattoos covering his arms and legs. Frank is handsome, has long flowing hair, is wearing sunglasses, tee shirt, faded Levis. Charlie has a stubbly beard and dark, unkempt hair and keeps stopping to stare at the beautiful buildings surrounding us. There's a scattering of the architectural boils that arrived in the 1960's, but most of the buildings in Oxford's bustling streets are from calmer times. Even the council offices appear to be a haven of peaceful study. Wherever I look there are leaded-glass windows behind which gentle academics must be pondering the timeless mysteries of life. Or perhaps just downloading porn. It's nice to be in a town that has character; it's so different from many concrete city centres, a lovely place to stroll on a warm and sunny afternoon.

I asked Scott if they had done their soundcheck.

'Naw, we don't bother, our road crew does them for us. It always sounds different when the crowd is in anyway. We never do them.'

This was more like it, that heavy metal attitude. To hell with spending hours fiddling with knobs and monitor levels. Just go for it.

Scott started Anthrax in Queens, New York, in 1981. At the time, heavy metal music was an underground cult; nobody would book them. Scott rented church basements, put on gigs and friends would come. Word got around fast. He reckons the media have always been hostile to heavy metal – when techno-music enjoyed a brief moment in the spotlight some of the music press loved gloating that bands like Anthrax and Metallica were doomed to failure.

I don't know why I never listened to heavy metal. I guess when I was younger I was too busy trying to pay the mortgage, bring up my kids and run my company, or perhaps all the paraphernalia and body art put me off. Sometimes guys that worked for me would turn up on a Monday morning, their arms lavishly tattooed with fire-breathing demons, chains freshly drilled through their nostrils and dowel pins inserted in their still-bleeding ear lobes and I'd have to explain to them that even though they were nice removal men they were frightening the customers. Then there was head banging. The sight of all those crazed kids swinging their noggins back and forth – I mean, come on . . . it was a joke, right?

I'd always reckoned the 1980's was a dark decade in music. It seemed to be a choice between brain-melting guitar riffs or smarmy crooners. One minute we had The Who, Zappa, Stones, Hendrix and Cream, and just as we were thinking that they had built the solid foundations on which music could only keep getting better we suddenly had Haircut 100, Flock of Seagulls and Tenpole bloody Tudor.

Anthrax have come a long way since their early days rehearsing in freezing rooms and have a massive worldwide following; they've sold more than 10 million records. Any business that starts from nothing and has turned over, I guess, at least a quarter of a billion dollars, is very successful by any measurement. In an industry that has always preferred bands that release catchy tunes and advertising jingles, Anthrax is unlikely to be pick of the week on Terry Wogan's show or fight off requests from *Hello* to photograph their weddings.

The band has been around the world – how many times is it?

They stopped counting after 50 tours and 32 countries. Scott loves to travel, enjoys getting to know cities thousands of miles from downtown LA where he lives. Paris is one of his favourites; he feels at home there. As a kid growing up in Queens he used to stare across the East River to the lights of Manhattan, couldn't wait to ride alone into the big city, find his way around by himself. When he talks there's no bullshit; he's seen and done it all but never tries to impress anyone. He doesn't wave his arms around or tell tall tales, he speaks quietly and articulately; you could be having a chat over a fence with your next-door neighbour.

Tonight's gig is at the Zodiac Club, a much smaller venue than they would usually play. They are almost at the end of a six-week tour headlining huge venues all over Europe and had a few spare nights so they decided to throw in a gig – a party really – for some of their fans.

And I'd never even heard them.

It's been a hard tour covering a lot of road miles and the band are looking a little tired as they sit in the small, hot dressing room, picking at snacks and fruit. They are slim, don't look like they eat very much. Scott is about to do a radio interview with a likeable little guy who looks like the midget on that old Doors album cover. Heavily tattooed and wearing his favourite ripped Anthrax tee shirt, he has prepared reams of questions.

He switches on his digital recorder. 'Tonight I'm delighted to have with me Scott Ian of Anthrax. OK, Scott, going back to nineteen-eighty, to the very beginning . . .' he starts confidently.

Scott looks at the wad of paper, thick as a telephone directory, and smiles. 'You want to go over the last twenty-five years in twenty minutes?'

About half an hour before the band is due on stage, singer

Joey Belladonna and guitarist Dan Spitz wander into the dressing room, they've been for a quiet dinner somewhere. Both of them left the band 10 years ago, this is a reunion tour and they are enjoying being back on the road. Joey has been playing in his own band around New York State; he is slim, tanned, with long, tumbling dark hair and the sort of rock star good looks that the spotlight will pick up and carry all the way to the back of the hall.

Dan is a tiny guy with a pointy little beard and gold-framed glasses, which he holds up to the light and meticulously cleans. It takes him about five minutes to get the lenses just right, polishing, examining them, finding a little smudge of grease and repolishing. Then he takes off his shirt; he has a superbly toned, muscular body, surfer abs and stacked shoulders. He got it that way by following a strict daily routine doing precise exercises with heavy rubber cables; nothing Dan undertakes is done haphazardly.

When he left the band, he gave away all 53 of his guitars, put music out of his mind altogether and turned his attention to becoming a master watchmaker, eventually being invited to Switzerland on a scholarship at the jewellers' equivalent of Harvard. When he qualified, he had become the only American licensed to service the most expensive watches in the world. I am looking forward to hearing him play; chances are that anyone who pays that much attention to precision is going to be playing some stunning guitar. He glances at my watch, an old stainless steel Rolex that I bought years ago and that I'm very fond of, but which got beat up on climbing trips.

'Hey, nice watch, man.'

'Yeah, but it's not right. I can hear something rattling inside it.'

'Let me see.'

I hand him it, he takes off his glasses and examines it.

'Yeah, it's the automatic winding mechanism. I have my tools in the bus outside. I'll take a look at it later.'

This is not what I expected of a heavy metal band that has released albums called *Spreading the Disease* and *Fistful of Metal*. I asked him if he is glad to be touring again. His eyes steady, he speaks quietly.

'It's time to destroy people once again.'

What the hell have I let myself in for?

Charlie sits quietly in the corner by himself and starts warming up, tapping rhythms on a rubber drum pad. Frank sips a Diet Coke, tries to open the window a little more; it's getting very hot in here and sweat begins to glisten on a large tattoo on his arm, a drawing of his murdered brother. Six months earlier CNN reported:

> *COLUMBUS, Ohio. December 8. A 25-year-old man stormed the stage at a heavy metal rock concert in a night club Wednesday night, shooting and killing Pantera guitarist 'Dimebag Darrell' Abbott and three others. . .*

I decide to leave the dressing room and keep a safe distance while the band get revved up, ready to go on. In a few moments, I imagine they'll be putting on leather warrior outfits and hitting exotic chemicals, hoovering up lines of speed, or sucking on superfat doobies, even though there's no sign of anything stronger than a cold Budweiser. As the start time of 9pm nears, bottles of single malt are unopened; nobody has lit even a cigarette. I'd told a few friends I was coming here and left details of my next of kin; they'd all wished me luck.

So where's the mayhem?

Outside the dressing room a short passageway leads to a

door into the hall. I'd decided to go to the back of the crowd to listen to the band - one thing for sure, it was going to be mighty loud. As soon as I open the door a huge wave of heat swamps me. The place is packed, absolutely crammed. No way through.

A few weeks earlier I'd been to see Oasis, a band I really liked, but, Christ, the crowd . . . every one of them seemed out of their minds on cheap wine, sulph and ecstasy. It felt that a face-slashing was only a few chords away. Tonight, the crowd are packed far tighter, the atmosphere is like a nuclear generator. Deep, growling riffs hammer from the speakers, the hall is sauna hot and pulsating with energy, almost everyone is dressed in black.

There's a heavy steel barrier across the front, bolted solidly to the floor. The soundman's father has come to see the band, and he's standing at the side, a worried expression on his face. He points towards four beefy, sweating security guys, muscular arms, hands on hips, standing behind the barrier, between the packed crowd and the stage. He shakes his head and says, 'They'll earn their money tonight.'

Was the club in Ohio just like this?

I go back to the dressing room; the door is open so I glance in to see what's happening. I can feel the buzz from outside, can hear the loud hum of the crowd but in the dressing room all is calm, just Joey doing voice exercises and Charlie hammering the drum pad.

A photographer is in the corridor, checking his digital cameras. He works for a Chinese heavy metal magazine. He tells me the band is very big in Beijing. 'Anthrax are great to photograph. So many bands are a pain. Most of them only let you take pictures during the first three songs and you mustn't use flash.'

'Bands only allow pictures during the first three songs?'

'Yeah . . . that's the usual rule. You're allowed the first three then you have to fuck off.'

'But why is that, and why no flash?'

'Well, I guess they want to look their best. As the gig goes on they sweat a lot and can look tired, and flash shows up all their lines and wrinkles, makes them look old. Some of the big stars, especially the older ones, won't even let you near the stage. You're only allowed to shoot them using a very long lens from the sound desk at the back of the hall so that it softens their features.'

'What about Anthrax?'

'Naw, they're cool. They don't care, they don't have all that bullshit.'

I keep glancing into the dressing room. *Where's all the leather and chains and make-up?* I remembered seeing Kiss in Tampa. They were dressed like an intergalactic circus show, more make-up than Coco the Clown. But Anthrax are wearing the same shorts and tee shirts they came in. Not a drop of stage paint.

This is not what I expected.

Then suddenly it's showtime. The crowd roars. The band run on stage.

And then it happened.

11

BRUSSELS

Anthrax

CHRIS is an old road dog. He's seen it all in his 27 years as a roadie, or tech to use his job title; drum tech to be exact. He's been around the world countless times – guys who find their lives on road crews are like the buccaneers of yore, always restless, constantly on the move. If, like Chris, they are from New Jersey – *Noo Joisey* – then expect no mercy; if you can't take the banter you're in the wrong job.

We're sitting upstairs on the ferry from Dover to Calais. Scott, Frank and Charlie from the band; Chris and the other guys from the Anthrax road crew. Oxford is hours behind and we're heading for Belgium. It's some bleary-eyed hour; I don't know . . . maybe 4am. The tour bus is locked up below deck; the ship's stewards don't let anyone up or down once the boat has pulled out of port. The ferry company prefer that their passengers pass the voyage within easy spending distance of the bars and gaming machines.

Chris is bored. He looks around the near-empty lounge. His gaze locks on young Tom, the most recent recruit to the Anthrax family, the new guy who works the onstage monitors.

'Well, Tom. *Tommy boy*. How long ya been on the road? Six months, huh? Getting to be a real veteran, yeah?'

Tom grimaces and tries to ignore him. Chris grins and tosses an empty bottle at him; it's plastic, it won't hurt.

'So ya learned all your stuff from *books*, Tommy boy? Straight outa *college*, ain't ya, Tommy Boy?' Chris laughs and we wait to see Tom react. He has to learn not to rise to the bait, it's just banter to help pass the hours.

'Fuck off.'

'*Whoah*, Tommy. Now that's not nice. Hey, *Tommy boy*, that was your mom and dad at the gig tonight, wasn't it?' Chris's eyes are locked on his prey now.

'You know it was.'

'Well, Tommy boy, just imagine what they're doing right now. In a big bed in their hotel room. Just picture them, Tommy. Can you see them doing it?' Chris laughs.

'Fuck off, you cunt.'

Everyone laughs. And so another 10 minutes of the journey drifts by.

After a while, I ask Chris what other bands he's worked for.

'Aw shit, I dunno. Been doing it so long I forget. So many. There's one American tour I been told I did that I don't remember a single night. I been with this band a long time.' He stares in the air for a moment, yawns, takes off his cap and runs his fingers through his long hair, then glances at his hand as though it has been bitten. 'Aw yeah . . . I do recall doing one with Aerosmith.'

'How was it?'

'Shit. The Aerosmith *po-leece* were looking out for us to keep us in line. The *band* had stopped doing drugs and drinking so the whole fucking crew had to do the same. No one was allowed to do anything. Fucking pussies.'

Whatever story he tells, even if the band have heard it a hundred times before, they tune in all over again. There's always someone like Chris with a touring band. If you want to spot him just look which way the chairs are facing, see who everyone is listening to. But don't let his manic laugh and jaunty denim cap fool you; he is highly skilled. There's nothing he can't do with a drum kit: build it, take it down real quick, tune it – a difficult job that many drummers haven't a clue how to do. Every night he sets the drum mikes just so, he knows exactly how Charlie wants it to sound. He bolts each drum at precisely the height and angle Charlie likes. He can fix anything, can even re-chrome the hardware if that's what's needed. Guys like Chris are in short supply these days.

Charlie and Frank have bought shit-flavoured coffee at the self-service counter and they offer everyone a taste. No one fancies trying it. Scott slumps back in a deep chair, gazes at the milky dawn light slowly filtering through the windows, then closes his eyes. Everyone is tired, but Chris keeps us laughing. The boat is quiet; apart from a gaggle of girls on a school trip, it's pretty much deserted. They're stabbing their pink coloured phones, sending and receiving a constant stream of texts, and, judging by their Robbie Williams and Justin Timberlake ringtones, they're probably not heavy metal fans. Perhaps it's just as well: *Hi, Mum, we're on a ferry with Anthrax. They have a really cool bus with beds. One of their roadies is really funny.*

At last the boat meanders into Calais and we are allowed below deck to the tour bus where Joey and Dan are fast asleep. They'd decided to catch up on sleep; what the hell, ferries hardly ever sink. As we pile into the bus, the driver asks Scott what time the band can check into their hotel, the Sheraton at Brussels airport.

'Twelve,' Scott answers. 'How long will it take you to drive there?'

'About three hours.'

Scott glances at his watch. 'It's only seven o'clock. That will get us there too early.'

'Do you want me to stop somewhere?'

'No, just drive slowly. We can only sleep if the bus is moving. The minute you stop we all wake up. Just keep it moving.'

As we left Oxford, Dan told me that at home he can never sleep, never settles down much before four in the morning, but on a tour bus he can sleep 10 hours straight, as long as the damn thing is moving. It's like being a baby in a pram, that reassuring rocking motion as the bus rolls along the highway.

Summer is festival season, and all over Europe bands are coasting along motorways from gig to gig. Support bands are crammed alongside their beat-up guitar cases trying to grab a few hours shut-eye in little minibuses; some of them even carry tents and camp backstage at the gigs. Headline bands like Anthrax are sleeping soundly in air-conditioned tour buses. All of them quietly moving through the twilight hours from one huge festival stage to the next.

Tour buses have been used in America since jazz orchestras first took to the road. Some were comfortable, others were torture, sweat-boxes with oily clattering engines and wooden seats, bouncing along rutted, dusty roads to gigs in little towns in Georgia and Tennessee. I once read about a guy who played guitar for Muddy Waters and did so many road miles in a cheap bus that by time he was halfway through the tour he could hardly sit because he had haemorrhoids like plums.

In America, bands live in tour buses for months at a time; nowadays they are air-conditioned, luxurious, cheaper than hotels and flights, and a much easier way of covering the long road miles. In the UK, despite the short distances between towns, rental costs are much more expensive and only bands with the backing of major record labels can afford them. I once managed to see inside BB King's bus – it's like a presidential palace. Little Feat always hire the same driver and gleaming red bus. You can see it at the back door of any of their gigs, it's home to them. If you are ever in Nashville and want to see what kind of luxury big bucks will buy, go to the parking lot behind the Ryman auditorium or Grand Ole Opry when someone like Toby Keith or Dolly Parton is playing and ask the driver for a quick look inside.

Anthrax's bus is very comfortable. On the upper deck it has deep couches, television, DVD player, CD player and a bar. Downstairs is a kitchen and two long rows of curtained-off bunk beds, like the inside of a submarine. But apparently this is not one of the higher-spec jobs; the band is staying at hotels most of the tour. The road crew use the bus more than the band, they have to get to the gigs early to set up the equipment. Once the band has been dropped off at the Sheraton, the crew will head straight for the festival site and start work.

There is a little toilet at the back of the bus, so I nip in for a pee. It smells like a tent for geriatric elephants. It's not the band's fault; for some reason it has no ventilation. In the TV show *The Osbournes*, there is a touching scene where young Kelly tells Sharon she doesn't want to go on a cruise ship because she can't manage for a week without going to the bathroom. Sharon is bewildered until she realises that Kelly thinks that boats have the same rule as all those tour buses she has grown up in: *No shitting in the bus.*

I clambered into my bunk and lay down on the thin foam mattress, pulled the curtain shut, looked up at the underside of the upper bunk, then fell into a deep sleep. Sure enough, the rocking movement of the bus is very relaxing. When I woke a few hours later we were parked at the Sheraton.

It's great to have a long, steaming shower in my room, then

sprawl on the comfortable bed while I have a look at the notes I've taken. When I write something down I can read my handwriting perfectly; a few hours later it has changed into gibberish. I spent a frustrating hour trying to decipher *Anthrax ghrted hjii shee ookme thhhee gheke* then gave up and went downstairs to the restaurant. I stared at the menu; the hotel had no pity on the hungry traveller – a tiny cup of coffee cost €5 a hit.

Scott was sitting alone at one of the tables, and I joined him. I mentioned that I noticed no one had been drinking or getting wasted last night.

'Yeah, well, you learn. You feel shit enough after a night with hardly any sleep, you don't want to make yourself feel worse by having a hangover.'

'Have you always laid off like that?'

'No, of course not. When you're young. . .' He smiled. 'The first time I was in London I met Lemmy from Motorhead in a bar near the Marquee and was dumb enough to try to drink as much as he did. I ended up in hospital with alcohol poisoning.'

'Did you ever wreck hotel rooms, do the sort of stuff heavy metal bands are supposed to do?' I thought back a few years. I destroyed a few myself, even when I played in a fucking folk-rock group. Hell, I even demolished one when I was playing in a band backing a famous kilted Scottish singer, although I made sure he got the blame.

Scott sipped his coffee, looked into the little cup, and signalled to the waiter for another. 'Sure, but when you realise you're just going to get a huge bill you stop all that. Years ago we were on tour with a band called Slayer and staying in the same hotel in Indiana or someplace. We all used to be into paintball guns so one night we ended up on the roof, blasting them at the big Hilton sign. We thought it looked much more colourful, a big improvement, but in the morning we had to pay $15,000 damages. You learn not to do that shit any more. Costs too much.'

Two guys come up to our table, one tall and slim, the other short and fat, his skin covered in fiery tattoos and a lavish collection of spots – *plooks*, as Glaswegians call them. His head is shaved to the nut except for a purple-dyed tuft above his eyes. His pal has waist-length hair. There is a smell of freshly smoked hash from their ripped black tee shirts and knee-length shorts. They are covered with more metal piercings and studs than a Masai warrior. They're clearly not Mormon missionaries.

'Hi, Scott, we are your drivers. The festival is about an hour from here.'

Scott tells them they are way too early and to come back in four hours. They apologise, smile politely and wander off. I catch a glimpse of one of them opening his tobacco tin and guess they won't have any problem whiling away the time.

It's six o'clock and the band's two minibuses are parked at the door of the Sheraton, the drivers waiting patiently with a faraway look in their eyes. We jump in and roar off down the tree-lined E19 motorway. It's a nice drive, passing the place where the Battle of Waterloo was fought, heading south to the little town of Dour.

The Stones have Mick and Keith – the Glimmer Twins; Aerosmith have the Toxic Twins, Steve and Joe; Anthrax have Scott and Charlie, the BlackBerry Brothers. They are hooked on the instant emailing capabilities of the little cellphones, which they call CrackBerries because they are so addictive. All the way to the gig there is silence as messages fly from their fingers to all parts of the world. Their phone bills must be fearsome.

After an hour or so we pull into Dour and it looks like the

whole village has been taken over by the festival. The artistes' area is in a school house about half a mile from the stages, so we wander to the Anthrax dressing room. The guys dump their bags then head downstairs to the canteen and join the queue for pasta and meatballs or rice and vegetables, or maybe some of that salad there, whatever looks good. There's a strong smell of grass; the band glance in the direction of the smokers, then push their chairs nearer a gentle breeze coming through the open doors leading to the playground.

After lazing around for a while they decide they want to hear a band that they reckon are worth checking out, so we climb into one of the little vans shuttling back and forth to the backstage area of the festival site. It looks like there are about 50,000 people out front, perhaps more. One of the support bands is blasting away on the main stage, the one Anthrax will be on in a couple of hours. I can't wait to see them again. *Was what happened last night just a fluke?*

The band they want to hear is getting ready on a stage further along the festival site. The drummer has the largest pile of gear I've ever seen: a kit with every size of drum imaginable, bells, marimbas, little bangy things... Is he actually going to hit all that stuff? About 100 yards away on a covered, raised platform, deep in the packed crowd, the soundman is speaking into a microphone on his desk. The people out front can't hear him, but his voice comes clearly over the onstage monitors as he runs through a check with the drum tech, who is banging each drum in turn, then adjusting the position of each microphone, a little closer or further away: *A little higher with that snare mike* ... They've been at it for almost an hour.

When everything is sorted, the band walk on and start playing. It's like a mixture of heavy metal and free-form jazz;

sounds very complicated. Frank knows the guys in the band and tells me that they learned it by breaking it all down into two-minute sections, then rehearsing each part for six hours at a time. I haven't a clue what it's about, but the crowd seem to enjoy it.

We find a shuttle bus and return to the schoolroom and I ask if there's anything I can do to help. I'm not used to being in a dressing room unless I'm playing in the band and I don't want to feel like a hanger-on. The band had a tour manager, but they haven't seen him since Zagreb a couple of weeks ago where he was stranded after losing his passport.

'Hey, it would be great if you could find us some water and organise a bus to take us back down,' says Scott.

'And some Red Bull,' adds Joey.

I leave the band to get changed. *Will it be leather warrior outfits tonight? Will they put on a load of paint?* I find one of the drivers and ask him to reverse his minibus to the school door and keep it there ready for the band. He pulls out a huge joint, lights it and asks me if I want some. I smile, *no thanks*, and wander across the schoolyard, past open-air communal showers. A reggae musician is standing naked in the steamy spray, humming contentedly in the warm evening air. A child stares at him, fascinated, then her mother gently takes her by the hand and leads her to the schoolhouse.

A girl is sitting on the ground, leaning against a wall, staring into space, her eyes heavy. She is smiling, listening to her iPod, slowly nodding, lost in a wonderful world of her own. It all reminds me of Roskilde in Denmark, a festival I played with the Incredible String Band when we headlined there. It seems only moments ago, although it must be more than 30 years.

I go back to the bus, and make sure the driver is more or less on this planet. It's time to go. The band come downstairs – they are wearing shorts and vests, street clothes. We drive down the road, past little two-up, two-down brick houses, like an old Yorkshire mining town, and pull into the dusty area behind the main stage, which is built from timber and scaffolding, with a heavy tarpaulin roof. It's a lovely, clear evening, no chance of rain. I can sense the huge crowd out front, can *feel* them watching the stage, waiting for Anthrax. *This is it*.

They run on stage and . . . and it happens again.

I've been putting off describing this because it's so hard to explain what Anthrax sounds like, what they do. Let's start this way: I've seen hundreds of bands, including a lot of the megastars. I saw Zep when they were young and at their best; the Stones several times since 1966; Marley, The Who, Dylan, Springsteen, The Eagles, U2. . .

I have never experienced anything like Anthrax.

The moment they hit the stage the power of Scott's chords blasts into the crowd and the band explode into life. It's like a rocket taking off. I'm standing at the side of the stage, and even behind the huge PA, the power of their playing is something I've never heard before. The way Anthrax play is unnerving but exhilarating, it's like they are creating raw energy. Something very different is going on here. It is like grabbing a power line and trying to hold the jerking ends as they twitch and spark.

Frank stands with his legs wide apart, his Fender way below his waist, his head swinging back and forth, body swaying wildly, long hair slashing the air all the way down to his ankles. Charlie is hammering his drums, driving the whole thing in an eruption of energy; if you were standing right in front of him it would feel like a hurricane. Dan and Scott are screwing out thick, low, growling guitar chords, sometimes slow, then furiously fast, frantic but controlled. Together they sound like some sort of vast powerful engine. Joey screams the vocals, gulping from cans of Red Bull, working the crowd but also part of it. They love him; he's one of them.

Gig reviewers always seem to put in negative comments or smart-ass remarks. There's probably some professional reason they do this, perhaps they think they'll sound gushing if they praise the band, or maybe it's like Hugo said in Ljubljana, *It's dead easy to write something critical.* I don't know – all I can do is write down exactly what is charging through my mind, try to catch a few of the thoughts that are racing by so fast.

We all know that music affects our emotions; rock music and sex have been joined at the groin since *Good Golly Miss Molly – she sure likes to ball.* In the 1950's, 'rock and roll' was slang for shagging, which was why so many radio stations banned it. Scottish armies have always used pipers and drummers to fire up teenagers to the point they could march straight into searing walls of whitehot bullets. Mozart can inspire the weary, or calm the troubled mind. This we all know. But when I hear Anthrax play live there's only one conclusion I can come to: it's a completely different art form. This is way beyond what I'd always thought of as rock music.

They are hitting dormant neural pathways in my brain, something is being released inside my head. I don't know what it is but the instant they start playing the same rush of energy I felt last night in Oxford is surging through my body again. It's like the feeling I used to get when I was rock climbing on some insane cliff-face, when I had finally reached a tiny but safe ledge hanging above a desperate, jagged void.

Christ – it just keeps building.

It's like the feeling when you peer over the edge of a near-vertical wall of ice and frozen snow and you know you are crazy even to think about it, you know you are not good enough on these stupid skis to do this, that if you lose it for an instant you will hurtle to the bottom and bones will shatter but ... *fuck it* ... you breathe deep ... and look straight down again ... and another last breath ... then you launch yourself at it ... and now it's too late ... you are racing down so fast, so very fast ... and suddenly you feel you are part of these awesome white mountains and glaciers, you belong here.

I've never heard anything like it.

Or when you are on a mountain bike powering down a crazy track, and you know one slip and your skull will be caved in like an eggshell but you feel so totally in control that suddenly you are freed from fear, from all your fears, and in one massive rush of insight, you know why you were born.

When you see how much these guys put into playing, when you see Scott and Frank and Dan pulling every last ounce of energy out of their bodies, when you see Charlie driving this wall of sound you realise that if you believe in something you have to give it all you've got. *It's gotta be that way, to hell with anything else.* When you reach your crossroads, when your moment comes, when you know the time has arrived that will decide whether the rest of your life will be a rut or a highway, you have to use every scrap of energy you possess. If you don't, you will live to your last breath knowing you robbed yourself, knowing that you had more to give but you held back.

I look at the vast crowd and suddenly realise why all these people are leaping in the air, jumping, dancing, why they are bouncing off each other – *moshing*. This is primeval energy, the same force that made African jungles throb, that coursed in the veins of American Indians. It is the driving force of life itself. Now I see why the band don't drink or take drugs before they play. It would be senseless, dope would cut off their minds from their muscles, would stop the force exploding from their amplifiers, this pure energy vibrating and surging from the stage.

It's like someone has detonated a nuclear charge in my head; I can feel every nerve tingling. I am so fucking alive.

I'm standing beside Tom, who is working the onstage monitors, watching the guys for the tiny signals they make. Joey glances upwards: he wants a little more vocal in his monitor. Scott touches an ear; a bit more guitar. No one else would notice, it's almost telepathic.

From behind the amps, Chris grins at Tom: *Let's hope Dan doesn't try to sing, hope he'll stay away from the mikes.* Dan is a genius, his fingers flashing up and down the fretboard, even builds his own amplifiers, but Tom says microphones and Dan are like matter and anti-matter, the two must never meet. The crew were joking earlier that they should put a jolt of electricity through any mike that Dan goes near, just in case he gets so carried away that he tries to sing. But, Christ, he can play guitar. Screaming runs, blindingly fast, structured and precise, clean yet distorted, every note fits on top of and meshes with Scott's churning, gnawing chords deep at the very heart of the band, everything driven relentlessly by Frank's surging, low bass riffs, and Charlie's thundering rhythms.

Suddenly a slight nod and a gesture from Joey catches Tom's attention – one of the stage monitors has blown. Tom grabs a spare with both hands; it's bloody heavy but he is oblivious to the weight and rushes onto the stage, pulls the plug out of the wedge-shaped speaker cabinet and plugs in the new one. Then he drags the broken monitor to the side of the stage and dumps it behind the sound desk, so fast that it's done before anyone realises what's happening. One of the PA company's roadies yells at Tom: *What the fuck d'ya think you're doing?* This equipment is the best in the world, it's worked perfectly for all the other bands. He grabs the monitor, sticks a lead in it and presses his ear to it, then realises that, sure enough, the speaker has died. Sounds like a few bass notes too many have blasted the thing clean off its bolts.

Scott is having trouble with one of his guitars; he's hammering the strings, trying to get more sound from them. He's sweating so much that the pickups have drowned – they are fried, barely twitching. He whips the guitar off and hands it to his guitar tech, who is standing behind his speaker cabinets, constantly tuning Scott's guitars, ready whenever he needs them. Scott pulls on another guitar and his sweat immediately drenches it too but somehow it works. There's not the slightest drop in energy, the set powers on, nobody is daydreaming.

I've never seen a crowd react like this, they're not letting up. Not for a moment.

All pro bands know how to involve the crowd, get them leaping around, it's part of the job, but this goes way beyond anything I've ever seen before. Now I understand what this music is all about, what it does. Anthrax is the last band to play tonight, and everyone in the crowd must be exhausted after being on their feet since early morning, fuelled only by festival hot dogs and way too much beer. But they seem transfused with fresh energy and surge towards the stage; the level doesn't dip for a second.

Every band I've ever seen has had a slight lull mid-set, when the audience settles back, catches its breath, whatever. Bands know this will happen, and structure their set around it, maybe play a slow song or something quieter. But it didn't happen in Oxford last night or here in Belgium tonight. From the minute

Anthrax starts playing, the crowd go wild, like a wall of pure energy.

Suddenly I realise why Anthrax people never need to explain why they love this music, why it is so different to anything else. They *know* why. They don't need to justify themselves to anyone. They *know* what is going on, why they love the power of this playing.

What the hell are they are tapping into? Maybe the Catholic Church realised something about music all those centuries ago . . .

The gig is over. The band come off stage for a moment; the deafening roar of the crowd is pulling them back on. The band is behind the amps, no one can stand still. Yeah, they're going to play one more song, they'd play all damn night if they could.

Frank turns to me, hands me his bass.

'Hey, man, come on and play.'

For the first time in my life, the first time ever, I hesitate. I look blankly at him. . .

'Come on and play, just go with it. . . '

I hesitate again, Frank grins and then he's back on stage; the moment has gone. I feel like a fool. I should have done it. I will never hold back again.

I'll never forget this moment.

The church was wrong about devil's intervals. Music can never come from evil. If there is a hell it will be a place of endless darkness and soul-gnawing silence.

I think I'll skip the tattoos, though.

12

WREXHAM

Hayseed Dixie

TWO weeks later I was still jumping up and down whenever I heard the first few notes of an Anthrax track blasting out of my huge old-fashioned speakers. My neighbours in the quiet suburb in which I live didn't share my enthusiasm and I was in danger of being served with an ASBO. Besides, there's only so much adrenalin an ageing body can handle so I decided to take a little trip to the tranquillity of the Welsh hills.

I had been in Wales twice before; the first time many years ago when I got lost heading to a festival at a place called Shepton Mallet, near Bath. I'd gone with an Australian guy I met when he came to collect his sister who worked at a Glasgow pub where I was playing. Two minutes after dropping her off at her bedsit, we jumped into his ancient rattling Land Rover, lit a fat joint and bounced off into the night in a southerly direction.

We had no idea where we were going. Back home all he had to do was follow the road out of town in either of two directions and he hadn't grasped that not everywhere is like the outback. After a long night's drive we parked in the shadow of a Welsh coal bing, sleeping the sleep of the mortally stoned, before eventually finding our way to Somerset. We gatecrashed the festival, hooked up with a couple of beautiful hippie chicks and spent the rest of the weekend, mellow and happy, listening to Led Zeppelin,

Canned Heat, Captain Beefheart and I can't remember who else. It was very pleasant.

The second time I was in the land of green hills and village choirs was when I played Cardiff with the Incredible String Band. We were doing a British tour and our support act was a group called McGuiness Flint who had released a catchy tune called 'When I'm Dead and Gone' and, much to their surprise, found themselves at the top of the charts and appearing on *Top of the Pops*. Hundreds of school kids came to see them and stayed to hear us. It was interesting to look out from the stage and see this strange mixture of bearded hippies packed in beside teenagers dressed like the Bay City Rollers.

We always ended the gig with jigs and reels, played at breakneck speed by Robin Williamson, a great fiddle player, one of the best in the world at that stuff. The kids loved it and charged to the front of the stage, leaping around and having a great time. They noticed that we had no stage security, the Incredible String Band were so used to playing to stoned hippies that it had never been necessary. I mean, how many pug-nosed bouncers do you need when the worst that might happen would be someone throwing a few daffodils up at you? Before anyone knew what was happening, a huge swarm of kids had jumped up beside us, knocking over amplifiers, drums and guitars. As photographs will prove, Robin in those days looked like a blonde Greek god, and I will never forget the startled look on his face as he disappeared under a pile of schoolgirls.

I decided to go to Wales again, to an AC/DC convention featuring an insane group called Hayseed Dixie, a bluegrass band from Nashville, shit-hot players each and every one of them. We live in a golden age of music. In the wave started all those years ago by Beatlemania, music shops are selling more guitars than ever before, with the happy result that there are countless great musicians ready to play for us. The only drawback, from a musician's point of view, is that it is very difficult to earn a decent living because there are so many great players competing for the same gigs. And besides, most people have limited income to spend on listening to bands, no matter how good they are. Consider the Hayseeds: world-class musicians, yet when they tour every cent has to be carefully managed.

The band was formed by John Wheeler in 2001. He owns a recording studio in Nashville, knows the music business inside out, and has the good old-fashioned Tennessean ethic of self-sufficiency and hard work. The Hayseeds were doing quite well in America, had recorded their albums in John's studio, but he had spent years trying to find a record company in the UK that would release them. They all turned him down. No one was interested, even though John was offering them a finished product – they wouldn't even have to finance the recording costs. 'The problem is that record companies are run by forty-year-old guys who try to figure out what young people want to hear, and they haven't a clue. They're afraid to try anything different. They just wait to see what is fashionable then jump on the bandwagon.'

Aching with frustration, John eventually brought the band to England to play some gigs, paying for everything himself. This would be his last attempt, it was all or nothing. He finally managed to find a small company that would distribute Hayseed Dixie's records in the UK, and when local radio stations began playing them, the band suddenly found themselves in big demand. As John says, 'There's a saying in Nashville that overnight success takes about ten years.'

John knows that too many bands have embarked on trans-continental jaunts, checking into the kind of hotels that have thick bathrobes and lavish room service, and guzzling steak and lobster dinners every night only to be handed a bill by their record company at the end of the tour for stomach-churning sums of money. I know a guitar player who had to cough up $22,000 at the end of a two-month tour. The Hayseeds ain't gonna make that mistake and would sleep in their minibus if they had too. But, hell yeah, they like to enjoy themselves; they are experts at it. They even carry their favourite bourbon, Knob Creek Tennessee Whiskey, which they say is the best in the world.

Stacked backstage behind most big-name bands is a mountain of aluminium flight cases for all their gear. The Hayseeds carry exactly one guitar, one fiddle, one mandolin, one banjo and one bass. There are no roadies. John changes his guitar strings every night himself. 'You either change them before the gig or you'll have to change them during it when they break.' It's just another boring task that needs to be done, often while he is doing press interviews.

Managing a band, organising tours, and being the lead singer, guitarist and fiddle player are all demanding jobs. John does them all. If the alternator packs up in the hired van (as it did) and you have to drive without lights along the motorway to get to the gig on time then you just do it. When some sonofabitch smashes a side window in Cardiff and you have to shiver for the next five hours as you drive through sleet and rain to the next show, then you get on with it and don't complain.

It is fortunate that the sonofabitch in question didn't get caught by the Reno Brothers Dale and Don Wayne, the banjo and mandolin players in the band, who always work together. 'You hire one of us, you hire both.' They are a pleasure to meet: polite, relaxed and good humoured, speaking in a soft Tennessean drawl, but you get the impression they are nobody's fools, their pappy taught them good manners, but not to allow anyone to take liberties. If the bold Taffy had been a minute later thieving from the van there would have been something other than a welcome in the hillsides for him, that's for sure.

The band believe in playing fair. They encourage fans to record bootlegs of their concerts; even tell them how to get the best quality and invite them to share the recordings with friends, but warn them that if anyone tries to make money by selling them they can expect 'a good old-fashioned Tennessee butt-whuppin'.

John Wheeler has a lot of respect for the Reno brothers. 'It's only when you're on the road with someone that you find out what they're really like. You can hire someone who seems just fine but when he's gone a few nights without sleep that's when you see what he's got. Some guys get very bad tempered, they can't control themselves, they lose it altogether.' On this tour, he says, it's been a month since he's had a full night with his head on a pillow.

The Hayseed Dixie story is that of four dungaree-wearing rednecks who 'hail from the fertile valley of Deer Lick Holler, deep in the heart of Appalachia'. One day a travelling salesman's car hits a tree. In the wreckage they discover his collection of AC/DC records. As their biography says, 'All they had to listen to them on was an old Edison Victrola that only played at 78 rpm, but the boys all agreed it was some mighty fine country music. So, in memory of the stranger who had perished the boys set about learning these songs.' They play them at the next barn dance and farm-folk for miles around can't get enough of it. The legend is born.

The band have built a huge following the old-fashioned way, by playing anywhere and everywhere – in the UK, all the way from

Shetland to Cornwall. Hayseed Dixie's gigs have the atmosphere of a hootenanny, a rollicking old-fashioned hoedown. It's all about hard-working folk having a good time, there's lots of talk of 'fine-looking titties and ass, corn liquor and beer'. John yells like a preacher, 'When you go to meet your Maker make sure you ain't sober.'

The fans join in, dressing up as straw-hatted hillbillies. Some of the girls wear their hair tied in bunches, have bright red cheeks and mascara plastered around their eyes, tiny shorts and low-cut denim tops – the bigger the breasts the better. Political correctness is for northern folk. As John says, 'No one leapt out of their wheelchair just because Nancy Reagan told them they are physically challenged and not disabled.'

He reckons musicians should stick to what they're good at, is doubtful about the motives of some stars yapping about politics. 'You want to change the world, then run for president. Making people think they have done something to help world poverty just by wearing a rubber band at a rock concert in some muddy field is fooling them. What's that gonna do for kids in Africa?'

Headlining the AC/DC convention is their 37th gig in six weeks; tomorrow they face a five-hour drive to the south coast of England, then they'll fly back home to Nashville for a recording session before coming back to Europe a couple of weeks later and starting all over again. 'We love playing, we do every gig for free. We get paid to travel, that's the way we see it.'

If you have been in America and watched CMT, the Country Music Television channel, you may have noticed that many country bands are actually rock musicians. They are great players but they are fooling no one by slicking back their chest-length hair and wearing neatly pressed blue jeans and smart jackets. They have realised that making a living playing head-banging riffs is as likely as being paid to drink Budweiser. And so they have found gigs backing the new wave of country megastars; slim, Hollywood-handsome guys in check shirts and Stetsons, like Keith Urban or Brad Paisley, or one of the gals, like Gretchen Wilson, who, unlike their predecessors, have their own ideas about givin' all their love to just one man.

Whenever these guitarists think they can get away with it, they'll whip up the sort of raunchy guitar solo that only used to be played on Thin Lizzie or Bad Company tracks, but to make sure the good ol' boys don't pile their records on a bonfire, they'll also lay down some great twangy Fender Telecaster. Slick slide players, who used to crank out "Rollin' and Tumblin'" in steamy blues bands, are now in big demand in Nashville. I love hearing rock musicians playing country. But how does the reverse sound – country musicians playing rock? The Hayseeds play the chord-crunching songs of the Australian heavy rock masters AC/DC in good old-fashioned bluegrass style, the purest form of country. How would the denim, leather and tattoo mob at an AC/DC convention react? It sounded like a lot of fun.

I decided that if it was going to be relaxing I sure as hell wasn't going to drive to Wrexham. I hate driving. No one in his right mind wakes up, yawns, claws himself, stretches, and with an enthusiastic grin happily joins the daily traffic jam, inching slowly forward in a funereal pall of carbon monoxide while listening to talk radio winding everyone up with inane phone-ins. If I can catch a quiet train, one that isn't full of rampaging and vomiting drunks, is clean and leaves and arrives more or less on time, I am very happy. I enjoy stretching out with a good book and large cappuccino, glancing out of the windows at lush green hills drifting by, while on the horizon convoys of trucks and cars battle for space on the M74. Yeah, that's the way.

Buying a train ticket over the Internet requires patience – far more than I have – let's say no more. I gave up after an hour and tried booking through the nice lady at the call centre. It was going just fine until she told me she was in Bombay and it would take a week for the ticket to arrive by post. And then there's the automated helpline. Remember not long ago when we all gathered round the TV to watch *Star Trek?* When he wasn't punching hell out of aliens, Captain Kirk would speak to the Starship Enterprise computer, which responded in a silky and attentive female voice. How wonderful it will be, Trekkies and normal people the world over would say, when we can talk to computers! That's exactly what happens now, yet instead of being awed we just want to smash the damn phone. So I still had no ticket – no matter how slowly I spoke, the computer couldn't understand my Scottish accent.

I gave up and early next morning caught a cab to Central Station where I managed to buy a ticket from a very helpful human who kindly gave me a printout of my journey telling me which stations to change at. I didn't even have to queue – just presented myself at the window marked 'Immediate Departures'. I was on my way, even had time to pick up a large coffee. Joy.

And so to the gig.

Wrexham University is one of those modern campuses, just beside the local football club's impressive stadium and handy for pubs and supermarkets. Everything a hungry, thirsty student needs. I met up with John just as the Hayseeds had finished the soundcheck. They had booked cheap rooms in the student accommodation block, as had I, and we wandered over to collect our keys. I know my bones are getting on in years, but how anyone can comfortably sleep in a bed that hard is beyond me. The pillow was like a folded newspaper and the mattress as unyielding as mahogany – perhaps to discourage the students from long humping sessions. Oh well . . . only one night.

I dumped my stuff and as I walked back to the hall got talking with a guy called Cocker the Rocker who was wearing all the AC/DC regalia: leather waistcoat, frayed jeans, cascading hair, tattoos and a fox's tail hanging out of his pocket. I asked him if he'd been to one of these conventions before.

'Yeah, this is my annual holiday. This weekend. It'll cost me a couple of hundred quid. That'll do me. It's a great atmosphere. Great people.'

'You been into AC/DC for a long time, then?'

'Yeah, I used to go t' Wigan Ballroom when I were young, for the soul nights. Geno Washington. Them people. But there were always fights, skinheads, it were a very tense place, you never knew when there would be trouble. Then I went to a heavy metal night, it were full of bikers and Hell's Angels and everyone was like family. Fantastic atmosphere, really friendly. It were great. I've been a fan ever since.'

He told me he was unemployed. 'I collapse, pass out. I know when it's going to happen, like, but I can't work. I'm dyslexic but I did an adult education course and learned to write. I write stories. I send them through internet t' other AC/DC fans.'

'What kind of stories?'

'Well . . . one of them is Ralph the Fish who is mad about undersea bikes. And the Crimson Pirate and Blood River. Lots of people get eaten by crocs. It's a goodun' that is.'

The entrance to the hall was busy and there was a cheery, friendly atmosphere as old friends met up and recalled happy tales of head-banging gigs, and solemnly reminded one another that this was the 25th anniversary of the passing – actually the choking in his own vomit to be frankly, although not unsympathetically, factual – of Bon Scott, AC/DC's original singer. Many fans regard Brian Johnson, his replacement, as a newcomer even though he's been with the band for a quarter of a century. When Brian invited the Hayseeds to play at a house party in Carolina, they were delighted to do it free; he slipped them a tip as they left – an envelope containing $5,000.

Inside, the place is buzzing. Tables with long-haired, extravagantly tattooed guys in denim jackets, smoking little roll-up cigarettes, selling AC/DC stuff, rare records, bootlegs, tee shirts – what they call swag. Wild women with raucous laughs and rattling coughs, a few of them old enough to remember AC/DC's first tours, bare bellies dangling over tiny denim skirts, black tights, chains, studs, body art. It seems everyone knows one another, like a family gathering. Pints of frothy beer and smiling faces everywhere.

While one of the support groups were blasting out AC/DC songs, I had a coffee backstage with the band. They say they 'love playing England and can now tell Australian from other British accents'. They tell great jokes and stories, there's no pre-gig tension or the inspirational huddles a few young superstars indulge in. They reckon too many modern bands are 'whiney'. The Hayseeds like to sing 'manly-man songs, not girly-man stuff'.

The Reno brothers are tuning up, sipping cold beers. Their father played with Earl Scruggs and co-wrote 'Duelling Banjos', that anthem of the south. Both brothers are left-handed but their paw insisted they learn to play right-handed because good left-handed banjos and mandolins were impossible to find. Dale tells me of the time he played at the Grand Ole Opry in Nashville and a famous female country singer grabbed him by the plums and said, *Hey boy, kin yew fuck as well as yew kin play?*

Dale grins, then lets rip one of his long and deep, beer-fuelled, world-famous belches. He reckons if they gave medals at the Olympics for burping, he'd walk away with the top prize every time. I'm proud to be able to belch loudly when the occasion demands, but Dale's is exceptional, rolling like thunder around the small room. If I might offer an opinion, it seems to me that the difference between men and women is clearly the life-long pleasure a man derives from the unrestrained expulsion of gas. From the first surprised grin of delight as a baby, to his last lingering farewell fart, what other activity unfailingly offers so much simple joy?

The band's usual bass player, Jake 'Bakesnake' Byers, is otherwise disposed and is absent from this tour. Seems that he was doing some much-needed repairs on his mother's home in Florida when a hurricane hit. Next day, when Jake examined the house for damage, he discovered that by the grace of the Good Lord the storm had blown a new roof onto her old house. So he was staying there until he had nailed it down good. At least, that was his story.

Filling in for him is Jason D. Smith, who has just finished changing his strings. He pulls them, getting any stretch out of them so they stay in tune in the heat and sweat of the stage. He also is left-handed but plays a right-handed bass upside down. The youngest member of the Dixies, on leaving school he worked for exactly one week in the Gibson guitar factory in Memphis, then walked right out the door when offered a job playing in a country band for a month-long tour that eventually lasted 10 years. They all love this life, wouldn't want to live any other way even though they know it's hard, almost impossible, to make big money in a bluegrass band. 'You have to be one of the chosen few, someone like Alison Krauss.'

Time to play. They stride on stage, rolling on their ever-present beer cooler filled with longnecks. To roars from the steaming-hot packed hall, John announces that they are 'here to testify! Here to *TESTIFY!* There's only four things worth singin' about. Drinkin', cheatin', killin' and HELL!' Then they belt into their version of AC/DC's 'Highway to Hell'. The fans bounce up and down, loving it, punching the air, yelling out the chorus.

There is currently a view– thoughtful and well-researched in my opinion – that rock music is directly descended from Scottish musicians who escaped to America at the time of the Highland Clearances. A few humourless souls scoff at such a notion, but they probably also believe the world was created 4,000 years ago. I like the idea of a wee Glasgow plumber and a big teuchter crofter meeting on the sailing ship to the New World. With nothing more than the clothes on their backs and a guitar and a fiddle, they formed a folk group, busking on the heaving deck to make some beer money. They eventually found their way to Appalachia where they'd heard there was good money to be made working on farms, and at weekends found themselves gigs at barn dances, playing the old songs everyone had loved at the ceilidhs back home. Southern musicians like the Carter Family, hearing how good these tunes were, changed them around a little, recorded them, and called it bluegrass music.

Then another wee Glaswegian, an electrician, got a job rewiring the house of a dance band guitarist called Les Paul. Twang! In no time, they'd knocked up the first solid-body electric guitar. Of course, no mention could be made of the wee Glaswegian in the history books since he'd been working for cash – doing a 'homer'. According to enlightened opinion, as soon as Gibson put the guitar into mass production, bluegrass split into two streams: mellow country music for the white folks, and, for black musicians who liked louder and raunchier music, the twelve-bar blues, the heart of all rock music. What is less widely known is that this itself was descended from Presbyterian hymns – spirituals – that God-fearing Scottish plantation owners had taught their slaves to sing in the evenings to discourage wild fornication. Thus all the ingredients were gathered, and the stage was set for the inevitable: bands such as AC/DC, who – and this cannot possibly be mere coincidence – are also Scottish emigrants.

Musicologists and academics therefore owe a debt of gratitude to Hayseed Dixie for distilling rock music, tracing it back to its source and bringing together the two streams that sprang from the original music. It's like the Knob Creek corn liquor the Hayseeds brew in the hills of Appalachia, different from the original Scotch, but pure nevertheless.

The circle is unbroken.

13

HAMBURG

Eminem

I'M sitting in a busy airport, my flight is delayed and I've drunk far too many espressos to be able to have a wee snooze. So I'm going to rant a little.

I strongly believe that if aliens ever land, the first thing they will notice is how musical are the inhabitants of this otherwise savage planet. When we speak they will hear the sounds we make as song, of that I'm sure. We are so used to hearing only words, we don't notice the lilt, the ebb and flow of the voices that carry them. We don't hear speech as music. But it is.

Another thing, before the caffeine wears off. Possibly because of the way we were taught at school, most people I know regard William Shakespeare as long-dead and boring, interesting only to dreary academics too dull to be computer geeks. A teenager once told me that theatre actors were just losers who weren't good enough to get parts on daytime television, and that poets were all saddos lucky to get jobs writing crappy verses for birthday cards. Yet, like all his friends, he loved rap music.

In his day, Shakespeare was a star. He played to packed, beer-swilling hordes who loved a good, rowdy gig. He was just like a modern-day rapper. So I really wanted to see Eminem in Hamburg, on his European tour. But, like Chuck Berry, he didn't turn up either. Oh well.

That's my flight being called now.

14

EDINBURGH

Antonio Forcione

I LOVE Edinburgh. It is so old. No matter how often I go there I always notice something I haven't seen before: some ancient building, hall, church, bank or forgotten statue tucked away in a leafy corner or down a grassy lane. It's like dipping into one of those beautifully photographed *National Geographic* books and finding a fascinating new picture every time. I know nothing about architecture, but always get a warm feeling when I'm walking along Edinburgh's cobbled streets, staring up at its lovely old stone buildings.

Take the train to Waverley Station, climb the well-worn steps to Princes Street then glance up at the clock on the towering Balmoral Hotel. The hotel used to be owned by British Rail and has always set the huge clock five minutes fast to help travellers catch their trains, which I think is very thoughtful of them. Turn and look at the Scott Monument, like a rocket aimed bravely at the stars. It's quite some tribute, a lot more impressive than the Booker prize or whatever they give writers these days.

Turn round and there, not far away, is the serene, craggy mountain known as Arthur's Seat, like a watchful lion guarding the finest urban park in the world. The Queen thinks she owns it and we Scots are too polite to tell her otherwise. Holyrood Park is a little piece of wild Highland landscape, like Scotland in miniature, and it's right in the middle of Edinburgh. It has hills, little lochs, glens, ridges and cliffs, all packed into a small area. Arthur's Seat is 350 million years old and although it is 823 feet high, it's a nice easy stroll to the top from a little loch at its foot. On its west side, it has vertigo-inducing cliffs with terrific rock climbing, provided the park police don't catch you. There are even the remains of Iron Age hill forts. People have been spending their weekends wandering happily up and down Arthur's Seat for at least 4,000 years. If I lived in Edinburgh, I'd go there every day.

Thankfully, I'm not one of those middle-aged men who frequent public lavatories, but if you would like to treat yourself to a five-star pee, stroll round the corner to the North Bridge and enter the old *Scotsman* newspaper building, now a very fancy hotel. Its restaurant is impressive enough in itself, the sort of calm, dignified sanctuary where I'm sure the Queen Mother might have enjoyed a cup of finest English Breakfast tea with a wee nip in it, a Dunhill and the *Racing Post*. But the toilets are exceptional. Down an ornate staircase that would not be out of place in Buckingham Palace, they await your convenience, gleaming marble, chrome and polished wood. Even the paper towels feel thick and luxurious.

A little further uphill is the Royal College of Surgeons' building in Nicolson Street, discreet yet important, almost frowning as it looms over a £1-for-everything shop on the other side of the busy road. Yet even that building has something going for it. Above the shop's gaudy sign there is a lovely stone façade, like an elderly duchess embarrassed because her knickers are on show.

Wander up the ancient Royal Mile, then down to The Mound and the National Gallery – it's only a short distance. The gallery is in the heart of the city where it belongs, surrounded by the trees and lawns of restful Princes Street Gardens. If you pause for a moment beneath its stone pillars and high angular doorways it would be easy to imagine you are in Ancient Greece. Travel writers often say that Edinburgh is the Athens of the north, but it's not. Athens is the Edinburgh of the south.

On a warm and sunny afternoon, it's great to cross Princes Street with its grand department stores and stroll aimlessly around the broad, tree-lined streets of the New Town, glancing into solid Georgian residences, stealing glimpses of high, elaborately corniced ceilings, neatly ordered bookcases, deep, well-worn leather sofas, and tasteful décor: restful, warm colours. Compared with the bustling streets and alleyways of the High Street and Grassmarket, the New Town is spacious and unhurried, resting amid quiet, well-tended gardens.

Just a few minutes from the marble pillars of Queen Street is Moray Place, a semi-circular terrace that I wandered into one day and just stopped and stared. It is so unexpected; it seems too distinguished to be in a northern city. There is something haunting about it, as though it holds the spirits of the noble citizens who dwelled behind its doors in a bygone age.

At night, glittering with a million lights, cities always look exciting and Edinburgh has a beautiful skyline, as captivating as that of New York. I love walking towards Waverley Station in the chill of a starry winter evening, looking up at the ancient castle looming darkly as it watches over the black, jagged tenements of the Old Town – skyscrapers when Manhattan was swampland. Shining brightly like candles in the towering black walls are little square windows, hundreds of years old, glowing warmly against the cold, northern sky. I often wonder how many folk have passed their years in those rooms, and about all the things that must have happened in them. The people who live in them now sleep in the same bedrooms as the long-gone tenants of the past, looking through the same old windows onto the same ancient alleyways, squares and tiny shops.

Edinburgh also has the oldest pubs in the world.

When I was a teenager, every Glasgow schoolboy wanted to brag about doing a pub-crawl along the brightly lit bars of Rose Street and just managing to lurch onto the last train back, the good old vomit express. Of course, Edinburgh folk liked to think they were much more *refined* than the uncouth hordes from Clydeside. Glasgow was a dirty place of clattering machinery, noisy shipyards and smoke-belching factories; Edinburgh was quietly dignified, the nation's capital city. Glasgow had Hampden, but Edinburgh had Murrayfield, the home of Scottish international rugby.

In the 18th century, great minds in Edinburgh laid the foundations of the modern world, and its bankers created the solid framework for commerce. An Edinburgh academic called James Hutton studied the rock strata around Arthur's Seat, figured out how they had been formed, and earned himself the title of the father of modern geology. Voltaire said the world looked "to Scotland for all our ideas of civilisation", and he knew his stuff. Scotland had the finest education system in the world; every successful company in the British Empire depended on Scots accountants and lawyers to keep them right. Restrained and diligent by day, at night they gathered in the pubs like polite schoolboys going out after a rugby match to get rat arsed.

In the 1700's some Edinburgh poet wrote about how its citizens loved to binge-drink together, whatever their day jobs: beggars and bankers, street traders and economists gabbing over whisky about politics and wild, wild women. The poem ends with a highly satisfying description of a communal session of 'pishing and spewing'. The chat must have been brilliant. If you had wandered into the old White Hart Inn in the Grassmarket, you might have been bought a wee dram by Robert Adam, David Hume, Adam Smith or Sir Walter Scott. *And would you like a wee bag of nuts with that, Sir Wattie?* For a while, Burke and Hare were shady patrons who mysteriously seemed to get through a lot of drinking partners, and apparently William Wordsworth and his sister Mary were a good laugh once they had a few drinks in them. *Hey, Wullie, how's that poem about daffodils coming along? Think Interflora might buy it?*

The inn has been serving thirsty travellers for at least 500 years, and probably since the 13th century. It's a lively place still, with a welcoming fire and someone strumming guitar and singing rousing Scottish folk songs; when all those voices drift out into the night air, you can't help wanting to join in. There's always a clutch of American tourists, keen to see the place where Robert Burns last embraced the fair hand of his mistress Nancy in 1791, before he went back to his long-suffering wife, as most married men usually do. But at least he had the tenderness to write her a wee poem and chose the finest word ever found in a love song:

'Ae fond kiss and then we *sever*.'

If you enjoy company, the best time to see Edinburgh is during the Festival, the biggest arts show in the world. It's a combination of several: the highbrow Edinburgh International Festival, which hosts ballet, classical music and acquired-taste stuff; the beating drums and skirling pipes of the Military Tattoo, which sells out faster than a Beatles reunion; the vast, anything-goes Festival Fringe; the Film Festival; and the Book Festival, the largest of its kind anywhere. I went there almost every day to casually move my book from a lonely shelf in the shadows to bask beside Harry Potter and Dan Brown in the bestsellers display.

The Festival starts in the long, hot days of August when the sky is blue, the air is warm and it's after ten before the sun finally yawns and dips out of sight for a wee rest. Och, I suppose it does rain occasionally – OK, sometimes every day. But glance at the smiles and gentle touches between happy people as they sip cappuccinos in the sunshine and Edinburgh looks like the easiest place in the world to fall in love – well, at least for a few weeks. When I was young and playing in a lusty rock band, we always tried to get gigs in Edinburgh at the time of the Fringe because it was packed with heart-stoppingly beautiful girls, many of them drama students. It lasts until September, and when you leave the final show you can usually feel the first chill wind of autumn sweeping across the Meadows near the city centre, blowing away all the brightly coloured leaflets and posters for another year.

The Fringe uses great venues – I can't think of any city with so many old and interesting places to hold a play, concert or those baffling, one-woman shows, all of them within walking distance of each other. Anything is allowed, no censorship. Jerry Sadowitz, a weird Jewish-Glaswegian who makes Billy Connolly sound like Prince Charles, comes every year. He is rated in the world's top five close-up magicians and performs card tricks of bewildering skill while ranting about poofs, suicide bombers, cunts from London, Glasgow Pakistanis, and people from Newcastle: 'Kill them all.' He says people from Birmingham are the lowest of the low: 'These bastards marry someone from fucking *Dundee* so they can move up the social scale.' Everyone knows what his show will be like, but some buffoon always buys a ticket so that he can heckle him (big mistake), or another struts out while yelling abuse (even bigger).

There are so many shows that some struggle to sell more than a handful of tickets, but Jerry enjoyed a sold-out run in his chosen venue, the cloisters of the College of Divinity, a breathtaking building where the General Assembly of the Church of Scotland have their annual get-together. If Jerry was put off by the looming presence of the grey statue of John Knox, the great Presbyterian reformer, he showed no sign of it. After a verbal blitzkrieg, he ended the show by dropping his underpants and displaying his tackle to the crowd, not something, I imagine, that the good Moderator of the Church has ever done to get a laugh.

Of the huge number of comedians appearing at the Fringe, one of the best is Adam Hills, an Australian. He is a terrific storyteller who doesn't tell jokes in the old-fashioned man-walks-into-a-pub style. He happens to have an artificial foot. When he was told that Disneyland discourages 'physically challenged' people from being photographed with the Mouse (apparently they don't want kids to think Mickey can cure them) he grabbed his camera and caught the first plane out there. He is very funny, sending up Disneyland, Americans and President Bush but without the usual tedious malice. There is something very likeable about Adam, the audience warm to him immediately – it's a pleasure to be in the same room as him. He makes his point without poking anyone in the chest. If he ever decides to become a politician, I'd vote for him immediately.

He sells out almost every show at the most prestigious Fringe venue, the Assembly Rooms, a beautiful building lit by glittering chandeliers. The queue starts early and, while waiting in the line outside, one of my favourite sights is the sun setting behind the dome of New Register House at the end of George Street. After the show, if it is a dark and misty night, the luminescent green dome looks as if it is floating high in the air like some sort of UFO.

One of the joys of the Fringe is to spot tomorrow's stars playing in tiny venues that are almost empty. Every well-known comic did the Fringe before they became famous: Peter Cook and Dudley Moore, John Cleese and the guys from Monty Python and, more recently, Jack Dee, Dara O' Briain, Eddie Izzard, Ed Byrne, Jeff Green and Michael McIntyre, the funniest comedian since Billy Connolly. Some shows are runaway successes, others forlorn failures; artistes hire venues and pray for good reviews that will bring in the crowds. Many years ago Malcolm le Maistre, who I played with in the Incredible String Band, put on an excellent comedy show he had written. Apart from friends and relations, all of whom were on the guest list, I think only two people came to see it and they were both jakeys who had got lost trying to find their weekly AA meeting. We lost a fair amount of money, but it was good fun.

Another time I saw a show by a guy billed as a hilarious stand-up from Los Angeles. The posters were filled with quotes from triumphant reviews of his show the previous year. Unfortunately, he'd since suffered a nervous breakdown and, as part of his recovery, had written an hour-long monologue recounting in terrible detail every last twitch, every sleepless night of his torment. Expecting jokes, the bewildered audience soon began shifting uncomfortably in their seats. When one confused girl started laughing, he turned on her and demanded to know what was *so funny about having a fucking breakdown?* It's all part of the charm of the Fringe; you never know what you will see.

Every year, two Australians turn up to perform a show called *Puppetry of the Penis* and cavort around bollock-naked, twisting and wrenching their tadgers into shapes resembling hamburgers, the Loch Ness Monster and other objects. It sells out every night. I wonder if they have children back home? *Daddy, what do you do for a living?* What do they say when their little ones ask them to speak to their class in school? *But all the daddies give a talk about their jobs...*

In the Renaissance, many musicians made pilgrimages to Edinburgh. There's a great piece of music by Italian composer Barsanti, who arrived in Edinburgh in 1735 and stayed for eight years, playing in pub jam sessions with the local muzos. It is a nice fusion of Venetian baroque and Scottish jigs – fairly gets my feet tapping.

Edinburgh has always attracted great musicians and one of the best to play at the Fringe is another Italian, Antonio Forcione, who I shared a table with in Henderson's, a busy basement restaurant in Hanover Street. It's just a short walk from Princes Street: self-service salads, nut roasts, oatmeal haggis, sweet potato and bean casseroles, proper fruit desserts, that kind of thing. Pine tables worn shiny, a little wine bar, a guy caressing piano keys, some tables tucked underneath low arches – mind your head. If you go there during the Festival there's a good chance you'll bump into some of the performers. It's the Hard Rock Café of the vegetarian world – it was always Robin Williamson's first stop when he got back to Edinburgh after a long tour.

Antonio is from a little village on the Adriatic coast. When he was young he wanted to be a footballer, until one day his father gave him a guitar. He started like most kids, strumming along with Beatles' records; and he learned very quickly. He was soon playing in local bars – he was always late for school on Monday. By the age of 13, he was touring Italy with his own band. He eventually moved to Rome where he studied classical and jazz harmony, and began composing complicated pieces but playing them in a way that non-musicians could enjoy. He uses all sorts of tricks: bending strings, popping out harmonics, rapping and tapping the body of the guitar like a drum– he's been described in the music press as 'the Jimi Hendrix of acoustic guitar'.

He is slim, intense, and almost vibrates when he talks about guitar playing. 'As soon as I began, I realised I was scratching the surface of something great. The guitar has infinite possibilities. Discover them. Play things you don't know. Music is auto-biographical; composing is the most rewarding thing I can imagine. Performing is a combination of three things: technique, creativity and delivery. It is like circular energy surrounding you. You must learn to extend this out to the audience.'

He's attacking a plate heaped high with celery, carrots, nuts and fresh-looking green stuff – Henderson's has this healthy eating idea really figured out. When Antonio first arrived in London he couldn't speak English, fed himself by busking in Covent Garden, was 'discovered' by a TV company, and has been touring the world ever since. Like all professionals, he has many funny on-the-road stories, and we chat about the old idea of musicians paying their dues and all those kids nowadays who dream of leaping to overnight fame through shows like *American Idol* and the *X Factor*.

He sips sparkling mineral water, looks at me and shrugs. 'Who *wouldn't* want to be a guitarist touring the world? To succeed in music you have to do something outstanding; you have to work at it, you have to stand out. Being a professional musician is a hard, winding road. What other business would anyone work at for twenty-two years before becoming successful? You are alone, stuck in Istanbul airport and your passport is missing. You are due to go on stage in Hamburg and your instruments haven't turned up. You need a great deal of passion for this life, you can't be half-hearted or you will become bitter.'

Music is a language, a complex tongue that requires a special talent to become fluent in. So here's the thing about Antonio. Many guitarists have slogged through countless hours of practice to perform cascades of arpeggios, scales and rhythms. They leave the audience in awe, but feeling very little – remote spectators of technical wizardry. There are some guitarists who put life into only a few phrases, like the emotion that BB King can squeeze out of four simple notes. But there are very few who can play staggeringly complex guitar pieces with real feeling the way Antonio does. And he's not one of those musicians who take themselves way too seriously. 'Everyone has greatness within them. Search for it. But it is good to put in a little sparkle of humour.'

That night, I went to see him play at the Assembly Rooms. He has a multinational group: Russian accordionist Igor Outkine, Brazilian percussionist Adriano and Nigerian cellist Jenny Adejayan, each bringing some of the world's great music. A concert by Antonio is always a treat, one of the gems of the Festival – in 2001 he won the Spirit of the Fringe Award – and the hall is packed every night. His playing is exquisite, especially one of his pieces, 'Touch Wood'. If you could capture the sound of breathing and heartbeat and blood gently pulsing through your veins it would be like this. He ends the set with a 'classical' version of 'Smoke on the Water'; everyone loves it.

After the show, I wander along Princes Street, among crowds of people walking to and from shows, laughing, talking – accents from all over the world, like songs drifting in the warm night air. The bars are busy, folk on the pavements reading leaflets handed out by performers, everyone relaxed and enjoying this warm, summer night. I can't think of any other city with so much to see, and, high on a hill in the heart of it, overlooking it all, a castle with a 900-year history.

I love this small country. It's got the most beautiful mountains, lochs and glens in the world. And it's got Edinburgh.

15

REYKJAVIK

Franz Ferdinand

AS I walked towards the station to catch the train back to Glasgow I noticed a lot of people jumping up and down, trying to catch a glimpse of the bandstand in Princes Street Gardens. Franz Ferdinand were on stage, but you could only get in if you had a ticket, and these had sold out in seconds. It's a great place to play – I did a gig there once and loved looking from the stage up to Princes Street, even though only a few people and a dancing, wined-up alkie had come to hear us. Tonight, the organisers had put up a tarpaulin screen so that no one could see Franz Ferdinand from the street.

My younger son, Alan, had told me about Franz Ferdinand and how good they are, but when I listened to them and tried to catch some of the buzz surrounding them, I couldn't share his enthusiasm – maybe I was getting too old. They got big, really big, on the back of one exceptionally strong song, 'Take Me Out', that seemed to be playing on almost every TV show I switched on, here and in America, even as background music to sitcoms and sports programmes. The world is so hungry for new music that one killer song is all a band needs to go from playing for free in half-empty pubs to pocketing a million-pound cheque for headlining Glastonbury.

Songwriting is at the heart of any successful band. It is a

difficult thing to do, very few people can write strong material. Many top artistes only became successful when they were smart enough to recognise their limitations and hired professional writers. In 1967 Elton John advertised in the *NME* for a lyricist and has worked with Bernie Taupin ever since. It's a great job if you have the gift.

Countless musicians can play the notes and all the twiddly bits, and there are millions of would-be songwriters trying to be the next Coldplay, but even their most heartfelt efforts do no more than clog the Internet with dirges that are about as interesting as a blocked drain. Thousands of songs are technically flawless, beautifully recorded, sung perfectly and intertwined with wonderfully skilful playing, but are as appealing as a week-old Big Mac. The writers may have been to music college, have studied the work of everyone from Lennon/McCartney to Springsteen, know exactly what a good tune should sound like, and their tunes often have all the right ingredients, yet they have no spark, no life.

The fascinating thing about songwriting is that it is based on trickery, it is musical sleight of hand, like a good card trick that is baffling until you see how it is done. Most successful songs are so simple they can easily be picked out on the piano by any 10-year-old kid stabbing one finger at the keys. Good composers are like magicians in that they disguise this by clever arrangements and adding crafty guitar parts and little musical phrases – hooks – that divert the listener's attention from the basic simplicity of the song. It's very clever. I wish I could write songs.

Radio 1 and MTV can make a band with the right song world famous in weeks. Often bands have been struggling for years, then manage to come up with one song that does more for them than a decade of slogging around the country. Bands are also well aware of the world-wide marketing power of the Internet – the Arctic Monkeys are generally regarded as the first band to become huge stars this way. They played their first gig in 2003 and soon began giving away their CDs which their fans circulated on the Internet on sites such as myspace.com. This created a street-level buzz and before long they were packing venues all over the country, normally impossible for a band without the backing of a record company PR machine. This got them noticed by Domino Records who signed them in 2005 and released 'I Bet You Look Good on the Dancefloor' which shot to No 1. Plenty of people have the same idea – overnight myspace.com had grown to over 140 million subscribers including four *million* bands – 250,000 in the UK – all of them clamouring for attention. The Internet is not just flooded, it is submerged in a sea of would-be rock stars.

Not very long ago, the Musicians' Union ran a campaign with the slogan 'Keep Music Live' because they were worried that computers and DJs would soon replace bands. The opposite happened; there are countless new venues opening all over the world, desperate for exciting new acts. Consider Franz Ferdinand's short career: in 2002, they played nine gigs, all in Glasgow. The following year, their lives had changed forever – 67 gigs in nine countries. In 2004, they played 198 gigs, collecting 28 more stamps on their passports, and 2005 saw them do 97 gigs in 23 countries.

It's a great life if you like being paid to travel to exotic lands and stay in fancy hotels. Who wouldn't? So there are more bands desperate to make the big time than ever before, although to many the music is entirely secondary – they want to be professional stars rather than professional musicians. They will play anything they think will get them noticed, much like those washed-up celebrities who eat spiders and creepy crawlies to get their faces back on national TV.

All over Britain, playing fields and football pitches are weed-covered and silent while the suburbs thump to the sound of music. Everyone knows someone who plays in a hopeful unsigned band and, for a few, global fame is just a song away. Right now, eking out a tin of beans in a dingy bedsit, there is a scruffy kid who won't be able to walk down the street next year without being mobbed. It's very exciting. There are even rehearsal studios everywhere, complete with all the shining new equipment any aspiring band might need. Back in the glory days of rock music there was nothing so posh. We used to set up our peeling, battered amps in rented student flats, jam a few coins in the electricity meter and make as much racket as we dared until we were forcibly evicted.

Not too long ago, yelling fathers chucked their sons onto the street because they wasted their time playing guitars instead of studying or finding 'proper jobs'. A university degree was once a passport to a good job and many graduates would tell you it still is, provided your ambition is no higher than scanning videos in Blockbuster or flogging car insurance from your own little cubicle in a call centre. Many parents now think the music business is no more insecure than any other career, and offers the possibility of far higher rewards. Some desperately push their kids to be performers: *Hey, Dad, can't I just be a plumber?* Others simply want to be *supportive*. If their little darlings believe they were born to be stars, their doting parents are convinced the cosmos will grant their every wish and all their dreams will come true – even if tubby Tarquin sings like a frog with a smoker's cough.

If they took 10 minutes to find out the piddling income of most professional musicians, even that of many well-known ones, they would realise that there are far more lottery winners than millionaires in the music business, but somehow all those pop stars make it look so easy. *Our Tarquin is every bit as good as him!* Some smart-arsed mathematician has proved that filling out a winning lottery ticket is as likely as walking up to a stranger and guessing their telephone number. The chance of making the big time is much harder – you need a lot of talent too. It's got almost nothing to do with luck.

Many people seem to believe that all that stands between them, or their children, and world fame is luck. But if you look at any of the really successful bands, they are so much better than everyone else. Were the Stones just lucky? U2? The Beatles? Springsteen? When they wrote those great songs, was it all down to luck? Luck has very little to do with it. Luck is winning the lottery. At best, luck might get you into the right place at the right time, but you have to be talented enough to deliver the goods when you get there. But there's no shortage of dreamers, which is why Simon Cowell has gleaming Bentleys, Aston Martins and Ferraris in the garages of his homes in Holland Park and Beverley Hills. *American Idol* is by far the most popular TV show in the USA, with news channels carrying daily updates. Recently, one of the *judges* sobbed on screen when her favourite contestant was voted off.

So is it surprising that colleges now run full-time courses in rock music? Cynics call them 'degrees in dreams'. There is an endless supply of hopefuls learning how to be recording engineers, performers and songwriters. Brimming with youthful confidence, they know they don't have to be signed to a record company to make the big time, they can walk into their nearest Oxfam, buy an old Mac, take it back to their bedroom, load it up with a programme called Protools and record their very own CD.

There are just enough big winners to create the illusion that anyone can do it, like Mylo, a talented musician from Skye, who recorded his million-selling 'Destroy Rock and Roll' in a rundown tenement flat in Partick, Glasgow. Up until then, when U2 came to town he couldn't scrape up the money for a ticket; suddenly they were asking him to remix their tracks.

Hundreds of thousands of bands release records on their own indie labels, but almost all of them sound alike, imitating whatever band happens to be trendy at the moment. Producing a professional-sounding product can be expensive, but some parents have very deep pockets. All over the country, bands are giving away their CDs at gigs, hoping they will be heard by a management company who will sign them to one of the major record labels.

Every night of the week, in every city, unsigned bands are playing showcase gigs arranged by small-time promoters who hire pubs, clubs and just about anywhere with a stage large enough to hold a drum kit and a few crappy amplifiers. The promoter gives the band tickets to sell, telling them he expects them to shift at least 20. The band that sells the most tickets gets to top the bill. New bands hope that a talent scout will come along, see how good they are and all their dreams will come true. Promoters know that most bands will only be able to sell tickets to their friends, and so they put on as many bands as possible – four or five each doing a half-hour set is usual.

When The Beatles started out, they had to play five-hour gigs in tough Hamburg clubs, and most of the older rock stars have similar backgrounds. Many new bands can play for only half an hour; they don't have enough songs for any longer. It's like that wee Japanese guy who was signed by a top agent after being spotted on the driving range where he could whack the balls for miles but had never actually played golf.

For the promoter, there can be serious dosh. On a ticket costing £6, he will let the band keep £2, although most bands give their tickets to their pals and pay the promoter themselves. They figure that Sony BMG or Island Records are always on the lookout for new talent so it's worth the cost. The promoter pays the venue about £150 for the hire of the room and equipment, so if 100 people come, he will clear £250 for his night's work. Some promoters have exclusive deals with several gigs, and are constantly searching for willing bands to play, often recruiting them by sending out random emails to bands on myspace.

There is nothing new about heavyset promoters making money out of musicians, but here's the thing. Go to any of these gigs and you will see dozens of doting mums and dads cheering on their Tarquins. Rock bands used to play gigs to get away from their parents. Rock music was about not trusting anyone over the age of 30, and wanting to die before you got old. I can't imagine young Mick Jagger's mother shaking her ass and dancing around her handbag when her son played at the old Crawdaddy Club.

The other thing that is instantly noticeable is that when a band finishes playing, they and their friends often walk out, as if to show their contempt for the other bands. When I was a young musician, if you carted out your gear while another band was playing you'd have had a mike stand crammed high into your bowels. Bands who have done a few of these gigs often insist on playing second or third when there is most likely to be the maximum number of people present. Playing last usually means playing to their pals only.

There's nothing terribly wrong with this, at least it gets musicians onto a stage and, since all the gear is provided, they don't have to drown themselves in debt buying equipment, as young bands used to have to do, which was what actually started the punk movement – bands rebelled by playing cheap guitars through Woolworth's amplifiers. There's a sort of socialist equality – anyone can now headline some of the most prestigious venues in the city just as long as they can persuade enough pals to come along. The majority of bands are young, often not old enough to drink in the venues they are playing in, but many are, frankly, sad old farts still dreaming they could have a life that doesn't involve going to a boring office every day.

For many ageing musicians monthly showcase gigs and myspace are their last hope of fame, their last throw of the dice. Now that they are married and have kids and a mortgage, going on the road is pretty much out of the question, but every dark and wet morning as they drive to work they fantasise that the right person will hear one of their songs and it will be picked for the next James Bond movie. Dreams don't half die hard. But the inescapable fact is that almost all great rock songs are written and played by hungry, horny, inner-city, penniless 20-year-olds, not paunchy middle-aged insurance salesmen stuffing their mouths with pasta in warm, comfortable suburban homes. Watching some of those guys strutting around the stage in front of their pals from the golf club is like seeing some fat git posing on a Spanish beach in a tiny thong. You just want to give his blubbery arse a right good skelp.

Thankfully, at least some of the people playing unsigned band nights are young, enthusiastic and ambitious musicians who have worked hard on their music. Glasgow has so many bands playing live gigs that you could go into the city centre every night for a year and not hear the same one twice. Most are dire, simply lapping up the applause of their mates, but some are very good. A few are exceptional.

So for Franz Ferdinand to make the giant leap out of such a deep pool of obscurity into the dazzling light of world fame, they must have something really special going for them.

And they have.

I had always fancied a wee trip to Iceland. When I added up the cost, however, it was always cheaper to go climbing in Spain, skiing in Italy, or even flying to sunny Florida for a week. But when I found out that Franz Ferdinand were playing in Reykjavik I decided to find some way of getting there that didn't involve melting my credit card. I have a pal who is the editor of a newspaper and I asked him if he would be interested in a travel article. He wouldn't commission me, but as long as I met my own expenses he would have a look at my offering. If it was readable he'd use it. So far so good.

Icelandair does weekend breaks from Glasgow but they are priced on the basis of two people. I emailed their booking department and told them I was going to Reykjavik to do an article – how much would it cost for one person? A very kind man replied with the offer of a free flight. *Yes!*

I thought I'd chance my luck a little further and contacted Franz Ferdinand's management and asked if it would be possible to get a ticket for the gig. They passed my request to the promoters in Iceland, a local record company called 12 Tonar, and an email promptly came back telling me to call at their shop in the town centre. The street name was unpronounceable, but they told me I'd see a hill with a gleaming white church that looks like the Apollo moon rocket. Standing in front of it is a statue of Leif Eriksson; the shop is just a little way downhill from it. *We will have a ticket waiting for you, together with a strong espresso, the best in Iceland.*

And so next morning there I was, checking in at Glasgow airport with a happy smile. No queue at the Icelandair desk, and the helpful lady quickly sorted me out with a window seat – I wanted to see all those hills in the Highlands that I loved wandering on.

Unfortunately it was cloudy until the plane was over . . . what sea is it? It's a long way north whatever it is. And then the seat belt signs were switched on and we were gently coasting down to Keflavik airport. When you fly into most cities you will see some familiar landmark, something you recognise that gives you a little surge of warmth. As you approach Heathrow it may be the towering stands of Twickenham, the striped, lawn-like pitch of Fulham Football Club, or the Serpentine as it curves lazily through Hyde Park. Possibly it's the rolling Campsie Fells or fertile green fields of Ayrshire when you approach Glasgow, or the proud and ancient castle as your plane gently descends to Edinburgh. I can't imagine any Icelander sighing contentedly when he looks down on the ochre, mossy volcanic desert of south-west Iceland. It is the most barren-looking, bleak landscape imaginable, not a tree or bush to be seen – NASA used it to train astronauts for moon landings.

Keflavik airport is quite a distance from Reykjavik but Icelandair is very switched on with transport. A large luxury coach was waiting outside the terminal, ready to take passengers directly to their hotels. There was a line of hopeful taxis but with a bus service this good they were in for a long wait.

Reykjavik is like Fort William, but colder, if such a thing is possible. The main street in the older part of town is nice in a timber-and-corrugated-iron kind of way, two-storey shops and houses, many looking like large huts, although some are painted pretty colours and have lovingly tended gardens. I don't spend more time in shops than I absolutely have to and it has been a frighteningly long time since I have had any desire to go clubbing, but I am told Reykjavik is great for both.

Icelanders love good coffee and when you look in every other shop window you see locals sipping creamy cappuccinos and chatting happily. All very cosy and welcoming, especially when a skin-stripping breeze is whipping across the bay, as it was. I stopped at one of the many coffee shops in the main street where I was served a small cup and half a pannini thing with a little cheese and tomato for the equivalent of just under £10 – but I think we all know that Iceland is not coy when it comes to prices. I sat at the bar beside a guy who was drinking steamy espresso and reading the local newspaper, nodding and chuckling to himself – a contented soul. When I passed three hours later he was still there, cup in hand, utterly absorbed in the strange hieroglyphics on the page.

Sometimes it's very nice to do a bit of organised sightseeing and I took a coach trip so that I would have something to put in my travel article. Once you get inland, Iceland is a huge playground, all sorts of natural stuff going on, like thermal things bubbling out of the ground, providing hot water for everyone's baths. There is steam rising out of fissures in the rocky landscape, and spouting geysers and cascading waterfalls and smoking volcanoes and groaning glaciers and a huge national park where the prime minister has his summer residence, and when he takes his daily strolls he chats amiably to tourists. He doesn't need bodyguards; everyone likes him. Oh, and there's skiing too, but I never saw that, but I will some day, soon I hope, because how cool would it be to ski on a mountain inside the Arctic Circle and maybe even see the green glow of the aurora borealis dancing across the starry sky? And in June I'd love to cycle under the midnight sun on all those empty roads through vast silent lava fields and sleep in a tent high on a mountain, looking towards the North Pole, beside crystal-clear streams tumbling over gleaming white pebbles, and hear real salmon jumping in the night. *Splash!*

Iceland also has its own special horses, although they have four legs, big teeth and a tail and love to whinny and shit like any others I've seen and I can't remember what the wee tour guide woman said makes them unique. Something weird about the way they run. And there's the Mid-Atlantic Ridge. I loved that. Iceland straddles two tectonic plates, the North American and the Eurasian, one riding over the other. You can see where it is happening, a long, high, stern rock face, pushing across the land like a northern invader, and I had a great time stepping from one continent to the other until the harassed tour guide came looking for me.

But enough of this meandering . . . I was here to see Franz Ferdinand.

They were playing at Kaplariki football ground, the home of a team who were at the top of the Icelandic league. I like football grounds very much, especially older ones that have character – so many British grounds are now almost identical. I could take a cab there for the equivalent of about £35, but I enjoy travelling on public transport in foreign towns. Actually I get quite excited travelling on public transport in the UK too, because I'm never sure where I might end up or whether I will be mugged on the way. Anyway, for less than the price of a coffee I caught a bus from the town centre and asked the driver to tell me when we reached Kaplariki, but he seemed a tad bewildered by my accent. Fortunately, a young girl overheard me. 'Is it for the Franz Ferdinand concert?'

'Yes.'

She smiled. 'I am going there too. I will tell you when we get there.'

As we travelled through Reykjavik's quiet suburbs – they seemed to spread a long way, a bit like Auckland – she told me that she was Norwegian and had decided to spend her postgrad year learning Icelandic before eventually, she hoped, finding a job in tourism. Apparently Iceland has the most highly qualified tour guides in the world – she already had a degree and could speak three languages. After about half an hour we needed to get off and change buses. Her boyfriend was waiting for her and we caught a taxi the short distance to the gig. When we got to the football ground, we arranged to meet afterwards to share the cost of a cab back to the town centre. It's nice to be in such a friendly country.

The hall was hot and packed, breathing space only. I sat sweating at the side, sipped a Coke, and waited for Franz Ferdinand to appear. What would they sound like? I'd listened to their first album and it was very good but I always prefer to hear bands play live. Suddenly dazzling spotlights flooded the stage and they bounded on. Alex Kapranos marched to the front, his old Fender Telecaster slung low, waving as the huge crowd surged forward. Then he held up his arm, grinned and yelled into the mike, 'Hi, we're Franz Ferdinand, and we're from Glasgow!'

In countless articles about Franz Ferdinand I had noticed that the writers studiously compared them to other groups who, they claimed, had been 'influences' on the band. Yeah, I know these guys are highly trained journalists who have vast stores of musical knowledge. But the more I read, the more irritated I became.

For a start, many of the bands they talked about were limp, dreary and barely successful groups that most people had never heard of, or had long forgotten, obscure bands of passing interest and limited talent but which intellectuals in later years would elevate to some imagined plateau, to be discussed knowledgeably, as if comparing paintings in some pretentious exhibition. If you are cornered by one of those guys in a west end coffee shop and there's music playing, you need to be able instantly to name three other bands that it sounds like. It's all become terribly serious.

On the first Beatles records, such as 'All My Loving' and 'Can't Buy Me Love', George Harrison played country and western guitar solos and half the first two albums were covers of other people's songs, but no one pontificated about it; all that mattered was that electrifying sound and the clarity of vision of being young – teenagers heard their records in a way that no adult could.

Sometimes I wonder if the critics ever just listen? I suppose they are wary of phoneys – so many new bands are utterly contrived, they've studied rock music, they think there is a blueprint for success, and their managers have choreographed every move they make on stage. Many new bands are dumb enough to believe that the public are fools and all they have to do to become stars is dress up in whatever clothes their stylists tell them to wear, throw some songs together by slightly changing the best riffs from other bands, and spend a lot of money on self-promotion.

So it is so refreshing to see Franz Ferdinand.

Every song the band plays passes the fairground test. Go to any carnival anywhere in the world and listen to the music being played beside the spinning wheels, the roller coasters and dodgems. Only the best music makes it to the funfair; carnies know exactly what draws the punters, what makes the fun seekers roll up. Spotting records with fairground magic is instinctive; it's their daily work.

Every song I ever heard at a carnival vibrates with excitement. You can trace it all the way back to Phil Spector, 'Be My Baby' and 'Da Doo Ron Ron', and Buddy Holly, and The Beatles' records, when the backing music suddenly became as exciting as the vocals. They are all different, but they all have it; the music combines with the smell of carnival oil, the electric heat of shining steel, the sparks, the glittering colours clattering round the tracks. You can taste fairground music, it's more than sound, it's alive, it widens your eyes, makes your legs twitch, your back tingle, you want to jump a ride and let it hurl your body over bends and loops under lights so bright that you forget about your boss telling you: No dice, son, you gotta work late. You feel the richest guy in the world, your girl is at your side, it's Friday night and you've just been paid; you got 50 cents more than you're gonna keep. Carnies are no fools, they know exactly what songs to play, and nothing too long either – the punters expect a one-song ride for their money.

As they started 'Take Me Out' with its great walking bass line – 'I know I won't be leaving here' – I could hear what makes Franz Ferdinand so special, why these Icelanders were dancing to them just like hundreds of thousands of people all over the world. Can you recall the first time you heard the warm, unmistakeable, so electric jangling sound of a Fender Telecaster? That's the sound of Franz Ferdinand, each song brand new and fresh but somehow familiar, as though it always existed. If you are a guitarist, think back to the first moment you held an electric guitar in your hands . . . the feel of the shining, lacquered wood, the smooth contours of the body so snug against your thigh, the tingling excitement as you plugged it into a quietly humming amplifier and hit a string, then turned the volume control all the way up and played a chord . . . Were you trembling? Remember the rush of energy, the surge of power that great sound filled you with? That anything was possible?

Alex Kapranos is such an obvious star – the test of star quality is to look at a photograph of an unknown musician and be able to remember his face a week later. There is something about guys like Bowie, Jagger, Bono, Marley and all the rest that is way beyond just being photogenic. It's as if you've always known them. Alex is like that, as is the band's music. See one picture and you will always recognise him; hear a song once and you can hum it.

I spoke to him after the gig; he's a nice guy who is perhaps a little surprised by the band's phenomenal success. 'We're just playing music that we enjoy. We're friends, we sit round a table in the flat, drink a bottle of wine and write songs. Bands were taking themselves far too seriously, staring at their feet when they played. People were going to gigs and just standing around. Then they'd go to clubs afterwards so they could hear something they could dance to.'

Franz Ferdinand love playing and watching everyone having a good time. They write great lyrics, but realise that no one ever rushed onto a dance floor just because a song had clever words. They have rescued music from becoming the preserve of balding intellectuals with stiff bones who would rather talk than dance – all those failed popstars, those tubby Tarquins who became music critics.

16

SARASOTA

BB King

IT was time to cash in some of my Air Miles on a flight back to Florida. When I owned a removal company, the local garage gave me Air Miles every time the trucks filled up. We got through a lot of fuel. I no longer had the headache of running a business but I still had the Miles.

There are many reasons why I love Florida: the soft, pinkish light at dawn, the glorious, balmy sunsets. It has a sub-tropical climate with lush plants, all sorts of vibrant, beautifully coloured flowers like orchids and things, gnarly mangrove trees with intertwined roots like an elf's fingers dipping into steamy, shallow lagoons, and there is something wonderful about watching a long, lazy alligator slipping into the smooth, silky water of the jungle-like rivers and backwaters that are a long way from Disneyland. I love swimming in the ocean, warm even in November, although now that fishermen have been banned from using their boats close to shore it's wise to stay out of the water at night, which is feeding time for the sharks that hunt much nearer the beach; all those extra fish make easy prey. The way a shark sees it, at night there are only two things in this world: other sharks and food; if you aren't one you're the other.

I even love the late afternoon thunderstorms in summer; when it rains in the southern States it really rains. None of the flaccid Scottish drizzle that seems just an irritant until you discover you are chilled and wet through and you'll never feel warm until you have a hot bath. It's proper rain in Florida, the kind you see in old Raymond Chandler movies, bouncing off the pavements and clattering on your roof, and the lightning is spectacular. The superheated air gathers in tall, ominously black thunderheads then sparks and explodes and lashes the sea like elemental demons. It's great to park at the beach, sipping an ice-cool drink while watching a dark storm raging above the ocean, hurtling javelins of electricity into the frantic water. One of my most exciting moments was a few years ago when I was sitting in my car about 20 feet from a tree that was instantly turned to charcoal.

In late autumn and spring, the thunderstorms and hurricanes have gone; every day is glorious with the humidity kept low by cool air slipping down from up north, as Floridians call pretty much anywhere else, usually with a wave of their hand and a smile. Deep blue sky, hot but not clammy, everyone wearing shorts and tee shirts, ideal cycling weather. Just what I needed to get fit again.

I love cycling, especially in America. You can nosey around places where you'd be arrested in a heartbeat if you were on foot, especially on Longboat Key. The local retirees can get a little jittery if they see anyone under 55 near their home other than a Mexican mowing their lawn or a college kid cleaning their pool. Someone from the Neighbourhood Watch would notice a scruffy Scotsman wandering along the street, admiring the houses, wondering how many millions it would take to own a gaff like theirs with sighing palm trees at the front and curved, custom made windows overlooking the sparkling sea. The island has its own police force and in the time it takes to speed dial 911, you might get to meet them. But they see cyclists differently.

Or they don't see them at all. You can cycle in Glasgow streets where the local junkies would leave you naked and penniless if you were crazy enough to walk. If you are on a bike, they just don't see you. Being invisible has a downside, though, because car drivers don't see you either. I am terrified cycling in Glasgow, the traffic is more dangerous than New York City. I don't know whose bright idea it was to narrow Glasgow's main roads – making them narrower doesn't mean that double-decker buses and delivery trucks shrink to fit them. By comparison to Sauchiehall Street, Broadway, Columbus Circle and Fifth Avenue are a cyclist's paradise, even in the sweltering heat among all the honking cars, dented, swerving yellow cabs and wailing ambulance sirens. Motorists in America don't dare knock over a cyclist.

If our government leaders were serious about solving the chaos of city centre traffic, they could take a trip to Disneyland or any of the big American theme parks, with their satellite car parks and excellent shuttle-trolleys, and see what public transport and intelligent traffic management is all about. But I'm wandering off the point.

When you are cycling, you can casually stop and have great conversations with people. If you are slowly pedalling through a park it's easy to talk to strangers who might otherwise blast you with mace and call the cops if you as much as glanced at them. Being on a bike separates you from street lunatics, somehow you must be safe. It's like strolling along with a friendly little dog that people just can't wait to pat. People smile and talk to you.

I'd propped my bike against a lamp-post and was slowly baking in the sun on Sarasota Main Street at one of those seats-in-the-street cafés that serve langoustine and scallops with

Chinese lettuce and balsamic vinaigrette, whatever that might be. Real foodies learn very young to appreciate all that stuff, these strange-sounding plants and sea-animal products, but it's a lost cause on me. I never get tired of Scottish porage with banana, and poached eggs on rice are a feast. I am easy to please food-wise. They serve properly made Italian coffee, though, something that is not easy to find in America.

I was sitting at a table, in my cycling shorts with the padded arse, sweat dripping off my nose, drinking dark brown coffee and eating one of those high-protein bars to try to build back some muscle, and the waiter, with the kid-on French accent, was looking at me as though I had just crawled out of a dumpster. An unshaven guy wandered slowly along, breathing heavily, looked at the empty chair beside me and asked if he could sit there for a moment. He was wearing a blue shirt embroidered with the name of the nearby hospital and the baggy cotton trousers they issue to patients. He had a plastic name tag around his wrist and a stained dressing on his arm. He'd taken a stroll from the ward to get some fresh air and stopped at a convenience store to buy a coffee, the cheap kind that you pour from a jug stewing on a hotplate into a white Styrofoam cup and get a couple of coins change out of your dollar from the bored guy yapping on the phone behind the cash register. He looked tired, his face lined and drawn, his eyes squinting in the bright midday sun.

At the table next to mine, two white-shirted lawyers shifted irritably as they drooled over their $35 salad lunches and inched their chairs a little further away. If the guy noticed, he gave no sign of it. As he lit a cigarette I noticed his hands. They were trembling slightly but looked strong, like a carpenter's hands. You could tell at a glance from the tanned, calloused skin they had spent most of their working life under the sun. He looked at my bike, sucked the smoke in deeply and thought for a moment.

'I used to cycle. A lot. For my college team.'

'You don't do it any more?'

'I get around on a bike. I don't have a car. I was on it when I had a heart attack. The cops said it was a seizure but I knew it was a heart attack.'

'When was that?'

'I'm not sure. About four days ago. They took me to hospital. They lost my bike. Four days. Maybe more.'

He drew deeply on his cigarette and the two lawyers at the next table glared at him. I hate smoking, I had a hell of a job giving up two packs a day and I've spent too many hours choking in smoky rehearsal rooms and pub gigs ever to want to light up again.

'You had a heart attack less than a week ago and you're smoking?' I grunted. 'You're asking for another.'

He looked at me, his face curious. 'What . . . is it smoking that does it? Gives you heart attacks?' He seemed genuinely surprised.

I looked at him. Was he serious? Did he really not know? 'Well . . . *yeah*.' My voice was heavy with sarcasm. 'Of course smoking gives you heart attacks.'

He looked at me; there was an almost child-like innocence in his eyes. 'Are you a doctor?'

I suddenly realised how bloody pious I sounded. I knew nothing about this man or what had brought him here, what he had done with his life or what had caused him to collapse that day on the street.

I smiled at him. 'No. I'm sorry. I'm not a doctor. What about you, are you working?'

'No. When I got out the army I had a couple of jobs, good ones too, but my mother got sick and I had to sell my home to care for her. She lived in Boston. But my brother and I never could get along and we had a fight and I been on the street since. I know I was drinking too much. I came here, I needed to get as far as I could from the winter.' He dragged deeply on his cigarette and slowly blew out the smoke, as if reluctant to part with it.

Suddenly the stench of a hot, pungent fart drifted across our faces. The sort of fart that only a huge suburban American breakfast followed by a heaped $35 salad lunch can release. The guy screwed up his eyes, waved his hand in front of his face and turned to one of the lawyers. 'Hey, pal, you need to take some Mallox. You got a real problem with gas. I'm trying to drink my coffee here.'

I was still laughing as I cycled back over the new, gleaming bridge across Sarasota Bay to St Armands Circle, an enclave of expensive shops, jewellers and upmarket restaurants set round a manicured little park with shady trees, stone benches and statues of performers from the old Ringling Brothers Circus. There used to be a great coffee shop where I often stopped for a cup but it had just closed. It had been owned by a man and his younger, very attractive wife who wore loose fitting low cut little tee shirts. She was very friendly, with a lovely smile, and enjoyed chatting with the customers. This did not please him. One day I greeted her with a cheery good morning and his eyes flashed at me like Exocet missiles. I thought it best not to go back.

The staff at the local Starbucks were much nicer than her husband. Every morning they'd make me a 'heart-starter', one-to-go with the extra shots the way I liked, and they always had a welcoming hello. It turned out that the guy in the other place was a more troubled soul than anyone realised. He bolted onto the wall of the coffee shop a clamp with a surveillance camera so he could keep watch on his wife when he was at home. Then one night the torment ended. He strangled her in their garage, crammed her still-breathing body into the freezer and locked the lid. Then he turned on the engine of his car and sat there, gripping the steering wheel until his life was gone too.

Bad things happen in Florida, like anywhere else, but good things happen too. The music bars are fantastic. There used to be a great live music scene in the UK. When I was a teenager, every church hall, scout hut and youth club had bands on Saturday nights that played Stones and Beatles songs at a volume that didn't leave your ears ringing for the next two days; music that everyone loved to dance to. If they were short of money, the guitarists plugged into small amplifiers, triangular-shaped, distorting 15-watt Watkins jobs covered in blue cloth and cigarette burns. If they could rustle up the hire purchase, they bought smoothly humming Vox AC30s just like George Harrison's, or Selmer Truvoices with little green lights pulsing at the front, the same kind of amps that Keith Richards and Brian Jones used. They played cheap Hoffner and Burns guitars, gleaming with red and black varnish or, if they were very lucky, sunburst Fender Stratocasters and white Telecasters that are worth big money now, if they managed to hang on to them after their wedding days.

But then an electrical engineer called Jim got talking to Pete Townshend and built what became known as the Marshall Stack, two towering cabinets with four big speakers bolted inside each and a heavy 100-watt valve amplifier piled on top. It was the most powerful guitar amplifier ever made; perfect for rock music at huge venues like the Hammersmith Odeon, or the Isle of Wight Festival, but devastatingly loud in small church halls. Trying to imitate their heroes Hendrix and Clapton, local bands blasted themselves off the little stages with tortuous wailing feedback and screaming 20-minute guitar solos.

The youth club organisers – no-nonsense church elders in tweed jackets and thick glasses – threw the bands onto the streets and welcomed in eagerly waiting mobile discos that, with one easily turned down volume control, quickly took over. The live music scene in the UK has never been the same since. Even today most pub bands in Scotland seem to feel naked without staggeringly large PA systems operated by haystack-haired, hearing-impaired sound men sitting 20 feet away at mixing desks bigger than the one used at Woodstock. It's a pity.

But small-venue live music is still thriving in America, especially in Florida where many excellent musicians, finally accepting that their chance of the big break had slipped away, decided that living in the sun and playing for fun and a few dollars in bars was far better than trying to hustle a deal in the shivering streets of Greenwich Village, or having to work day and night to pay the crippling apartment rents of Los Angeles.

These guys know how to play and have seen and done it all, like the car salesman who played with Danny and the Juniors in the early 1960's when they had a big hit about going to the hop. There was a huge music scene in LA, everyone loved groups and many film stars' homes were like communes with their own bands. He told me about a movie star who auditioned a guitarist for a band at the house she was renting. He was hopeless and, besides, no one felt comfortable when he looked at them with his weird, staring eyes, spooky even by LA standards. The film star turned him down, saying he wasn't good enough. Her name was Sharon Tate; his was Charles Manson.

The bar band scene in Florida has many great musicians, which is another of the reasons I like going there. And one of the best is Twinkle.

Twinkle is a blues singer.

She's, oh, almost 40, beautiful in a natural way, her face fresh and clear of make-up, looking even better now that she's washed the peroxide of her youth out of her shining, dark brown hair, and it tumbles onto her slim shoulders. She was *almost* a huge star, she'd backed Rod Stewart at Madison Square Garden, sung the Stars and Stripes to 75,000 Miami Dolphin fans and come this close so many times, but time has pretty much run out, at least as far as record companies are concerned. She's still got the voice, can still make your spine sweat, but ever since Ancient Greece the public like their stars to be teenagers and that's that.

She can always pull in a good crowd when she plays in Sarasota, including one guy who you might think is a little too devoted – he's filmed every gig in the last 10 years. He stands there at the front of the little stage, gripping his video camera, oblivious to the crazy Florida fun lovers dancing all around him, high as they are on gulps of tequila and a little weed, their skin tanned and warm with the heady aroma of coconut oil. No matter how rowdy they get he never misses a beat, films every note she sings; when he gets home he'll watch again every move she makes.

She's good. Very good. Her voice is like Janis on a good night. When she's really on form, you remember why blues music always sounds best in small, hot bars. Especially when played by people who have nothing to prove, who are there because it's what they were born to do; because they feel and love it. Right now she's singing 'Stormy Monday', that old standard so many people have slaughtered, but she gives it new life, she knows what being a dollar short of a two-dollar drink feels like.

The crowd mills around, an unusual mix. Young execs throwing back Southern Comfort to give a little edge to the cocaine they snorted in their Hummer, ready to par-tay – *well, all right!* Yelling young mothers who have left the kids with their men for a change, and are happily dipping and swaying in their short skirts and tiny tops, proudly showing off their 30th-birthday-gift surgically revitalised breasts. A fat, balding, used-car salesman, grinning to his small, chubby wife, celebrating his on-target bonus; if he makes it again next month, they'll take that three-night Caribbean cruise they've always wanted. There's even a tall, slim cowboy waltzing the floor with his woman, his arm curled down behind her back, fingers pointing at the floor, left hand holding hers high in the air as he gently spins her round, his gold-stitched leather boots gleaming in the red and blue spotlights. Everyone is smiling.

The slow blues finished, it's time to play something fast and Twinkle grins, waving to a friend in the crowd near the front. She catches his attention and nods sideways at the stage, her eyebrows raised in a question, then she smiles and looks at the crowd, throws her long hair behind her shoulders, arching her back like a cat, her tanned, naked stomach flat and tight between the sweat-soaked, tied-off shirt and her low-cut denims. There's something about her smile, something about the way her warmth fills the room. Maybe you would still see this if she was on a big stage in a huge arena, perhaps her soul would reach across the gap, but here in this small, hot bar she is so close you can almost feel her breath softly brush your skin.

'OK, now I'm going to get a great friend of ours to play with us. He's a guitar player. Come on up. . .'

I don't catch his name but he looks an unlikely musician. Fat, stumbling and awkward, like he's had way too many beer and pizza dinners. He bumbles towards Twinkle's guitarist who takes off his old Telecaster and hands it to him with a friendly smile. He picks up the guitar, slips the strap over his shoulder and sits the Tele awkwardly on his large stomach, then looks around as if he's never been on a stage before, as though suddenly realising he is facing a packed, expectant crowd who want to hear what he can do. He looks embarrassed, with big, rolling eyes, puffy cheeks and a goofy grin.

The drummer glances at the bass player, holds his sticks in the air, raps them together, 1-2-3-4, then cracks out the intro to 'Rock and Roll' by Zeppelin. Exactly on cue, the guy hits the riff, perfectly in time, the hot, crystal-clear sound of the Telecaster exactly right. His eyes shoot open, he turns and looks at the old tweed-covered, steamy Fender amp as if baffled that he is making this exquisite sound, and then he turns to the crowd and grins like a schoolboy as they roar and yell encouragement. He looks so happy.

Then Twinkle is singing: *Been a long time since I rock and rolled.* We are packed against the front of the low stage, grinning, breathing hard, strangers with hot skin pressed close together, all of us staring at her, at the film of sweat glistening all over her skin, at the way she throws her hair from side to side, how she closes her eyes and smiles as she screams the words *I can't count the tears of a life with no love.*

And the guitarist, his legs doing some kind of uncontrolled, disjointed twitching, completely out of time to the music but somehow wonderfully in rhythm. But it's Twinkle we keep looking at; when she sings it's just so damn good. And I'm sure, when I see the wide eyes around me, that I'm not the only one that feels that way. She thrusts her right leg forward, grabs the mike stand and the crowd jump and yell and cheer as she sings the end of the song: *It's been a long, lonely, lonely, lonely time.*

Then they drop into a slow blues, the fat guy gently stroking sultry three-note chords on the neck of the warm, mellow guitar, the bass softly strolling, pulsing with the bass drum, and when she sings I swear I can feel her voice deep in my stomach; the way she moves, the way she waves her fingers. Every man and woman in the hot, smoky bar is staring, all of us held by this slim woman; we're going nowhere, not now. She sings with such tenderness it's like a feather on your flesh, then her voice soars, like a call from a cabin in the backwoods, and everyone in the place is quivering.

> *I may be too much woman for you, baby*
> *But when you touch me you start a fire so strong*
> *I may be too much woman for you*
> *But honey we gonna find out*
> *Before too long. . .*

As she grabs the high notes, the fat guy closes his eyes, a blues wail rips clean out of the old Tele, and we look at her and, yeah, no bar band anywhere in this world has ever looked or sounded finer.

Next night BB King was in town and I went to see him at the Van Wezel, a huge, sterile, purple-coloured concert hall, inspired, they say, by a sea shell picked up off the beach by the wife of the architect. While waiting for the man they call the grandfather of the blues to grace the stage, I watch everyone settling into comfortable, well-cushioned seats and stretching their legs in anticipation. There's the those-and-such-as-those section right in front of the stage, silky Armani suits, Sex-in-the-City shoes, diamond-studded Rolexes, bleached teeth frozen in botox smiles. Some of them will have million-dollar boats tied up at the Longboat Bay Club; their kids train with the best tennis and golf stars in the world at the 300-acre IMG sports academy just a few miles north off Highway 41.

If you look further back, you'll see the guys from nearby Bradentown, or B-town, as some call it, which has street names like Martin Luther King Boulevard, a tough neighbourhood where many families somehow get by on welfare or minimum wage Wal-Mart jobs. These guys are proud of BB, he's one of them, they are going to have a *good* time tonight and they wait patiently, joking and laughing with their huge, melon-breasted wives with beautiful African smiles, their massive hot asses stretching their velvet pants to bursting point. They fan their faces with their concert programmes, even though the air conditioning is way up high, dry cool air pouring over us.

There's a large pair of white knees right behind me and I turn round. A heavily built tattooed woman is sitting beside a wiry Hispanic man with twitching hands and darting eyes. She has the muscles of a weightlifter, calf-high Doc Marten boots, legs that look like the brushes in a car wash, and tiny, bone-tight shorts straining around her thighs. She's wearing a tee shirt with the words *Harley Davidson – helping ugly people get laid since 1920.*

There is a shifting at the end of my row as one of the fattest women I have ever seen edges along to the empty seat beside me. She lowers herself into place, arranges her folds around her and when she catches her breath she starts talking to me, almost yelling, and I can't help liking her. She doesn't give a rat's ass about her size. *Hey,* she says, *I couldn't care less about these scrawny rich bitches down front.* If I want to know what a real woman is like, she tells me loudly, I can go back to the trailer park with her tonight. She throws her head back and laughs with shoulder shaking guffaws.

BB is 79, he likes to pace himself, sits down when he plays.

He takes it easier these days, chatting between songs, and sometimes during them, about the old times and joking about the helping hand that is Viagra. The audience nods, smiles, laughs, as if listening to a much-loved grandfather telling his story. He sings 'The Thrill Has Gone', but we all know it hasn't. He closes his eyes, blinking out the sweat rolling down his face, tilts his head back and sings out of the side of his mouth, then squeezes one of his licks from the neck of Lucille, his black Gibson guitar, his fingers vibrating, hitting the strings so hard they almost snap, and everyone hears why he is the best blues guitarist ever.

Being a Glaswegian with no shame I managed to talk my way into his tour bus afterwards; I just wanted to shake his hand. *Hey, I'm sitting with BB King!* We chat for a while about Scotland; he likes to play there and loves the beautiful countryside. He is gracious and charming, quietly spoken. I tell him about Twinkle and he smiles, happy that the music he loves is still alive and well where it counts, not in huge concert halls but in small hot bars, his roots. Either that or perhaps he's thinking about what he could do with the little blue pills in his pocket. . .

Driving home, I pass the coffee shop. It's a hot night but I shiver. I can almost feel the cold silence of the darkness inside and the dead weight of the notice taped across the glass door. CLOSED DOWN.

17

MEMPHIS

Elvis Presley

A hurricane was coming. Wilma had already wrecked Cancun; now it was turning, aiming across the Gulf of Mexico for the Florida coast. The Weather Channel kept us on our toes with 15-minute updates and even the national TV stations had grim-faced newsmen scaring the shit out of us. Armageddon was fast approaching.

Americans always have a wary eye on the sky – every day there seems to be an approaching *major weather event* somewhere: tornados, hurricanes, forest fires, bone–freezing winters, torrential rain bringing floods of biblical proportions, blinding blizzards, building–toppling earthquakes and even the occasional volcano erupting. America has hot summers, beautiful autumn colours and Christmas-card winters; it has great weather but a terrible climate. Scotland has terrible weather but a great climate.

The last time I was near a hurricane – and 25 miles is way too near – the hotel I was sheltering in lost all power and within hours the smell of old bodily fluids was overpowering. And it was a top-notch place, the kind where they pay someone to turn down your blanket and leave a foil-wrapped mint on your pillow, and the rooms smell sweet and clean, with perhaps a hint of lavender – very restful. But when those big winds howl, the palm trees sway and buckle and the power lines crash onto pavements and even the best hotels are plunged into darkness. When their big air conditioners stop spinning, the hotels' mattresses and carpets soon give up their lustful secrets. On the plane to Florida, I read a magazine advertisement for a CSI-type fluorescent-light semen detector: *For your safety in hotel rooms.* What are you supposed to say to the manager? *Excuse me, but I've found traces of. . .*

Most homes escape fatal wind damage, the locals roll up in their trucks to Home Depot, buy every 8' × 4' sheet of plywood and take them back to nail over their windows. When every room is daylight-free, they shrug their shoulders, lock the front doors behind them and head for hurricane parties in the bars of the nearest Hiltons, Marriotts or Hard Rock hotels, safe havens where they sit out the storms happily mixing new cocktails. 'Dodging a bullet', is what they call it.

The cynical view of Americans is that they are all wealthy and have Olympic-size swimming pools, walk-in fridges, granite worktops and beds the size of tennis courts to accommodate their huge arses; nothing could be further from reality. Most Americans I know work desperately hard, put in much longer hours and are permitted far fewer holidays than Europeans. They have to pay for absolutely everything from their first drink of plain tap water to their last dying aspirin. And almost all of them do it with a cheerfulness that is humbling.

In Florida there are many old homes built of wood – garden sheds in the UK seem sturdier – and thousands of retired folk eke out their savings in mobile homes that become spectacularly airborne if the big wind blasts through their trailer park. Peaceful Nook or Shady Willows will suddenly look like an explosion in a tinfoil factory. Pleasant Haven by the sea becomes Pleasant

Haven in the sea.

As the hurricane centres watch the swirling storm and try to figure out where it will hit land – something that is almost impossible to predict – everyone living in an area that looks likely to be in its path is ordered to leave by the police. Even a rumour of mandatory evacuation causes all sorts of hassle. All the supermarket shelves are stripped bare in the mad rush to stock up with emergency supplies, and if you don't have a full tank of gas in your car you could be in real trouble. The freeways are jammed. When New Orleans was hammered, the roads were so blocked that it could take 12 hours to escape a few miles north on the freeway. Countless cars ran out of fuel as they inched forward to nowhere. It is not fun.

Tracking hurricanes is largely guesswork because they suddenly appear over the warm surface of the ocean as moisture is sucked up into the atmosphere, rapidly build up to devastating force and can veer off in any direction in a moment. It took only five days for Katrina to escalate from being a harmless tropical breeze far out in the Gulf to leaving New Orleans looking like Hiroshima. Sometimes it seems disaster is imminent and then the storm backs off and disappears. Sometimes it completely switches direction and takes out an entire town that thought it was safe. It's like a rabid pit bull.

I decided to get out while I could when I noticed that there wasn't a single bird on the beach. Gloomy silence. Usually there are loads of them, herons swooping and diving, little armies of sandpipers that chase each retreating wave then bang their beaks into the wet sand for whatever it is they eat before the next roll of surf tumbles in. The shore was abandoned, the salty air whipping the sand, a restless, moody ocean, the water grey and troubled. I remembered being in San Francisco and seeing a colony of seals that lives in the harbour, flapping and happily honking to the tourists. They always bugger off just before an earthquake; perhaps Floridian birds have the same inside knowledge. It was time to get out of town.

But where? I called my friend Keverley, an island girl, who has lived at the beach all her life. She sighed and told me I'd left it too late to leave by car – the I75 was jammed solid, like a cholesterol clogged artery. 'All them damn tourists are running scared, hauling their white Yankee asses outta here.' Either I caught a plane to someplace else before they closed the airport or I should 'hunker down and sit it out'. Hell, that's what she'd always done.

A Category 3 can tear your roof apart like wet tissue paper. If you were crazy enough to tie yourself to a lamppost and gawp at the storm, as some guys do – they're usually called Billybob or Leroy – it could rip the fillings out of your teeth. Wilma had built up to the dreaded Category 5, the most powerful force on the face of the earth. The state governor was on television, warning any residents who refused to evacuate that they better have some identification tattooed on their butts so that their next of kin could be informed.

The storm had wobbled and stalled for a moment but it was coming. No doubt about it; it was just marshalling all its power. The slight delay meant that one of the airlines, which keep flying as long as possible, still had a seat to Tennessee if I moved fast – it was the last flight before they locked everything down. I hadn't been in Memphis since I played there with the Incredible String Band so I thought I'd head for Beale Street. It would be a better place to spend a couple of days than clinging to the roof of my house if it got swept into the Gulf of Mexico.

It is easy to get around downtown Memphis; they have lovely old streetcars, some dating back to 1912, that are clean, reliable and a delight to travel in. For less than a dollar you can climb aboard and relax on shiny wooden seats and, as the trolley clanks along gleaming rails, enjoy gazing at the kind of brick buildings you see in old Humphrey Bogart movies, department stores, drugstores and small-town banks with unfamiliar names. You know you are in the Deep South and feel sure that, at any moment, guys in pinstripe suits and fedoras will emerge into the sunshine and stop for a shoe-shine while they read last night's baseball scores. I like travelling by streetcar, it's so much nicer than driving around frantically trying to hunt down a parking space.

Until about 1936 America had the best public transport in the world. Then a company called National City Lines was formed and bought up more than 100 trolley companies in all the big towns, and promptly closed them down. They ripped up the tracks and replaced them with roads – not a coincidence, according to conspiracy theorists, since NCL was owned by General Motors, Firestone, Standard Oil and Phillips Petroleum. Ever since, Americans have been dependent on cars.

Huge out-of-town malls with all the shops under the same roof and massive car parks killed off many town centres, but with the help of the streetcars, Memphis has been successfully regenerating itself. In 2000 they built the Autozone, a red and green, 14,000-seater ballpark right in the middle of downtown where the Memphis Red Birds play. No, I'd never heard of them either but it's a wonderful place; even when it's empty you can almost hear the crack of ball and bat, the cheers of the crowd as another home run clicks up on the electronic scoreboard. In Britain we often think American cities are dangerous and crime-ravaged, but I can't imagine many UK town councils would want football grounds to be built in their city centres in an attempt to

create a sense of community.

A few minutes' stroll downhill from the Autozone is Beale Street, with its bars and restaurants that have blues bands playing day and night. Some of them are very good, although many sound alike, playing the same walking bass lines and slinky three-note guitar chords. I don't recall Beale Street having so many bands when I played in Memphis because if it had I would definitely have jammed with them. When I was young I loved to have a few drinks and sit in with other bands, sometimes whether they invited me or not. Anywhere, anytime. It was great fun; I played with all sorts of people, from little pub groups to Rory Gallagher and Ritchie Havens.

A block away from Beale Street at the start of Union Avenue, is the Isaac Hayes soulfood restaurant and its glossy photographs of the leather-clad Shaft: *A complicated man nobody understood but his woman*, according to the song. Americans do like their theme-based eateries. Just across the street is Lansky's clothing store, where the founder, Bernard, was still working when he was 78 years old, although that is not at all unusual in America. Publix supermarkets employ many old folk as bag packers – they take the jobs because they are desperate for the health-care benefits. Bernard used to make all Elvis Presley's clothes, even letting him have a suit on credit for his appearance on the Ed Sullivan show when he was penniless, a wise investment as it turned out.

In the States, as in the UK, we find the same chain stores, multiplex cinemas and, on almost every corner, Starbucks – or Fastbucks as some cynics call it. Because many towns are now almost identical, anything slightly unusual can pull in bewilderingly large crowds. And so, if I might have a minute of your time, stroll with me through the portals of the famous

Peabody Hotel.

From early afternoon camera-laden thrill-seekers gather in the hotel's grand lobby and jostle into position near a small fountain, where ducks are splashing, eating, quacking, shitting, and doing whatever ducks do to pass their day. Long before the appointed hour draws near, two packed lines of strangely excited people form a corridor from the fountain all the way across the lobby to the elevator. At exactly five o'clock, a uniformed concierge appears, makes a little speech – there's too much *ooohing and aaahing* to hear what he is saying – then marches to the elevator with the ducks waddling in a line behind him. They get into the lift, the door closes and the smiling tourists applaud happily. The show is over for another day.

A couple of the porters working at the Peabody were from New Orleans and, like so many others, they had lost everything when Katrina wrecked the place. Memphis had welcomed them like long-lost brothers, finding them jobs and homes. The South can be a heart-warmingly hospitable place, but, judging by the large number of men shuffling around and sleeping on benches, Memphis already had plenty of its own homeless people, and if Fedex, who has its biggest base there, ever pulls out, the locals really will have something to sing the blues about. Hotels, clubs, bars and soul music museums provide limited employment opportunities, usually minimum-wage jobs.

If you are still with me, a fair distance up the street from the Peabody is our next destination. Elvis Presley first visited Sun Studios at 707 Union Avenue in the summer of 1953 to record – he said – a song for his mother as a birthday gift, although her birthday had actually been some months earlier. More to the point, the Presleys didn't have a record player, so it's likely he was trying to catch the attention of Sam Phillips, the studio owner.

When you consider that his face became the icon of rock and roll for all time, it is baffling that it took a year of frequent visits to the little studio before the record producer noticed him.

Possibly Sam had more on his mind. In 1951, he had recorded what he claimed to be the first rock and roll record, a song called 'Rocket 88' by Jackie Brenston, the sax player in a band led by Mississippi pianist Ike Turner, who later became famous as a wife-beater. The story goes that the guitar player's amplifier fell off the roof of the band's car as they drove to the session and Sam jammed paper into the mangled speaker cone as a makeshift repair. When the guitarist plugged in, the sound was like a blown truck exhaust. The kids loved it.

It's a good tale even if it seems unlikely. In those days amplifiers used glass valves and presumably any fall that wrecked the speaker would shatter them. Apart from that, if you cranked up any of those old amps much beyond halfway they would rasp like an old kazoo. It doesn't matter; Sam saw the potential in having a fuzzy riff driving the song and suddenly he was on his way to becoming one of the busiest record producers in the South.

Sam recorded many black bluesmen such as Howling Wolf and BB King. When he formed Sun Records as an independent label, he promised to record anything, anytime, anywhere. He took that a little too far in 1953 when he released a song called 'Bear Cat' featuring local DJ Rufus Thomas and was delighted when it shot to number three in the R&B chart. He barely had time to pour the champagne before he was served with a writ for ripping off the almost identical Lieber and Stoller song, 'Hound Dog', which had been a hit for Big Mama Thornton. He narrowly escaped having his arse reamed, as the legal term has it, which was fortunate in view of what was to come.

For a long time Sam had been looking for a white boy who could sing like a black bluesman, someone who could top the national pop music charts, so much more lucrative than those of the small R&B record stores of the South. On the hot, humid Monday evening of 5 July 1954, Elvis, guitarist Scotty Moore and double bass player Bill Black were trying to record a version of the Bing Crosby hit 'Harbor Lights'. It wasn't going too well, Elvis was nervous and sounded stiff. Yawning and frustrated, they took a break late in the evening, snapped open a few bottles of Coke. Trying to relax a little and lighten things up, Elvis picked up his guitar and started clowning around, twitching his legs as he strummed an Arthur Crudup blues tune, singing fast in a jokey, staccato voice. The song was 'That's Alright Mama'.

As soon as he heard it, Sam realised the skinny kid from Tupelo was exactly what he wanted. *Damn, he'd been under his feet all this time!* Just over a year later, Sam sold Elvis's contract to RCA for $35,000. Many people thought it was the worst piece of business in history, but Sam was street-smart. 'Selling Elvis to RCA made Sun really well-known. If I hadn't done that we probably would have stayed a little provincial label.'

Even though it is still a working studio – U2 recorded there with BB King – it opens every day for guided tours. I stayed for a long time, looking round the small 18' × 33' warehouse, with its white, acoustic-tiled walls and ceiling, staring at a photograph on the wall of Elvis, Carl Perkins, Johnny Cash and Jerry Lee Lewis standing round the piano, and the old amplifiers quietly humming on the same grey linoleum floor these guys stood on all those years ago.

Since I was in Memphis, I reckoned I should visit Elvis's home, Graceland. A pal, Tommy Cunningham, the drummer with Wet Wet Wet, had told me about the time they played at the

Pyramid, the huge concert hall overlooking the muddy old Mississippi. They'd been invited to a party at Graceland by Priscilla, Elvis's former wife. 'It was weird. Looking around, I kept thinking that Elvis must have shagged there or pissed here.'

Elvis's home is one of America's busiest tourist attractions; to many fans it is a pilgrimage. They form long, orderly queues at the Graceland visitor centre to catch a shuttle bus that drops them at the door of the house on the other side of the road, just a couple of hundred yards away.

It was originally quite a modest gaff, which Elvis bought in 1957 for $100,000. A few years later he added a gym with squash courts and weights machines and other muscle-building contraptions that set him back another $200,000. The house is pretty much as he left it, Formica-covered worktops in the well-used kitchen, and deep shag-pile carpets. As you might guess, there are hundreds of gold discs on the walls, loads of old television sets playing the shows he would have watched, and display cases with his stage clothes, those white, glittering jumpsuits that seem smaller than you expected. American tour guides know how to build to a finale and solemnly lead the crowd out to the garden, stopping at a monument beside the swimming pool. *And this, folks, is his final resting place. Let's take a moment.* Cameras click at the engraved stone: 'Here lies Elvis.' Hanging over it seems to be an atmosphere of heavy sadness – thousands of people have mourned here.

The area around Graceland used to be rural, farmlands with mooing cows, clucking hens, neighing horses and that sort of thing – perhaps even some ducks having a wee holiday from their jobs at the Peabody. But the suburbs have spread, so now the house is beside a busy road with Jiffy Lubes and discount liquor stores. A cab driver told me that the neighbourhood 'is not one you outta be walking in after dark unless you belong there'.

In fact, a large part of it seems perfectly safe because it is taken up entirely by the Graceland complex: Elvis museums, souvenir shops, food outlets serving peanut butter and jelly sandwiches just the way the King liked 'em– *burp! Uh, pardon me, ma'am* – and the predictably named Heartbreak Hotel. There's plenty to see – the films of him playing gigs in the 1950's are brilliant. I wonder if the people in those first screaming crowds realised they were watching the world's best performer; that they would never, ever see a more exciting star.

Elvis donated a lot of money to charity, and enjoyed buying things, liked his Cadillacs, Mercs and motorbikes. He even had two private jets, one of which has a sumptuous bedroom that you can go into and conjure up exciting and erotic fantasies. Just bear in mind that you are being watched on closed-circuit TV.

The religions of something like two-thirds of the people on this planet believe in reincarnation. They are convinced that the actions of a person in their current life determine their fate in the next. If this is true, he must have done some wonderful things in his previous existence to earn the fabulous life he did when, on 8 January 1935, he was reborn into this world as Elvis Aaron Presley.

18

NASHVILLE

Grand Ole Opry

EY, I really enjoyed writing that last chapter – made me feel like one of those travel writers. So here we go again. Songwriters reckon that all roads lead to Nashville. They might, but you have to find one first. It's as if the city wants to keep strangers out. *Another tune about a mean man and his cheatin' woman? We got enough, already!* I wanted to go by rail, drink coffee, watch the cotton fields drift by, hear that old train whistle a-blowin' at dusk, but for some reason there doesn't seem to be a track between Memphis and Nashville, so I drove in a one-way rental car along the I40. It's one of those vast American highways, 100 miles longer than the more famous Route 66, stretching through eight states from Carolina to California, a greater distance than London to Damascus. If you drove all of its 2,547 miles I bet you would have heard of every city on the way: Flagstaff, Albuquerque, Amarillo, Oklahoma City, Little Rock. . . It's exciting cruising along even a small part of it, imagining all those familiar places. Perhaps I'll write a book about it some day. I mean, no one's ever thought of doing that before, right?

As long as you know whether you want to go north, south, east or west, American freeways are usually easy to navigate, and there are plenty of helpful signs telling you Nashville is up ahead: 70 miles, 50, 30,10 . . . then nothing. You can see its skyscrapers, high on a hill to your right – *that's definitely it there* – and you assume that there will be a sign for downtown – there always is. But all of a sudden the only ones are for places like Louisville and Knoxville and. . . *Where the hell has it gone?*

This can't be right. There must be a downtown sign. You realise with a sinking feeling and a flutter of panic that Nashville is receding fast in your rear-view mirror. You have to pull off the freeway to do an about-turn, not always possible in America because there might not be an on-ramp to take you back onto the freeway. You could be driving into a *barrio* that doesn't exactly welcome outsiders. A pal once came off an exit in East LA and before he could get the hell out of there, some crazy asshole, who I guess had nothing better to do but lie in wait for a lost traveller in a big white Lincoln, shattered his windscreen with a well-aimed shot.

Having grown up in Glasgow, the great thing is that you have long since stopped worrying about what might await you in potentially hostile neighbourhoods. You have adopted a kismet attitude; if it's going to happen, *fuck it*, it's gonna happen. It doesn't really matter whether it's by the crazed knife of some Drumchapel drunk or the bullet of a Harlem headcase; you can only die once, and it will happen at the allotted time and not a moment before.

Sighing, I steered off the freeway and pulled into the dirt parking lot of an old railroad-car diner, where fat, tattooed truckers and bearded bikers were sucking up elephant-sized all day breakfasts. And if they damn well wanna smoke, they will. The kind of place where everyone looks up when a skinny stranger walks in – it reminded me of a Gorbals pub. I ordered a soda, to make me sound as if I knew the score, then asked directions from a guy sitting at the counter in oily dungarees, torn tee shirt and the name of a car-breaker yard on his greasy baseball cap. He looked up from his bucket-sized paper cup and assured me that *no, sir, you didn't miss the downtown sign because there warn't one*, then patiently told me how to get there.

Nashville is similar to Memphis in that it is redeveloping the downtown area, and will soon have a baseball park in the heart of town. The centre of Nashville is on a big hill and it's easy to get confused if your hotel is at the top, as mine was, since all the streets head downwards in four directions. Finding your way around American cities, which are usually built on a grid system of blocks 100 yards long, is normally easy, unless you are so fascinated by everything, as I usually am, that you forget which way you came from. *Did I turn left out of Starbucks or right? I know it was downhill ... eh ... where am I?*

Except for a trailer park which was now in lunar orbit, the hurricane over Florida had pretty much blown itself out, so before I went back I thought I'd do three things: see the Grand Ole Opry, which I had last visited when I gigged in Nashville with the Incredible String Band; look up a pal I played with years ago in an Irish showband; and go and hear some country bands – not well-known ones, with their Las Vegas-style extravaganzas, but the guys cranking out nifty guitar licks in the bars. But first I fancied a wee look in Gruhn's guitar store. I dumped the hire car at the Budget office and walked the short distance to the corner of 4th Avenue and Broadway.

George Gruhn knows all about 'vintage' guitars. When The Beatles and Stones became famous they created worldwide demand for Fender, Gibson and Gretsch guitars. I wonder if they were ever sent Christmas cards by the companies? Or a wee something a bit more tangible? At that time, guitars were not mass-produced by clattering machines in factories in Japan and Mexico, and old models, many of them hand-made from beautifully seasoned rosewood and maple, are very much sought after. A Stratocaster made by Fender before the company was taken over by the CBS Corporation in 1964 would have cost about £150 when new. If you had the same one today it could easily fetch £15,000 on eBay, especially if it has been lying forgotten and unused in its tweed case in some old dear's attic. If it had been owned by somebody famous, it could get a crazy price: Mitch Mitchell, who played with Hendrix, sold one of Jimi's at Christies for £100,000.

The pawnshops of Memphis and Nashville used to be goldmines glittering with cheap vintage guitars, ruefully hocked by musicians who had failed to make the big time and needed the price of a Greyhound ticket back home to their former day jobs. Then Ian Hunter of 1970s' band Mott the Hoople wrote an otherwise excellent book in which he bragged about all the unbelievable bargains he'd picked up among the unredeemed pledges. He gave the game away; the pawnshops immediately trebled their prices.

Nowadays, eBay and the Internet have made it almost impossible to find a cheap old Rickenbacker, like George used on 'Hard Day's Night', or a Fender Broadcaster, like Springsteen plays. And there are countless fakes kicking around, although if you have been playing guitar for a long time you can usually spot a phoney as soon as you pick it up. Old guitars have a very special feel. I would much prefer to have an old Telecaster hanging on my wall than a Picasso.

Gruhn's guitar shop had some beautiful instruments: *This Martin feels so good. And can I have a wee shot of that Les Paul Junior, please?* I drooled over them for several happy hours and tried to ignore my credit card, which was getting seriously excited, trying to jump right out of my wallet.

In the old days, twisting their radio dials and tuning into the *Grand Ole Opry Show* used to be the high spot of the week for hard-workin', God-fearin' country folk all over the South. It was broadcast live from the Ryman auditorium, a lovely old converted church on 5th Avenue. The audiences at the Opry had been entertained by the best country stars in the world and were not easily impressed, but when Hank Williams first appeared there they wouldn't let him leave the building until he had played six encores. That must have been some night. It was a strictly bluegrass venue; no drummers allowed. When Johnny Cash played there, according to the tour guide at Sun Studios, he threaded a dollar bill through his guitar strings and hit them, *chug-a-chug*, making a noise like a snare drum, and so was born the rhythmic sound that helped make him famous.

The Ryman is still used as a concert hall – Jeff Beck played there not long ago so I guess they've relaxed the rules a tad – but the Opry is now located in the world's largest convention centre, about half an hour out of town. The show is still broadcast live every Friday and Saturday night and anyone can listen to it as they sit a while on their porch, gently swaying back and forth in their rocking chair, sipping good corn whiskey or home-made lemonade, crickets chirping, the dawg snoozing at their feet. All they need is an old valve radio or a broadband connection.

The night I went it featured eight acts in a two-hour show. I'd never heard of any of them, but they were all excellent, taking it in turn to gather round a microphone in the middle of the stage and do their thing. When the mandolin player, guitarist or fiddler played a solo he simply stepped closer to it, just like they did back in the 1920's. While each band changed over, there was a live message from our sponsors read by a guy with one of those deep, rich voices that are perfect for radio: *Martha White biscuits – mmm*

– fresh just like mom used to bake.

It was packed with old people, some very old. Motorised wheelchairs, Zimmers, oxygen bottles on trolleys, lots of check shirts tucked neatly into long shorts, arthritic knees showing above pulled-up white socks and gleaming black shoes. The audience was getting on in years too. Every week, thousands of people roll up in gleaming air-conditioned coaches to hear country music played the old-fashioned way, just as they had always liked it. There's a real nice atmosphere at the Opry, like sitting in a room full of smiling grandparents. I liked it very much.

Afterwards, I caught the shuttle bus back downtown; it was time to walk the bars and honky tonks and listen to the *stories.* The folk songs brought to America in long-ago times by exiled Scots and Irish were like books before the days of paperbacks. They told tales, sung with easily remembered tunes, which is why they survived so long. Country music has preserved this tradition: the main thing about country songs is that they have to tell a story. *You have two minutes to make your point, boy, and the tape's running.* The format is to keep it simple: Don't bore us; get to the chorus.

Country music certainly doesn't deserve sneers that it's all about dead dogs and divorce. Being able to write good country music is a rare talent, and if you have it, glittering riches await. Every star wants to be in the Country Music Television top twenty, is desperately seeking the tune that will bring them a Grammy Award and place in the Hall of Fame.

Hank Williams was a master of the art, his songs are beautiful poems, often tragic, plainly told in less than 2 mins 40 seconds, not a word too many or few. *I'll be locked up in this cell, 'til my body's just a shell, and my hair turns whiter than snow.* Hooked on morphine and whisky, he led a short, unhappy life. *I've never seen a night so long, when time was crawling by. [I've] lost the will to live; I'm so lonesome I could cry.* He wasn't kidding, and died at 29 in the back of his Cadillac on the way to a gig.

The most successful country songs follow a simple structure; the writers have the skill of storytelling down cold, and, like traditional folk musicians, their songs reflect the times we live in. Toby Keith tells us with commendable honesty that he likes his women *rough* and has a *little Whiskey Girl*, with a belly-button ring, and a tattoo she only shows to him. There's nothing fancy about her. *She ain't into wine and roses, she cain't stand the thought of champagne.*

When two horny cowgirls offer to put a *big Texas smile on his face*, he manfully accepts but with the sensitive demurral that he's getting on in years, *not as good as he once was, but as good once as he ever was*. Not all Toby's songs are so tender, and in a similar vein to bloodthirsty Irish anthems, he released a battle-song aimed at the 9/11 terrorists, promising them that the USA would *light up your world like the fourth of July*.

On a cheerier note, former trailer park girl Gretchen Wilson just loves to *partay*, dressing in unbuttoned shirts and tight jeans to *watch the lil' boys come undone*. She's a self-confessed *redneck woman, hell, yeah*, who likes to drink beer all night from *a four-wheel-drive tailgate* and keeps *her Christmas lights on the porch all year long*.

There's Terri Clark, who tells us what we all suspected: 'Girls Lie Too.' She assures her man that his comb-over is sexy, that *his old grey sweat pants turn her on*, and when they go out to dinner she *loves Hooters for their hot wings too*. Of course, *size doesn't matter and that other guys never cross her mind – how could it be any better than it is with you?*

While stars of yesteryear such as Tammy Wynette were

content to stand by their men no matter what, Carrie Underwood is less forgiving and takes no guff when her man cheats with a *bleached-blonde tramp*. She digs her keys *into the side of his four wheel drive, carves her name into his leather seats* then, perhaps a tad excessively, slashes holes in his tyres before finishing the job by taking a *Louisville slugger to both headlights.*

I love it. Makes such a change from listening to skinny rock stars squealing *Oww, baby, pretty baby and Little girl ah lurve yew.*

I called my pal from my Irish showband days, and we met up on 4th Avenue. Almost every place was a music bar and we wandered in and out of them, listening to the groups, all of them terrific, earthy, gutsy, string-bendin' guitar playing, soaring pedal-steels, overhead fans whirring, beer-drinking, yelling, high fives. *Damn right, that's one ass-kickin' band.* A bit livelier than the air-conditioned Grand Ole Opry.

My pal has been playing in Nashville for 20 years but doesn't exactly have a work permit so likes to keep a low profile unless, of course, Dolly Parton or someone cares to offer him a gig. Although he's a superb guitarist, he's never made the big-time in Nashville, but hasn't given up hope. He writes and records his own songs in his small apartment, teaching guitar to pay the rent. 'It's very hard to run a band here,' he says, his Belfast accent still strong after all these years. 'You've got to keep the musicians busy, get as much work as possible, keep them earning money or they go and join other groups. They don't want to spend their time in rehearsal rooms. They want paid. A lot of the jobs are in bars and you're playing for what you collect at the door.' Every so often he'd nod in the direction of a bass player or a guitarist and mention the names of famous bands they'd once been in. 'Aye, him now, he's a great player, but he likes the whuskey too much. And, Jaysus, the powder that one's stuck up his nose!'

Next day I had a little time to kill before my flight back to Florida. I went for a walk and wandered into the very grand Tennessee State Capital building, an outstanding example of Greek Revival architecture, as it says in the guidebook, sitting proudly at the top of the hill in a sunny park with lovely views. It was cool inside, oil paintings, a beautiful staircase, white and black marble. I always get annoyed when I see the money that politicians lavish on their comforts but kept my mouth shut because there was a state trooper guarding the joint. He was big. Very big. He sat quietly behind a polished oak desk, bulging over it, making it look like something out of a nursery school. A brutal-looking firearm was strapped to his side where he could get at it quickly.

I was the only visitor. His fingers were as thick as hot dogs and he expertly searched me, gave me a pass, then sat down to continue studying a well-worn, large-print Bible, nodding his head every so often, reading aloud quietly to himself, sometimes carefully outlining sections of text with a yellow marker. The lighting was a little subdued, so he'd brought a frilly bedside lamp with the Wal-Mart price tag still on it. His huge finger moved across the page as he mouthed each word. Then he started humming, perhaps trying to write the song that would get him out of there forever.

Och, you never know.

19

ST PETERSBURG

Devon Allman and Dickey Betts

I LOVE outdoor gigs, especially on a hot summer night, but have long passed the age where the thought of going to somewhere like Glastonbury can raise a flicker of enthusiasm. It's the pain of getting there, having to park 20 miles from the entrance, trudging through hassling hordes of scaffy little ticket touts, pushing aside pickpockets and being pawed by hulking bouncers. It's the British rain, the greasy burger vans, the long, twitching queues to shit in a tin box overflowing with crap and ribbons of soiled toilet paper. I hate being on my feet for hours, wedged in a crush of swaying, shirtless, sweaty neds who love pishing in their pint glasses then throwing it over everyone; my knees are just too old. And my idea of a restful end to the day is definitely not wading through a dark field of mud trying to find my tent only to discover, as happened to a friend at T in the Park, a bunch of junkies had used it as a *cludge*, as a lavatory is called by genteel folk in Scotland.

In Glasgow, the sky hung heavy. The chill, wet winds of the north had stripped the trees bare and were twisting them to the ground, bending their branches like arm wrestlers. The long nights of winter had arrived. If the sun came up at all, it would poke its head up around nine, blink a few times, then bugger off behind the cold, dark tenements around noon. But here in St

Pete, in Vinoy Park where Laguna Avenue meets Tampa Bay, thousands of people are stretched out in beautiful sunshine, tee shirts, shorts. Florida in autumn is the place for open-air music.

Even though it's November it's hot, nudging 80, the air fresh and clear, low humidity, a gentle breeze drifting in from the bay. All the hurricanes have gone, the engine room of the churning Gulf calm and still again until next year. The steamy July swamp-making rains and dripping sweats of August are behind us. Every flower, tree and bush has gorged itself on the summer rains and is plump and lush, the sky is blue, the palms richly green. It's perfect, just perfect, and it feels so good to be sitting here. Och – sorry if I sound smug.

Devon Allman, son of Greg of the Allman Brothers, is on stage with his band, chunky chords, smooth slide guitar, wailing blues solos – they are good. He's a nice guy – I've met him a couple of times. He is slim, has blonde hair, good looks, and a great voice, everything he needs to be a big star on CMT but he prefers playing southern rock, loves to be on the road with his band, even if it won't make them rich. 'I'm not after stardom, I want to be making really good music that's soulful and powerful. I love the blues, I want to carry that torch.'

Some of the local restaurants have set up catering tents and for half the usual menu price you can try the best crab cakes, fried chicken and Cuban food you'll taste anywhere. There's also more than enough burgers, chilli and beer to keep everyone burping. A lot of folk have been drinking all day, but everyone seems relaxed, all here for a good time. Muscular black guys and bikers in studded, sleeveless denim jackets queue patiently for foaming Buds – bucket size – trading tall tales about their Harleys, falls that have stripped their butts to the bone, speed cops they have outsmarted, and roads to avoid: *Too many damn ree-tire-ees with white sticks.*

Trailer-trash gals, as they proudly call themselves, are cracking outrageous jokes about their dumb-ass men, as they blow Marlboro smoke above their heads, away from the people in the line behind them. They have babies on their hips and are clutching crumpled twenty-dollar bills to buy paper plates piled high with fried chicken, dawgs and beans.

At the side, just over there in the shade of the banyan trees, branches heavy with trails of Spanish moss, is a group of laughing Mexicans, kicking a soccer ball with their children. Running, jumping, beautiful brown eyes, huge smiles. They're having one day off from their cash-paid lawn-service and roofing jobs. Thousands have settled in Tampa, been here years although still only speaking *poquito* English, but their children chatter happily in the flowing accents of all American kids – ending every sentence on a questioning upward cadence – switching easily from Spanish to English. If they play their cards right, their bilingual skill could land them really good jobs when they grow up, that's for sure.

From his hot spot working the steel counter at the Starbucks trolley, my pal Jon waves to me, smiles and holds his hands apart the height of a tall cappuccino, his eyebrows raised in a question: *Extra shot?* I hold my thumb up – *thanks* – and stand at the side of the line; he'll get to me in a minute. Soon as he serves these good folks. *And how are we doin' this fine day?*

These good folks, tanned, old-money Floridians with expensively dressed children at their sides, wait patiently for a grande latte decaff, a chilled coconut/banana frappuccino, and two bottles of water, please: *No, Whitney, soda makes you hyper.* Their parents had been smart enough to buy up those old shacks and 1950s' cinder-block cottages that had been slowly crumbling on large, tree-shaded beach lots before the condo builders cottoned onto Florida. Now they spend their days checking their stocks and bonds, attending fund-raisers, sitting on the boards of homeowners' associations and helping out at the local botanical gardens and art galleries. Their gleaming, twin-Yamaha-engined boat is tied up at the wooden dock a short stroll from the park, ready, waiting. They'll listen to Devon Allman: *Hey, that boy can play! Wasn't his father married to Cher?* Then maybe cruise down to Siesta Beach for the sunset. *Feel that sand, children. Like sugar. Best white sand in the world is right here at Siesta.* Or perhaps a seafood dinner on the old pier at Anna Marie Island; it's not far and the kids like the hamburgers.

And sitting quietly in the shade is . . . I can't remember her name. She's from New York, where she worked for years editing textbooks. She was too close to the Twin Towers that September morning, and when the dust cleared she escaped to Florida, is the editor of a New Age magazine, has high hopes for a TV script she's writing and never eats anything that has been cooked. Wafer thin, with china-white skin and long, brittle black hair, she has formed a network of raw-food friends and they're hoping to open a restaurant here soon, like the one in LA. She says scientists have proved that raw food prevents ageing; she's sticking with it.

A huge swell of teenagers, false ID cards in their sweat-soaked, unbuttoned shirts are gulping Michelobs and dancing like crazy in front of the stage. They can drive at 16, fire XM-8 assault rifles in I-raq at 18, but it's illegal to drink beer until they are 21. Perhaps just as well.

Sinewy, skinny rednecks with sun-leathered skin, tattoos snaking over their flesh, dancing jerkily, sipping from frothing beer cans. Long-haired guys stretched out in canvas chairs, coolers at their side, booze in their huge bellies, lungs full of marijuana smoke, grinning, just grinning. Weight-trained college boys in tight vests slowly swayin' to the music with their beautiful girlfriends, perfect cheerleader teeth, sun-bleached hair, tiny shorts and tops – and who wouldn't want to show off those volleyball-firm muscles? There are security guards and a few cops here and there but they're having a quiet shift; nobody is going to cause trouble. Not today.

I'm here with Keverley, the island girl, and her husband Geoff, who used to be a roadie with the Incredible String Band. They enjoy outdoor gigs, did plenty before they got married. She worked for the caterer that fed the big stars who played Tampa Stadium. She'll keep you laughing for hours with stories about the *we wannas* some of them attached to their contracts. Like the diva who demanded a jacuzzi, immediately, or she'd walk right outta there. Kev managed to find a company who rushed over a stretch limo with a built-in hot tub. 'Wish I would've taken a picture of that bitch nekkid in the suds – it'd be worth a lotta money now.'

They weren't all like that. 'BB King – now he was a gentleman, talked with him a long time, made him a nice dinner. Rod Stu-urt, sittin' there in his little white underpants – whooeee! All he wanted was a cup of tea, he was a cool dude. I'll tell ya, country bands were the worst – all of them crazy with drugs.'

They have their two lovely daughters with them, 10 and 12, burning up Geoff's monthly allowance of Verizon minutes. He has a panicked look in his eyes. 'They never seem to be talking about anything, just nodding and saying *OK* and *yeah* and *whatever*. They can be with their friends all day then yack to them for four hours at night. Always got them damn phones at their ears.'

He shrugs, cracks open a can of Bud, takes a long pull, then smiles. 'Kids in America, they expect everything. When I grew up in England you had to work, had to do a paper round if you wanted spending money. Here, they see these TV shows about teenagers being given Mercedes convertibles by their daddies and think they'll get the same. On their sixteenth birthday they expect to look out the window and see a car in the driveway all tied up in a ribbon waiting for them. Not any old car, not a twenty-year-old Volvo. No. It's gotta be new, gotta be a sports car. It has to be red, has to be shining, have the insurance documents in it, full tank of gas, even a pair of sunglasses.'

Kev laughs, and tells him to *chill out, come do some yoga with me.* She sits on the grass, closes her eyes and it's *crouching dog* and *stretched-ass cat* or whatever. She trained in dance at school and still has the flexibility of a teenager. Their seven-year-old son edges close, says he's got something for her, farts in her face then, jangling on Pepsi and Doritos, runs off to cause chaos someplace else. On stage, Devon is playing his encore, hitting those big chords, his guitar screaming and, yeah, everyone is relaxing. Even Steve.

Steve hates rice.

He has a real problem with it.

He knows why.

He lights another cigarette from the butt of the one he just finished. He's not drinking; says he's learned better. 'My wife is a deputy sheriff and she gets embarrassed.' He wears cheap plastic glasses held together with sticky tape. They keep slipping down, and he pushes them back up with the tip of an arthritic finger.

I don't know him well, but enough to be wary. If he had anything stronger than a cola in his hand, I'd sit somewhere else. I'm enjoying listening to the bands too much. I don't want to be keeping an eye on him. If he's been drinking, there's plenty that sets him off. But nothing as much as rice.

He told me once, quietly: 'I'm half white and half Lakota Indian. Lakotas were Plains Indians and can't handle alcohol. Something in our genes. We get mean, really mean. I don't drink any more. Used to get into too many brawls, had fifty or more around town.'

He's 60, but still wiry, he installs heavy air-conditioning units for a living. 'At eighteen, I took a physical. There was a hunner' an' forty of us and I was the only one who passed. Then they gave me a mental test and I failed so I was in. They were looking for people who weren't right in here.' Taps his head. 'That's how I ended up in a special unit in Vietnam.'

His glasses slide again. He examines them. Sighs. 'It's amazing we had the arrogance to think we could get away with it, not get ourselves killed, but we were young and didn't know any better. We'd just go in there firing.'

He knows all about explosives and how to rig traps. *You find a flashlight on the ground, what's the first thing you're gonna do with it?* He still has nightmares. He likes to listen to southern rock music, it helps him relax. He's come to see Dickey Betts, and is happy to sit quietly in a chair at the edge of the crowd, smoke a few Marlboros, watch the sun go down, but he's got four bullet wounds that remind him about Vietnam. 'Even now I can't stand the sight of rice. I was in a restaurant, and a guy at the next table he's got a bowl of rice and he's talking in a loud voice, going on, telling his friends how good it is and all and I got mad. I grabbed his head and shoved his face in it and told him I'd help him enjoy it. My wife warned me – *never again*. I haven't had a drink since that day.'

The sun dips into the Gulf, slowly at first, and then suddenly it's gone. For a while the sky glows red and orange and yellow then it's night, dark, but still warm. I go for a little walk, look up at the stars and, *hey, look at the moon!* In Scotland the crescent is upright; down here it sits horizontal, like a silver smile. *Think I'll try one of those banana-coconut things, and maybe a slice.* Suddenly I realise I've lost my phone. In a panic, I rush back. It's got all my telephone numbers. I'm in real trouble if I've lost it. *You're so fucking careless!* I'm retracing my steps, searching the ground, looking everywhere, *some hope!* I reach the spot where I was sitting, and there it is, on the grass. Nobody's touched it. *Relax.* I'm grinning again.

The crowd roars as Dickey Betts and his band come on. He's a local, lives in Sarasota. They're playing those high, melodic, Tex-Mex guitar solos, right up the top of the fretboard, just like he did when he played with the Allman Brothers Band all those years ago. It sounds so good in this hot night, 20,000 people are on their feet, having a good time. *This is what an open-air gig should be like.*

He's doing a big-venue tour that will take the band all over America and Canada for the next year. He's got a great band: three guitarists, bass and a keyboard player whose fingers are flicking and stroking the keys of his Hammond organ, that rich, thick sound swirling out of those old Leslie speaker cabinets. They have a female singer; she was pounding congas in the last song but now she's got the mike and she's taken over the lead and . . . *I know that voice.* I know that high, raunchy voice, like Janis Joplin on a good day. I'm squeezing through the packed crowd – I need to get a little nearer the stage so I can see her. Is it who I think it is? *Yeah, it is!* I'm so pleased for her. She's finally hit the big time.

It's Twinkle.

20

ORLANDO

Little Feat

I'M relaxing in the deep passenger seat of a comfortable Ford SUV, coasting along the I4 with Geoff, talking about the 17 years he spent on the move with bands. He doesn't miss it now that he's settled in Florida with Keverley, living in a nice house on the bank of a slow river. The water is clean and silky, meandering through lush, subtropical woods. He's home nice and early from work every night, drinks a cold one, watches the hot sun drop behind the trees, then smiles as he flips pork ribs or freshly caught shrimp on his barbecue. He loves to hear the 'gators grunt at dusk. It's all so far from London and all those crazy rock and roll tours. But he remembers the days. . .

Like when he ran the onstage monitors for The Who, at that time the biggest band in the world. They'd hired Shepperton Studios for rehearsals, their huge PA was set up and switched on, stage amps humming, lights quietly buzzing, road crew at their positions, alert and ready to run through the show. The band wandered in, yawned, uncorked a few bottles of wine, piddled around for 10 minutes then disappeared in their limos. Their 20-man crew were left staring at each other, knowing how much money this had cost the band.

Geoff adjusts his Ray-Bans as we close in on a white Lincoln chugging along the outside lane. He glances at his mirrors, then zips by on the inside. An old guy is driving, steering wheel in a death-grip, staring ahead as if a blink will cost him his life. Geoff shakes his head and sighs. 'These old guys, they get up to fifty five miles an hour, switch on cruise control, and would die rather than give up their lane.'

Geoff always wears sunglasses. When he drove a truck for The Who, he reckoned that fatigue was caused by headlights shining in his eyes. Even on the darkest nights he wore them as the convoy rolled along the motorways of Europe. He had a lot of fun when he was young. He grins. *Damn, The Who were crazy*. There was the time they were playing at a football ground someplace in France. Each band member had a Portakabin to relax in, get changed, warm up for the show, or, in Keith Moon's case, host one of his parties. He's enjoying himself, pouring the best champagne for his showbiz pals. All of a sudden there's a jolt and they are falling on top of each other, lines of prime Columbian flying into the air, bottles and furniture crashing on them. Moonie had, as usual, done something crazy the previous night so one of the band had decided to pay him back. He'd jumped on the forklift truck the crew use to lift heavy equipment onto the stage, turned it round and quietly slipped the forks under the edge of Keith's Portakabin. Then he'd pulled back the RAISE lever.

'When The Who were playing it was incredible. They were like a battleship coming straight at you, nothing could stop them. The sum of the members was far greater than the individuals. No other band even came close. They were the greatest rock and roll band in the world. John would stand there, staring straight ahead. Keith would be going crazy, pounding those drums, Pete jumping all over the place doing that windmill thing and Roger...'

Geoff shakes his head and grins. 'When Roger got cranked up he used to whirl the mike thirty feet in the air. He'd throw it above the crowd then yank it back. He'd usually catch it but sometimes he missed. Once it hit him and cut his head. Blood everywhere. If it bounced off the stage it smashed, so I always had five spares ready.'

We pass the first signs for Disneyland and Sea World, which will be packed with people visiting the Mouse and the Whale. It's Sunday and the road is quiet. We would stop for a coffee, but Florida freeways only have rest areas with 75-cent vending machines. If you want something better than a plastic cup of powdered hot water you need to drive into the nearest town.

'We used to work long, long hours. We'd have the stage all set for The Who, then the support band would come along and ask for a soundcheck. *"Eh, sorry, guys, no, you ain't getting to do a soundcheck. Just isn't time"*. They'd get all bent out of shape with us, then stick their amplifiers in front of The Who's backline and I'd move some mikes into place for them. I did the monitors for Little Feat when they supported The Who in Glasgow at some big football stadium. They liked the way I worked the desk. They asked me to go to Australia and New Zealand with them, work with them full-time. I was only 19, but I knew how to give the band what they wanted. I was real good with sound.'

He toured with almost every well-known band in the 1970's and 1980's. 'When I was with Motorhead everyone working for them lived on speed. Piles and piles of amphetamine sulphate. Everywhere. It was fucking horrible, everyone going for days without sleep, nerves like piano wires. And the chicks they had hanging around, they were monsters. Horrible looking. Fat, tattoos everywhere, leather gear, ripped black tights. Acne and zits all over their faces from taking too much speed.'

He moves into the inside lane to overtake another slow-moving car. 'I did sound for them at a football ground in England.

They were *loud*. Some old boy called the police. He's yelling at them: *"Stop that racket! It's deafening, I can't hear my bloody television!"* He lived *four miles* from the gig.'

During his years on the road, Geoff never had a home; he didn't need one. Whenever he was on a break between tours he'd open his address book and start dialling. 'In those days I was always going somewhere. Always jumping on planes. There was a girl in Sweden, she was beautiful, I stayed there two weeks. Another in New York. . .'

In those days cocaine was everywhere.

'I had to have a clear head. Doing sound is a big responsibility, so I couldn't be goofing around. But one band used to have Southern Comfort and a pack of Malboro on each of their amplifiers. They'd take some of the tobacco out and pack them with cocaine. All through the gig they'd smoke them. No one in the crowd knew what they were doing. Thought they were just having a shot of whisky and a cigarette. They were always out of their freakin' minds. And they were a bible-bashing country band. Played good, though.'

Those days are far behind him. 'I bumped into one of those good ole boys last week and he's all cleaned up. He says, "Hey Geoff, you know you're getting old when the time between snorting coke and regretting it becomes almost instantaneous."'

As we pass the off-ramp for Kissimmee, he gazes at all the new hotels and condos. 'The cost of land has gone freakin' sky high. Used to be so cheap. I couldn't buy my house nowadays. Everyone wants to live in Florida, they're payin' crazy prices. But it's still the best place in the world. Anytime I go to London, as soon as the plane drops down into all those clouds and rain I want to turn round and come back.'

We've come to Orlando to meet his old pals from Little Feat, who are playing at the Hard Rock Café in Universal Studios. At the entrance we pick up our pass for the parking lot, make sure we'll remember where we park the SUV, then wander through the crowded park to the Hard Rock. The restaurant is big, but basically the same as Hard Rock Cafés all over the world. When they started hanging those beat-up guitars and old photographs on the walls, they must have known they were onto a winner. It has a plush air-conditioned theatre, looks like it holds about 1,000, and many well-known bands come to Orlando to play in it. The Hard Rock Café must have grilled a lot of cheeseburgers to pay for this place.

Other than The Beatles, I doubt any band is loved by as many musicians as Little Feat. Mention them to any old pro, and they will quietly smile: *Now that's a band.* They lost the central player, Lowell George, in 1979. Geoff was very friendly with him, and doesn't like to talk about it. 'I don't think he realised he was having a heart attack. He was in his hotel room. If he'd managed to call for help they might have saved him.'

The rest of the band are still touring, still sounding great and have a devoted following, which has become a world-wide community. They keep in touch by email and through the band's website; every gig is like a family reunion. If you come along you'll meet people from all over the country, each with stories of the friends they have made, catching up on news, and having a great time. Like Ray, who was with the US Navy. When he retired, he decided to drive all over America, seeing the band in as many towns as possible. To his surprise, he never had to check into a motel. He was welcomed by the Little Feat Family everywhere: Bob in Kansas City, Scott in Atlanta, and, in Houston, Miss Clara Belle. If he ever finds himself heading for Austin, Texas, Melissa and her husband are very gracious hosts. In San Francisco, he got to know Miss Lynn Hearne, one of the 'original' Feat devotees, who knows more about their early days than the band members.

In St Louis, some fans he'd never met before gave him the keys to their motor home. There are fans in small towns, places with great American names: Pozo, California, and in Atascadero, where Larry's door is always open. They all help each other – just like a commune but without arguments about who's making dinner tonight. If the band ever need anything, anywhere, they have a big family to call on.

When I went to Canada to speak at a book festival, I casually mentioned to a Little Feat fan that I'd like to get a photograph. Nothing special, a quick snapshot would be fine. As soon as I arrived, I was met by a very nice lady called Marsha Fadely, a professional photographer, and long-time member of the Feat Family. *Smile!* The band's keyboard player, Bill Payne, is studying photography; when the band play near her home, she takes him on her assignments.

Every February, the band host a huge party in Jamaica, the highlight of the year; people come from all over the world. But the fans do much more than socialise; the band are very involved with helping New Orleans hurricane victims and the entire Little Feat community does whatever they can. No one makes a fuss, or seeks publicity, they just quietly get on with it.

I'm looking forward to hearing them play, I never get tired of listening to them. Backstage we meet up with bass player Kenny Gradney. This is what it says on the sleeve notes of *Feats Don't Fail Me Now*, one of the band's early albums: 'Do not be deceived by nor take lightly this musicianship that one describes simply as bass.' On the third track, a great song called 'Skin It Back', his playing is perfect, absolutely perfect.

Kenny apologises; he doesn't shake hands these days, he has

trouble with pain in his knuckles. Guitarist Paul Barrere steps out of the band's big red tour bus, he's one of those guys who seem to light up a room, easy going, always smiling. He's been getting his fingers massaged, which helps before gigs, but he needs surgery to fix a tendon problem. It's scheduled for Christmas. He lights a cigarette and blows out a stream of smoke. *Cain't put it off no longer.*

It's great to hear Little Feat anywhere, but it's best somewhere hot. No one else plays quite like them, a mix of swampy Lousianna, Dixie swing and Memphis blues, with the laid back feel of Topanga Canyon in LA, where they live. They never play anything the same way twice. Paul says, 'We love to jam. We'd get bored playing the same way every night.' When you hear them, the rhythm hits somewhere deep down in your stomach, your feet can't stay still, your legs move, the music is so slick, and so very, very horny. Some of the finest looking women you'll ever see are dancing in front of the stage.

Tonight, on their last song, they get into a groove that lasts almost half an hour, way beyond the scheduled end of the show. They're jamming on a regular 12-bar sequence, and I doubt any other group in the world could make it sound so fresh. It's terrific to see musicians still enjoying playing as much as they did 30 years ago. Just for the fun of it, they bounce in and out of other tunes, old rock standards like 'All Shook Up', then back into their improvisations, each member playing solos, just as long as they want.

The Hard Rock Café auditorium doesn't have the sweaty feel of a southern rock venue, it's more like the sort of place that Streisand or someone would play, but the Little Feat Family turn it into a big dance hall. I look along the rows; everyone has tilted up their seat and is swinging along with the music. Even the uniformed Hard Rock Café staff are swaying. I catch a glimpse of Geoff: his eyes are sparkling, he can't stop moving.

After the gig, as we drive back onto the freeway, I ask him if he ever misses touring with the band.

'Hell, no. If I was still on the road I'd be rolling heavy flight cases onto trucks right now and having a 500 mile drive ahead of me. This way I get to see the band and I'm home in bed with my lovely wife every night.'

Then he slips on his old Ray-Bans, pulls into the fast lane, switches on cruise control, and grins.

21

MIAMI

Bang Music Festival

I'T'S an edgy town, Miami. As long as you're not the sort of person who worries about the possible proximity of easily irritated drug dealers, sipping café cubano at a street table on a hot, humid evening is a heady experience. It's great to lean back and watch the evening promenade of stylishly dressed suntans strutting along Collins Avenue. Just a block from the beach, close enough to hear the surf, it is an art deco nirvana, a stucco and tile paradise, a Disneyland for architects and fashion photographers. Every building is sleek and unique, glowing neon signs, metallic letters curling like vines around coconut trees. Each bar, café, shop and hotel is painted in the pastel shades of sunset: warm pink, pale blue, glowing orange; or of the ocean at dawn: green, turquoise, sandy yellow.

In a cold town the street would look tacky, but this close to the equator, it's perfect. Many American cities are being torn down and rebuilt, as if ashamed of their past, but downtown Miami has a sense of history; you can almost hear the laughter and Latino music of the 1920's, the sleek cars, throbbing engines, glittering jewellery, plunging necklines and sharp suits. Back then, its nightclubs pulsated with the excitement of the forbidden fruits of a different prohibition. The beat tonight is louder, perhaps the salsa is hotter, but the pulse of the streets is just as it always was.

It doesn't feel like the USA; Havana is only a fast speedboat away, nearer than Orlando. Most hotel receptionists have skin the warm tone of café con leche, dark hair, brown eyes, beautiful smiles. If you want a free upgrade to a room with a view of the sand, then all you need to do is learn to speak a little Spanish. Americans don't.

The sun only rises over Miami, never sets. It is a city for the young, even more so than Hollywood. In LA, they act life; here they live it. The buildings may be old, but everything else is cutting-edge.

As I stir my second coffee, I read the poster for an open-air gig at the beautiful, ocean-front park on Biscayne Boulevard. It features: Front 242, Chicks on Speed, Spam Allstars, Chus and Ceballos, Saeed Younan, ATB, Benny Benassi, Judge Jules, Bad Boy Bill, Jori Hulkkonen, Pete Tha Zouk, Axwell, The Scumfrog, Sebastian Ingrosso, Basti George Acosta, Amoine Clamaran, Brazilian Girls, Jose Padilla, Icey, Celeda, Sammy Peralta, Amramn Pena, Robert Rodriquez, Matt Martinez, John Acquaviva, and many others.

And I hadn't heard of one of them.

22

NEW YORK CITY

Average White Band

I DON'T like seaside towns in winter. There's the feeling that something is missing, the town is a shadow of itself, the laughter has gone, at least until next summer. There's something haunting about wind-whipped beaches and the troubled crash of surf pounding darkly below a moonless sky.

In Florida there is no winter, at least not in the way that most of us understand the word, but it can get chilly at night if the tail end of an arctic storm makes it all the way down from the frigid plains of Canada. I like winter to be winter, not a ghost. I love snow and ice and the stars when they look like diamonds frozen in the dark sky. The sun, cycling and swimming had worked their magic. I was feeling fit again, fit enough to go skiing. I couldn't wait. I had a last stroll on the beach, locked my front door for the first time in a couple of months, then, as I waited for my taxi, said goodbye to Ann, one of my neighbours, who had arrived yesterday. She's glad to be back in Florida; who needs another New York winter?

Lying quietly in her pram a half-century ago, Ann had been a beautiful baby. 'I never cried, never made a noise. Didn't bother nobody. I could hear all these sounds in my head, I thought they were like friends, I thought everybody could hear them. My mother was hip, she told me, ssshhh . . . don't tell nobody . . . it'll be our little secret. She took me to the orchestra when I was three. The moment I heard it, that was it. Those were the sounds I'd been hearing – an orchestra in my head.'

She's a very successful arranger and has composed music for TV shows and movies like *Supergirl* and *Transformers*. 'When I was seventeen I was playing piano for Judy Garland and I asked her, what is it that makes a song? Is it the vocal? Is it the arrangement, the lyrics, the music? And she looked at me and said "Yes". Then, after a long pause, Judy said: "It's the mood, Annie. It's all of that. When it all comes together, from the same place, well, that's a hit song."'

Ann smiles, then looks around, waves to an old guy in a wheelchair being pushed by a nurse. He doesn't register anything, or maybe his head moved just a little. 'He was a fabulous jazz drummer. Played the Johnny Carson show for years. He could really play, that guy.' She watches as his chair trundles along the street, then she turns back to me. 'But you see what Judy meant? It's all of these things. When it all comes together then you have a song.' Ann shrugs. 'Composers just hear these things, they're connecting with something. I don't know what, but songwriters just hear it a lot more clearly than most people. We're all drawing from the same well. When you hear a great song, you know it right off. It's somehow familiar, as though it was meant to exist. I think we can all hear these things, we just need to step away from ourselves. Stop thinking and listen to the music that's already there.'

My cab arrives. *Can you stop for a moment at Starbucks?* I can't leave without saying goodbye. *Sure, there's no hurry.* The sun is shining, and swarms of retired folk – snowbirds – have been arriving every day, settling into their condos for the winter, glad to escape the blizzards of New York State and Ontario. As usual I try to push Starbucks' door open; I always forget that all doors in Florida open outwards, so that the summer winds don't blow them in. Ryan is cranking out frappuccinos, chai tea and mochas. An old guy with a Brooklyn accent is asking him: *Hey, can I just have a cuppa cawfay? Just a regular cuppa cawfay? An' a bagel? Can ya do that for me?*

Ryan is a nice guy, friendly to the customers; I like him. He's a writer, like everyone else working the nozzles at Starbucks he's a gonna-be, on his way someplace else. He recently finished his first book he describes as 'an experimental novel in the style of the Dylan, Visions of Joanna time frame'. He's sent it to just about every publisher in America, but seems like no one's looking for 200,000 experimental words. He wrote it at night, eyes wide on the Southern Comfort and ephedrine diet. So he's changed tactics for his current book. He's switched to coffee and broccoli. 'Caffeine and brain food ... gotta keep them brain cells buzzing.'

I love New York City, even when it feels like the coldest place in the world. I guess it's something to do with super-cold air being trapped on the street far below the summits of the skyscrapers. Whenever I am in town, I look up an old pal, Onnie McIntyre, a founder member of the Average White Band. I first met him when I was a schoolboy. He was 17 and playing guitar in a 'beat group'. They rehearsed round the corner from the tenement flat I lived in, practising their songs in a dark, 18th century cottage owned by a very old lady who lived there alone. She rented out chilly rooms for a few pounds; downstairs the large parlour with the faded brown linoleum was for bands, and in an attic at the top of a worn wooden staircase, huddled around the gloomy light of a single lamp, a pale, bony woman in a black dress and shawl held seances. Every Sunday night I'd hear the thump of the bass drum and the twang of Onnie's Gretsch and rush round to watch them, hoping there wouldn't be too many grim-faced recently-bereaved lurking in the dark and dusty shadows of the vestibule.

Onnie was determined to become a professional musician. Like most working-class Glaswegians, his parents persuaded him to get a trade, so that he would have something to fall back on, and so he served his time as an electrician. But as soon as he could, he moved to London, as all musicians had to in those days, and that was that.

The years flew by and the next time I met Onnie was in the old Mayflower Hotel, just across the street from Central Park. It was the place to stay for bands who wanted cheap rooms, not as cheap as the infamous Chelsea Hotel in Midtown, but much cheaper than the Marriott or Sheraton. The Mayflower was one of those old-fashioned New York hotels; no two rooms were exactly alike, but they were all much larger than the neat cubicles at the Holiday Inn. They had flaking paintwork and embossed wallpaper that had long since been covered over with cream emulsion, chipped yellow skirting boards that seemed to reach knee height, ancient flickering black and white television sets, with tuning dials and rabbit-ear aerials. Bolted solidly to each bedroom wall were fat, painted radiators that creaked and groaned in winter, like an old man forced to do heavy labour, and square, window-mounted air conditioners that rattled furiously in summer, dripping as if pouring with sweat while they hopelessly battled the stifling Manhattan heat. They had deep, steamy baths with all the hot water you ever wanted, and some rooms even had little kitchens so that guests on a tight budget could rustle up their own fried eggs and crispy bacon rather than cross the street and walk a block down Broadway to the Milky Way Diner. The Mayflower was for people who checked their bills carefully, and many guests lived in the hotel all year; they felt safe there. Best of all, the rooms had terrific views of the park.

Onnie was staying in the Mayflower with the Average White Band. I was there with the Incredible String Band. It was a great time to be in New York; young Marley and Springsteen on FM radio, loads of beautiful girls who just loved Scottish rock musicians. At night the bustling streets felt much safer than Glasgow – even the subway, as long as you could figure out which stations the trains were going to. The bars stayed open until two in the morning and the friendly barman placed your tab on the table; you paid for your drinks *after* you had drunk them. I got to meet the New York Dolls and Bonnie Raitt when they were playing in clubs in the Village, and had a few epic drinking sessions with Rory Gallagher when he was playing in Central Park and nearby Long Island.

The Incredible String Band were busy breaking up, but the Average White Band were busy breaking big. They were playing at the Bottom Line near Washington Square Park and everyone who packed the small club knew that they would soon become one of the most successful groups in the world. They were young and determined, and very Scottish. Most mornings, they'd pull on their Adidas football boots and kick a ball around Central Park. Guys from 125th Street would watch, not realising they would soon be dancing all night to the music of these skinny white kids. *Hey, boy, what all is that language you talkin'?*

I've been to New York many times since those days, but always feel the same buzz of excitement when I'm on a plane coasting down to Newark and I see the Empire State Building, like the godfather of Manhattan, a grey tower soaring above the streets. I always feel that in this city, anything can happen. I'd arranged to meet Onnie on 42nd Street and caught the express bus from the airport terminal to Manhattan.

The air temperature has really dropped, the traffic cops are wrapped in balaclavas, coats, black leather gloves and earmuffs. They're hunched over, stamping their feet, it's a cold one. At the corner of 8th Avenue and 42nd, the freezing wind charges up from the river, catches a clutch of tourists and takes their breath away. They hold their hats, turn their shoulders into the icy blast, then laugh out loud; they can't believe how cold it is. New Yorkers crossing the street glance at them: *Yeah, try living in it*. There's solidarity among New Yorkers in winter, a shared tolerance of the flesh-stripping cold. In winter they swear they'll never complain about the sweltering heat of summer again.

My blood must be thin from the Florida sun, my stomach is shivering. I need something to warm me up. Now. In Starbucks, a neat line of camera-clicking Japanese tourists has filed in from Madame Tussauds on the other side of the street. They all want hot coffee and the counter is short-staffed. There's a man in front of them, his last remaining hair gathered together in a ponytail, marshalled against baldness like Custer's last stand. He has bony fingers with carefully trimmed nails, thick glasses, a brown tweed jacket and woolly scarf. He smells of something sweet, I don't know, maybe lavender water. He's clutching a laptop to his chest and asks the sweating guy behind the till to confirm that they definitely have wireless here.

'Good. You are sure? OK, then. I'll have a triple venti latte, half soy, half non-fat, no foam, extra hot. Decaff. And can you please make sure it's decaff?'

The guy at the counter glances at the thirsty queue stretching all the way to the door. Beads of sweat drop onto his damp shirt, his eyebrows rise, and he holds his hands out as if pleading for a little understanding here. He looks at the man, then in a loud voice says one New York word.

'*What?*'

Onnie arrives and we walk along to Lucille's Grill in BB King's blues club, which is quiet in the afternoon, and we can get a table. Dark wood panelling, the colour of mahogany, high ceiling, a stage in the corner. Onnie orders a catfish sandwich, cajun-style. *You want French fries wid dat?* The waiter bends the whole sentence upwards the way they do in New York. And I'll have the meatloaf, no onions please. The Average White Band are planning to record a CD here. It will be called *Soul in the City*. Onnie glances round the room. 'This may not be the best place to record a live show,' he says. 'New Yorkers are spoiled, they see so many great bands, it can be hard to get them going. We'll see. A couple of nights ago we played Washington DC. The entire audience was black and they sang every word.'

Despite living in New York since 1974, his Scottish accent is exactly as it was when he was 17. He asks if I have enough time before my flight to go to the Iridium Club on Broadway. 'Les Paul is playing. He's ninety-one, and still drives in from New Jersey to play on Monday nights. It's incredible, the guy who pretty much invented the electric guitar and multi-track recording and he's playing a few blocks from here. That's what I love about New York.'

A guy asks for Onnie's autograph and tells him how much he and his wife love the band; they have every record they have made. He chats to them for a few minutes while the waitress pours us some fresh coffee, then they leave, happy.

'There used to be a great club called the Lone Star Café. It was in a lovely white-brick art deco building on the corner of Fifth and Thirteenth. They booked the best blues and soul artists . . . Sam and Dave, Albert King, Wilson Pickett, Junior Walker and The All

Stars. Sooner or later everyone comes through New York City. I met James Brown there, and got to know his band. They told me that when "Pick Up the Pieces" came out, people thought it was them playing. They were saying: *"It ain't us! It's six white guys from Skatland!"'*

The band's drummer was Robbie McIntosh, and his way of playing was unlike anything anyone had heard before. 'He'd learned to play in the Boys' Brigade pipe band in Dundee, then at sixteen moved to London to work with Ben E King. He somehow managed to combine the precise rolls and crispness of pipe band drumming with his tremendous feel for soul music. He was unique.'

Apart from being one of the most-played instrumentals ever, 'Pick Up the Pieces' is famous for something else: The Chord. It's the intro Onnie plays, the most instantly recognisable chord in soul music. 'A lot of people think it's a minor sixth, or a raised ninth. I'm always getting asked what the Chord is.' As soon as you hear it, it makes you want to dance. The Chord is a beautiful clash of notes, leading perfectly into the jaggy sax tune. It reminds me of the way a good Highland ceilidh band plays the first chord of a jig or a reel and it immediately pulls everyone onto the dance floor.

Onnie learned to play soul music in Glasgow. 'Local DJs like Tam Ferrie were importing records directly from Memphis, Detroit and New York. There were all those clubs, like The Picasso on Buchanan Street, which had live music 'til the wee hours and was a haven for musicians. There was the Lindella, where Lulu used to sing when she was thirteen. It was at the top of a seven-storey building in Union Street and you had to carry your gear all the way up narrow stairs.'

Onnie pauses, takes a bite from his sandwich, it's good and

hot.

'The Maryland opposite Glasgow Art School used to be another great place, Alex Harvey used to play there with his big soul band. The guy who ran it, Willie Cuthbertson, brought in bands like the Bonzo Dog Doo Dah Band and John Mayall's Bluesbreakers. Geno Washington played there a lot, he was terrific, a proper soul show. On week nights, bands came up from London to the Barrowland Ballroom, everyone from Screamin' Lord Sutch to the Stones. I went to see them all. It was magic.'

When he moved to London, Onnie played in a Scottish band that backed American artistes touring Europe. 'We worked constantly with all sorts of people including Lee Dorsey, and The Drifters. We arrived in Berlin, and played three different clubs on the first night. We stayed up all night and flew out the next morning – we never even saw the Wall. Wee Glasgow boys backing The Drifters. . .'

In those days, he travelled all over Europe in cramped, draughty Transit vans that were always too hot or bloody freezing, piling in beside the equipment. 'You can do that when you're twenty, you think nothing of an eight-hour drive to a gig, then all the way back to London afterwards.' He still loves being on the road with the Average White Band, playing in places like Russia, Dubai and Japan, as well as touring the USA and Europe every year. 'But it takes careful planning, you get older, you want comfort, your own hotel room. If you have a night off, you'll find a good restaurant, order a nice bottle of wine. Being a professional musician can be a terrific life, if you can organise things to make it work. But it's not easy.'

The band records its own CDs and sells them through its website. 'It's impossible to get radio play these days. Practically all the radio stations have been bought by big corporations.

Everything is now totally driven by advertising revenue. They won't play anything new, not even Stevie Wonder's new album, only his old records.'

It's time to go, and I'm sitting in the Port Authority bus station, not far from Times Square. The service to Newark airport is cheap and reliable. It's also quick; the coaches have their own express lane all the way, and zip through the toll while cars can be snarled up in honking queues. There's a variety of people in the waiting room: tourists like me, New Yorkers who are going out to the airport to work or to meet someone, a couple of weary looking salesmen whose expense accounts don't stretch to the taxi fare, or who don't want to pay the extra $60 for a cab when the bus is clean, has an English-speaking driver and will get you to the terminal building on time and without getting lost.

A couple of older guys are sitting near me; heavily built, crumpled coats. I love listening to strangers talking, especially in this city. 'Yeah, I used to own a store in New Jersey. A pawnshop. Place was a zoo, a fucking zoo. One morning we find a stiff in the doorway; he's a bum, he's died there in the night. The last thing we need is the cops calling the place a crime scene and closing us for the day so we move the body to the lane out back. He was a corpse anyway, what did he know? What harm were we doing? No sense in losing a day's business, right?'

He sticks a cigar in his mouth, pats his side, then remembers he can't light up here. He sighs and puts it back in his pocket. He might have stepped outside but the sun has set, it's freezing and the air is thick with diesel fumes.

'It was a fucking zoo all right. You had to pay attention all the time. One day a guy stiffs me for two hundred bucks. Gave me a check that was no good. So two years later he walks right into the store. He thinks I won't remember. Lemme tell you, I never forget a face, especially if it owes me money. So I hit the electric switch and the door locks him in and I shove my gun between his fucking eyes and I tell him, *"Give me my two hundred dollars right now or I'm gonna blow your fucking head off"*. That got his attention. He pissed in his pants right there in front of me.'

Noo Yawk. Who needs television?

23

LONDON

Edwin Shirley Trucking Company

I WORKED with a lot of truckers when I had a removal company. They weren't fussy eaters. Before his last supper, wee fat Mick had loved his grub and was happiest when guzzling three Big Macs at noon. Big George did the long distance runs. Every Monday when he climbed into the cab of his Scania, he carefully carried a large pot of home-made stew that his wife had rustled up for him. Every night, he'd reheat it on the truck's little stove and, with a loaf of sliced bread, would make it last all week. I paid him daily food money, but he preferred to save that for pubs featuring exotic dancers. The drivers on local work had a favourite Glaswegian luncheon: chips lathered in thick, yellow curry sauce. They never tired of it. A fast route to a quick heart attack, but it tasted delicious.

And so it was that I found myself noticing with surprise the dining choice of eight burly drivers working for the Edwin Shirley Trucking Company as we sat backstage at the Sportpaleis stadium in Antwerp. But I'm getting way ahead of myself, so I'll explain what brought me here.

It is the shortest day, 21 December, a dark, shivering night in London. A freezing wind is howling into the loading area at the back of the Earls Court Arena. The steel doors are open because a gleaming grey Bentley is waiting at the foot of the wooden stairs that lead from the stage. Its engine is quietly ticking over. The driver has turned up the heating, but his window is down; he is alert, ready to roar into the night. His job is to get the star as far from the venue as possible before 16,000 people pour into the streets and traffic comes to a standstill.

A couple of muscular black guys are positioned beside the car. One of them turns and looks up at the white screens above the rear of the stage. Unseen by the audience, three techs are hunched over their computers, tapping their keyboards, silently operating the rear-projection units that throw the image of the star onto the 30-foot-high screens. It is a long way from the stage to the cheaper seats at the back, but everyone has a good view.

That's the last song; any minute now. The security guy nearest the stairs rolls his bulging shoulders, opens and closes his hands, clasps them in front of his hips and gently shakes out his huge thigh muscles, his weight spread evenly, the way he was taught in the Forces. The metallic voice of his supervisor is in his earpiece, but he responds only if he hears his name. He is focused, ready to help usher the star straight into the Bentley as soon as he comes down the steps. Every second counts.

The final words of 'Maggie May' are swamped by the clapping, chanting crowd. *More. More.* Rod Stewart grins, bows, waves, and as the crowd stamps and cheers, he runs down the stairs. His shirt is soaking, sweat streaming down his face, and he blinks as it stings his eyes. The security guy drapes a thick white towel round Rod's shoulders as the other quickly guides him into the car. Just in front of the Bentley, a policeman is sitting astride a powerful BMW motorbike. As soon as the car door closes, he twists the throttle, roaring down the exit ramp to the street, blue light flashing. The Bentley chases him, almost touching his back wheel, tyres squealing on the smooth concrete.

We want Rod! We want Rod! No one leaves, watching the stage, hoping. The band is still playing, dazzling spotlights sweeping the stage. *He must be coming on again!* This gives the Bentley just enough time to escape. Only when it is well clear does the band play the final chord. The hall lights begin to flicker on and the audience realises the show is over. Rod's management team has done it this way for years; all big-name stars need a similar routine.

Parked in a line at the back wall are three articulated trucks, *Edwin Shirley Trucking* in yellow letters on their purple, 45-foot-long bodies. Their back doors are open, steel ramps stretching down to the concrete floor. Standing close to the trucks is a group of 40 'humpers', mainly guys. They have been hired from an agency to help load the equipment. Near the front is a girl called Kasia. She is concentrating, watching the man with the walkie-talkie. She's been told to wait right there. *Don't be wandering around, don't touch anything unless you're told.*

Kasia is nervous, she's never done this before. Since arriving from Poland last week, she's managed to find a job in a run-down hotel: cleaning, making beds, scrubbing pots. It doesn't pay much and she'll be glad of the £40 she'll earn tonight. London is so expensive; she'll have to work hard if she is going to send anything home. She has a degree in mathematics, but her English lets her down, it's not so good. The accents of the humpers are nothing like the tapes she listened to every day in Warsaw. Cockney, Irish, Scouse . . . there's even some guy from Glasgow but no one understands a word he says. She shivers, the damp air blowing through the open loading doors is freezing. She just hopes she will understand well enough to do as she is told.

She glances around; all the humpers are wearing tee shirts with the words *Rod Stewart Local Crew.* Kasia's shirt is blue: she will be helping to load the lighting equipment. Green shirts are stage gear; red are PA. The guy with the radio comes up to them. They will be told what to shift and when. *OK, everyone got their safety helmet on?* Another gust of chill air blasts through the backstage area, it's colder than she thought it would be in London. *Listen and pay attention. Green with me. Blue with him. Red over there.*

He looks at the back of the stage. The band files down the steps. He turns to the humpers.

'OK. Go!'

Rod's road crew, seasoned pros from around the world, move into action. Fast but in control, speed without panic. The next gig is in Belgium tomorrow night, there's no time to waste. The trucks must be loaded quickly, but as quietly as possible: people living close to Earls Court Arena will call the police if there is too much noise. They have jobs to go to in the morning; they don't want to be kept awake by the clatter of flight cases being rolled into the trucks, or the throbbing of eight-cylinder diesel engines. The loading door nearest their apartments, the one at the left-hand side of the backstage area, must not be used after midnight. It will be locked at twelve, not a minute later. Rod's crew and the humpers must fill the first three artics before then. It's already after eleven.

The crowd is slowly filing out of the massive arena. Under the harsh yellow glare of the hall lights, it looks like an aircraft hangar. An army of cleaners has moved in, and the hall echoes to the clatter of seats being pushed up as they shove their brushes along each row, building neat piles of litter. A dozen men quickly clear away the front rows of seats to make space for two large cherry pickers. Puffing dark exhaust smoke, they lift four of Rod's techs up to dismantle spotlights bolted to a huge rectangular, steel frame suspended 40 feet above the stage.

'This place is terrible. It's so slow,' says Carl Tovey, Rod's stage manager. He still has a gentle Welsh accent even though he's been living in America for years. He looks up at the cherry pickers and shakes his head. 'It's so slow having to use them. The health and safety people in Earls Court don't allow our riggers to climb up on the beams like they do everywhere else. We have to hoist them up there and they must work from platforms on the cherry pickers. It's really slow. And they are bloody expensive to hire in.'

Carl oversees everything, nothing escapes his attention. He speaks into his radio, quietly and calmly issuing instructions. He glances at the lines of video equipment and computers and smiles. 'It's all very high-tech nowadays, far fewer nuts and bolts. But we still use gaffer tape.' He glances at his Rolex. 'Everything must be loaded and away by 2 am. It'll take the trucks about eight hours to cross the Channel and drive up to Antwerp. They have to start the load-in at the Sportpaleis at 10 tomorrow morning.'

There are cables snaking everywhere and rows and rows of flight cases to be packed. Each piece of equipment has to go in the correct one or it will be a nightmare setting it all up in time for the next show. I can't imagine how they can possibly dismantle this mountain of gear and load it in such a short time. But Carl's team work quietly and efficiently, just as they have done all over the world for the two years that this tour has been on the road. They have their routines well figured out.

The Edwin Shirley drivers stand by their trucks, ready. They know they face a daunting schedule. John Long is in charge, the lead driver. He lives in London, but spends most of his time on motorways, hauling sound equipment all over Europe. 'I've been with Edwin Shirley for twenty years. Before that I did lights for

Pink Floyd, worked for Thin Lizzie, tried my hand at tour management. Never worked at anything else. Never wanted to.'

He's been careful with his money, has managed to buy a holiday cottage on the south coast. He loves to go there, just relaxing, gazing at the Channel he's crossed so many times. It's good to stroll on the beach after the long miles of tarmac and constant thunder of trucks and amplifiers. 'I've worked for most of the big names, been everywhere in Europe. Been to Marrakech, Tel Aviv, Sarajevo. Had to drive across bridges the army had thrown up. Metal plates and girders. There's a lot more gigs in Eastern Europe now. They have roads, but not like we know them. Did Moscow with McCartney. Didn't like it. Needed armed guards everywhere we went. They drove in little Ladas in front of us. The promoter hired them to make sure we didn't get hijacked. They were Soviet military, armed to the teeth. Naw, I didn't like it there.'

John likes driving in France. 'Clean roads, good food and scenery.' Hates Holland and Germany. 'Nothing but traffic jams.' Scandinavia is much better. 'It's good, plenty of open roads.'

Mike Fisher is a newcomer; he's been doing this for eight years. He used to love roaring along country roads on his motorbike in the middle of the night until a tractor drove out of a farm and he didn't see it until he was part of it. Now he prefers being high up in the cab of his DAF truck. 'Sometimes it is very difficult – like in thick fog on the autobahn when they've dug up the road. They'd made the temporary lanes far too narrow. I nearly had a head-on with a truck coming the other way. He only had one headlight. Just loomed up on me out of the mist. A nightmare. It's knackering when it's like that. It's Red Bull and coffee that gets you through the night.'

Edwin Shirley is the UK's top rock music trucking company;

reliability is everything in this business. The equipment must be at every venue exactly on time. There's no room for screw-ups: a dozy driver could cause serious problems if he gets lost – a couple of hours could mean a stadium gig being cancelled. No one will listen to some lame excuse, not when 60,000 people are stamping their feet, yelling for the band.

'Except for very tight schedules like tonight, this tour is easy, only eight trucks,' says John, as he watches the first flight cases being filled with the band's guitars and keyboards. 'I did one with U2, it was a ninety-truck tour. Went to Israel with them. They used two complete stage sets, forty-five trucks each show. We were leapfrogging all round Europe.'

'Biggest I've done was Michael Jackson,' says Alistair MacKenzie, a Scot in his fifties. 'That was a hundred-truck tour. We went to Istanbul, and all over Europe. He was a very talented young man. He was supposed to do a show the day Diana died. She was coming, it was all set up. He pulled the show, cancelled it. The crowd were devastated; they were so looking forward to seeing him. It's a shame what happened to him. I think he's living in Dubai now.'

Gradually piles of dismantled equipment are neatly packed into foam-lined flight cases, which the humpers roll to the trucks, then clatter up the ramps. As soon as a truck is full, it leaves and another reverses into the building. Carl checks his watch again. 'We're going to have to close that bloody door.' He frowns, time is tight enough without losing one of the access doors. 'The last truck to load has to be the first to unload in Antwerp. It all goes in reverse order. Lights are last. We've got twenty tons of them to pack away.'

At half past two in the morning, the last piece of lighting frame is crammed into Alistair's truck. He closes the door, pulls down the steel locking bar, snaps in heavy padlocks, then yanks them a couple of times to make absolutely sure. It's an obsessive habit all cross-Channel drivers have. They have to be very careful that no one could get in the back of their truck.

I will be travelling to Belgium with Alistair and I climb up into the cab. It is warm and the air-ride seat is comfortable. He carefully steers the huge truck out of the building and inches down the tight ramp to the road. As we pull out into the dark, deserted London street, Kasia watches us leave. It's been a hard night but she managed it. She has to start work at the hotel in less than five hours. She yawns, then smiles as she accepts a cigarette from Mick, one of the humpers. He seems nice. Perhaps London's not such a cold place after all.

24
ANTWERP
Rod Stewart

THE streets of London are deserted at 2.30am, and Alistair settles comfortably in his deep, air-suspension seat, sipping a mug of hot coffee as he drives the long purple truck towards Kent where we will catch the Channel Tunnel train. It was freezing back there at Earls Court and I'm glad of the warmth in the cab, although Alistair keeps the heating turned down. 'It's too easy to fall asleep if it's hot.'

My seat also is adjustable, I'm amusing myself, finding endless combinations of height, rake and firmness. If I want, I can even bounce up and down with the bumps on the road; it's great, just like the funfair. The truck has a huge diesel engine, big enough to power a tank, but even though we are sitting right above it, I can't hear a sound.

'We have to use these super-silent trucks,' says Alistair. 'Some European countries have very tight noise laws. The police in Austria will put you off the road if they hear your engine.'

The cab is roomy, with a comfortable bed behind the seats. 'I sleep best in that bunk,' says Alistair, nodding over his shoulder. 'I've bought one of those mattresses for my bed at home.'

Alistair is 59 and doesn't look like a member of a touring rock and roll road crew. He has the strong accent of the Aberdeenshire village where he grew up and almost everyone worked in the fishing industry. As we coast along the M20 he tells me to look at the other side of the motorway. A long convoy of artics snaking along the road, all of them with foreign names painted on the sides. 'Most of the trucks you see in the UK now are from the Continent. We pay higher tax on fuel, higher road tax – the government seems to be going out of its way to put British trucks off the road. The Spanish have invested a fortune in their haulage industry. Just count the number of trucks from Spain you'll see tonight. When they come to the UK they take back loads that British truckers used to deliver.'

When he gets time off, Alistair lives in Ballachulish, a beautiful village overlooking Loch Leven, in the shade of the towering mountains of Glencoe. He met his partner in Germany and has learned the language. It's useful when he is on the road in Europe, as he is most of the year.

'It's good to be working again. This is my first tour after my operation.'

'Operation?'

'Yeah, heart surgery. I had a heart attack in Helsinki.'

I could almost feel the dead weight of the lighting equipment rumbling in the long trailer behind us, and glanced at the speedo. A steady 65 miles an hour. Our total weight must be about 30 tons. *Bloody hell . . . a heart attack? If he has another one now . . .* I glanced at him, and then at the motorway stretching out ahead. Huge trucks were thundering by on the other side, separated from us by a thin metal crash barrier.

His phone rings; John is calling. He left Earls Court before us and is up ahead. Alistair listens, then turns to me. 'There's some sort of strike at Calais and the ferries are off. A lot of traffic is diverting to the Tunnel and causing big delays. It could be as much as two hours. We have to be at the gig by ten in the morning. I can't see us making it in time. The gig will probably be pulled.'

'What happens then?'

'The costs are covered by insurance. Rod's production manager will decide. This gig was always going to be tight. Maybe when we get there they won't use all the equipment. Maybe they'll cancel it. We'll see what happens.'

As miles of dark motorway slip behind us, I stare out of the window, my seat gently moving up and down with the motion of the huge truck. It's very comfortable, feels like a boat, a road-ship. Alistair tells me he has managed to quit smoking – well, almost. He picks up a little cigarette he rolled earlier, looks at it, then puts it back on the shelf between the driver and passenger seats. 'My partner would kill me if she thought I was smoking again.'

I asked if he gets bored driving all the time, even if it seems like a glamorous job.

'People want to drive for Edwin Shirley because they think they'll be getting away from routine, but this is a routine job. We sleep during the day in our cabs, usually parked at the back of the venues. We load up, we drive through the night. On days off you might manage some sightseeing, but it's mainly routine.'

He carefully overtakes a beat-up camper van laden with snowboards, then glances at the clock on the dashboard. 'The schedules are very difficult. The Americans are the hardest to work for. Bon Jovi are good, they treat you very well, but most Americans don't understand that in Europe the law only allows us to drive nine hours a day. In America, truckers drive for as long as they can keep their eyes open. They think Europe is just a small place and expect you to make impossible deadlines. All it takes is a traffic jam and they are on the phone screaming *where the hell are the trucks?* If you lose a couple of hours stuck in a jam, that still counts towards your driving time. It's all recorded on the tachograph, there's no getting round it. And we can't do any more than sixty-five miles an hour. All British trucks are fitted with speed limiters by law. But we always get there. It's what we do for a living.'

We reach Folkestone and pull into a long queue of trucks waiting to get onto the train. John is several trucks in front and confirms that the delay is at least two hours. We were the last to leave Earls Court; fortunately most of the other Edwin Shirley trucks have already reached France. Alistair dozes for a while. I watch trucks passing us as they arrive from the Continent – I'm fascinated by all the foreign names, the countries they come from.

A security guy looms out of the darkness and knocks on the cab door. *All right, mate? Freezing tonight, innit? Coldest night yet. Never mind, soon be Christmas. I'll only keep you a few minutes, then you'll be on your way.* He scans the inside of the cab with something that looks like a fluorescent light, checking for any trace of explosives. *OK, everything's fine, thanks very much.* He glances at the queue in front of us. *You shouldn't be too long now.*

At last we get the signal to move forward. It's an interesting setup: the trucks drive into a long, narrow cage on a flat-bed trailer hitched to the train, then a little bus takes the driver to the passenger carriages at the back. The ramp leading into the cage is very tight. Judging by the number of dents on the steel frame of the cage, many drivers don't have the necessary parking skills – there are only inches to spare on either side. Alistair steers the huge truck slowly and carefully, it's impressive to watch. If you have trouble getting round the bends in multistorey car parks then this would not be the job for you.

Alistair continually checks his mirrors. I offer to get out of the cab and help guide him in but he's used to doing this alone. 'You have to get it just right. The edge of the ramp can catch the fuel tank below the truck and burst it. You have to be very careful.'

It's dark and cold outside. We jump on the shuttle bus, which quickly takes us along to the warmth of the carriage. Drivers are sitting at tables, and I can hear different languages being spoken. Some of the men are wearing thin denim jackets and tee shirts. They will be heading south, back to warmer countries. Others have parkas, fleeces, wool hats and oily, steel toe-capped boots. They're going east. They don't look very happy.

John calls to us, he's kept a seat. I notice that we can buy breakfast and ask if they'd like anything, but John grimaces. *No thanks*. They have eaten on the train before, so they have brought their own food. *Just coffee, then?* I collect some, but oh dear.

Travelling below the Channel is quick, if claustrophobic; takes less time than going round the Circle Line on the London Underground. I try not to think of all the water above our heads. *Och, what the hell. Hopefully Bin Laden hasn't planted anything tonight.*

We reach Calais at the other end of the Tunnel, the shuttle bus takes us along the line of lorries to Alistair's truck, and we wait our turn to drive out of the cage. I'd assumed that the EU had made road travel simpler, no passport checks or queues at borders, but some countries provide their own little irritations. As soon as we drive out of the port Alistair pulls into a truck stop and joins a queue of lorries.

'We have to stop here to buy a temporary Belgian tax disc. It's a pain, could take an hour when it's busy like this. There's no way round it. If we got caught without one we'd be put off the road. We can't buy it at the Belgian border. We can only buy it at this truck stop or by driving into some little village and trying to find a post office. Such a waste of time. Only costs a few euros for the couple of days we'll be here. A million-dollar show could be cancelled because trucks were stuck in a queue for a stupid tax disc. Germany started this nonsense. They have satellite boxes that fit in the cabs. You have to install them and then they bill the company for the miles you do. All these foreign trucks use Britain's roads for free, but we have to pay when we come here.'

Fortunately, the queue moves quickly and we set off again. Almost immediately, Alistair has to stop. Another delay. *What now?* Two hulking artics with German number plates have parked on the narrow road out of the truck stop, blocking one side completely. Everyone coming in or going out has to take it in turn to squeeze past. The drivers have drawn the curtains across their windscreens, probably fast asleep inside, must be using earplugs and sleeping pills, ignoring the blaring horns of the angry truckers.

Alistair shakes his head and points to rows and rows of silent lorries in a truck park, which is the size of a football pitch. 'Inconsiderate bastards. They should be in there, but it looks like it's full. You have to be very careful where you park for the night. There are gangs that will push a pipe into the ventilation intake on your cab, pump gas in to knock you out, then rob you. Your passport alone is worth a thousand quid to them. It's mainly asylum seekers, gangs from Eastern Europe. There's loads of them hiding in those woods over there. You can't risk stopping in lay-bys. The truck stop is patrolled by the police, that's why so many trucks are parked here. It's a real problem.'

At last we pull onto the dark motorway, which is quiet, not much traffic at this early hour. There's a steady drizzle, damp and misty, not ideal driving conditions. It's an uneventful drive into Belgium, which we reach as a wintry dawn gradually lightens the fog clinging to the trees on either side. Alistair likes this road; in summer it's very pretty.

At 10.30am we pull off the motorway and into the parking area behind the Sportpaleis. Rod Stewart's crew are here; they travelled over with the band in four double-decker tour buses. The band has been dropped off at the Astrid Park Plaza Hotel in Antwerp city centre, and are probably catching up on sleep. Rod will fly in by private jet from Stansted tonight, just in time for the gig; there's no need for him to be at the soundcheck, the band does that without him. They will come to the hall at 5pm; everything has to be set up and ready for them. Alistair says that Rod is going to Elton John's wedding today. 'He'll be in a merry mood tonight so it should be a cracking gig. He's always good, but when he's had a few he's brilliant.'

The Sportpaleis is a purpose-built arena, great for gigs but with the usual lousy access for trucks. Alistair has to inch the artic down a narrow lane and round a tight bend to get to the loading doors at the back. He sighs. 'Architects think of everything except how trucks will get near the place.'

Using his large rear-view mirrors, he carefully backs up to loading bay 14. Local humpers are waiting, ready to muscle in the equipment: long braided hair, tattoos, calf-length shorts, high-cut Doc Martens, hand-rolled cigarettes made with dark brown liquorice paper. He opens the back door of the truck, pulls out the ramp, the humpers run up it and start rolling the lighting rigs out as fast as they were loaded at Earls Court.

There are probably 60 or 70 people working – everyone is busy, everyone has a job to do. The riggers strap on their safety harnesses, climb above the stage to the trussing suspended beneath the roof then begin wiring up chain hoists. A total of 60 have to be to be set up, then they can start lifting up the huge follow-spots. Lighting techs with heavy torque wrenches hanging from their belts tell the local crew exactly where to put the flight cases, then start unpacking them, laying the lights in neat rows. Long black coils of thick electrical cable are piled on the stage, ready to be plugged in. There are 80 PA speaker cabinets. Some must be lifted above each side of the stage, the rest positioned carefully around the auditorium. Sound crew grab them as they are rolled in and begin clamping them together, they need to work fast. There is a lot of gear. It will take all day to set it up. At the back of the arena, six girls are using air tanks to blow up hundreds of balloons that will be dropped on the crowd during the last song. The cleaners will have a busy day tomorrow.

As soon as the Edwin Shirley drivers finish unloading, they park their trucks underneath the motorway flyover that runs behind the arena, and then come back inside, rubbing their hands. Rod's caterers have unpacked gas cookers and converted a couple of large rooms backstage to a kitchen and dining area. The drivers settle down for tea and bacon rolls. *Lovely. Just the job. Hey, Jo, you've done us proud this morning.* They relax for a while, read the *Daily Mirror* and the *Sun*. Then they yawn, stretch and go outside to the neat row of purple and yellow trucks, look doubtfully up at the traffic rumbling across the flyover, shrug, climb into their cabs, pull curtains across their windscreens, and settle down for a day's sleep.

I've booked a room at a hotel in the centre of Antwerp. It's easy to get to it; there is a tube station right beside the Sportpaleis. A clean, fast train whisks me into town. It costs one euro, and there are no buskers or drunks. The receptionist gives me the key to my room, telling me it is at the front of the hotel and has a lovely view of the busy square. She's surprised when I ask if I can change it for a room with a view of the dustbins; I haven't slept all night and the cars, buses and little buzzing mopeds would keep me awake. I've been looking forward to grabbing a few hours before the gig.

It's 7pm. I'm backstage at the Sportpaleis. In a large room on the left, Rod's production team has set up a bustling office: desks, phones, banks of computers. People coming and going, press photographers, reps from the local record company. The tour accountant, Sunil Sinha, is checking spreadsheets and expense receipts while a few of the musicians are catching up on their emails. Most of the band live in America. Keeping in touch easily with their families has made life on the road far less lonely than it used to be – remember all those whiney songs musicians used to write about being far from home?

In a large room on the right is the dining area. There are four long tables with tastefully arranged flowers, a television showing *Sky News*, and a few small palm trees. It feels like a cosy restaurant. Some of the band are eating, a few of Rod's techs are having cappuccinos and strawberry gateaux.

I'm sitting with the Edwin Shirley drivers, who are tucking in. Rod's caterers had all the ingredients delivered this morning and they cook everything fresh. This is the choice: Lobster; roast chicken with wild mushrooms and leeks; cauliflower and potato dahl, basmati rice and naan bread; tortellini with sun-dried tomatoes and basil. The dessert trolley is heaped with brightly coloured delights, everything from a guilt-free exotic fruit salad to what-the-hell, mouth-watering profiteroles, smothered with thick chocolate and cream. It's a band member's birthday – there's still some cake if anyone fancies it: *Go on, have a slice*. It's a long way from chasing a greasy fried egg round a plate of baked beans in the Watford Gap service station. Rod arrives, smiling and nodding hello to everyone as he walks to his dressing room.

It's 8pm: showtime. Rod's unmistakeable voice fills the arena: *And you wear it well* . . . The packed crowd are on their feet, waving their arms, singing; they know all the words. From the stage, the arena looks like a sea of tartan scarves and Lion Rampant flags. Huge halls built with concrete and steel don't have good acoustics; the sound usually bounces all over the place and it's the atmosphere that carries the gig. But Rod Stewart has being playing venues like this for a long time and knows how to get the best possible sound: he uses the guy who has the reputation of being the best soundman in the world.

Lars Brogaard, originally from Denmark, has been working with Rod for over 20 years. They have always used the latest technology, always seeking the Holy Grail of perfect live sound. 'There's only one guy's name on this ticket,' Lars says. '*Rod Stewart*. That's who they are paying to hear. You have to be able to hear him sing. I mix the sound with the voice way out front, the drums and bass right behind it, and everything else around it. Everyone comes to hear him sing, that's the most important thing.'

I've always been interested in sound equipment and decided to have a wee look at the gear Rod uses. I'd noticed that the stage amps – the backline – was a wall of white Ampegs. This surprised me because although they are perfect for bass, guitarists usually don't play through this type of amplifier. I wandered up to the back of the stage to check them out. All the amp heads and cabinets were empty. This is not unusual; many bands have dummy cabinets on stage, it looks good. Most of the Marshall stacks that rock bands often have lining the back of the stage are not plugged in. If they were, and the guitarist hit an E chord, the blast of air from the speakers would blow the band off the stage. But there were no other amps on stage, so what was Rod's band playing through?

Then I noticed something else. Out in the crowd I could hear everything loud and clear. But when I came backstage and stood at the side, there was hardly a sound. I could hear the drums, but they were very quiet; they were behind a thick plexiglass screen. I couldn't hear the guitarists or keyboard players at all. Rod has a mandolin player and I could hear her, but only faintly. The stage was almost completely silent.

It occurred to me that they might be not be playing at all. *Surely he's not miming to backing tracks?* Many stars do this nowadays. When you see singers leaping all over the place, doing dance routines, it's a safe bet they are miming. They'd be on their knees panting for breath otherwise. But out front, Rod's voice and the band definitely sounded live.

I went round to the other side of the stage. There were two large desks, from which sound men were running the stage monitors. I got talking with Davey Bryson who has been working with Rod for years. I asked him why the stage was silent, even though Rod had a 12-piece band.

'That's because we don't use any amplifiers on the stage.'

'What – none?'

He grinned. 'Nope. Not one.'

'Isn't that that kind of unusual?'

'Yeah. We do it this way because it gives complete control to Lars out front. The guitarists play through radio transmitters that send a signal to their amplifiers. We put their amplifiers in soundproofed cases and stick mikes in them, and that's what we feed to the mixing desks. All the musicians are fitted with in-ear monitors, like little headphones. They don't hear anything directly from their amps, they hear what we send them from the desk. They don't even work their own effects pedals. That's done by the guitar techs there.'

He pointed to the other mixing desk, where there were two more sound engineers. At their side was a rack of Marshall and Fender guitar amplifier heads but no speaker cabs. Cables snaked from the amps and disappeared into flight cases under the stage. I listened carefully and could just faintly hear the sound of the guitars coming from them.

'Rod also wears in-ear monitors and I control everything he hears. The other guys do the mix for the musicians. I only do Rod's. I know exactly how he likes it. If I didn't know how "Maggie May" is supposed to sound after thirty years there would be something far wrong.' He grins and moves a fader ever so slightly, his eyes never leaving Rod for a moment. 'He only has to give me a tiny nod and I know what he wants.'

One of the problems in getting a good live sound is that microphones are highly sensitive. As well as picking up the singer's voice, they also pick up some of the sound coming from the guitar amps. This tends to swamp the vocals in the PA. If the guitarist turns up too loud, as most do in the excitement of a gig, the soundman at the mixing desk at the front of the hall can only turn up the vocals, because he can't turn down the guitarist's amplifier. The more he turns the vocals up, the more the mikes pick up the guitars and the sound becomes a mess. Ringing ears for everyone. Rod's sound company has solved this problem by having a silent stage. Apparently Rod Stewart was the first person to do this. Lars controls everything the audience hears, like the sound engineer in a recording studio. I'm fascinated; I've always loved the way musicians instantly latch on to new technology, artistic minds working with science.

Later, I got talking with the guitarists and the bass player with the band. They admit that it was weird at first, only hearing their playing in their little earpieces, but they got used to it after a few gigs; it makes sense. It also allows Rod to protect his voice. He doesn't have amplifiers blasting behind him, so he's not fighting against the volume of the entire band. This is probably why he can still sing a two-and-a-half-hour show four nights a week.

It's great to watch him do his stuff from just a few feet away. He looks as though he loves every moment, strutting the stage, working the crowd, he's still at the top of his game.

The usual perception of successful musicians is that they are self-absorbed, convinced they know best, are arrogant and demanding. Some may be, but of the musicians I've met this is true only of those who *failed* to make the big time. The guys who succeed usually know what they are good at, concentrate on that, and allow others to guide them and advise them on their weaknesses. They don't think they know it all. For example, when they make records, they hire the best people to mix for them; they'll happily use songs by other writers. I've known a lot of guys who were very talented but have been playing pub gigs all their lives because they won't listen to anyone else, they insist on trying to control every aspect of the creative process. Being successful in the music business is invariably the result of hard work by a team of people.

In the morning I caught an early train to Charleroi airport for a flight back to Scotland, listening to my iPod as I looked out at ghostly Belgian fields, dark with mud. We live in a world filled with music; in every country on our troubled planet everyone loves music. It's as though every style of music is a small stream, a part of something far greater. And you never find anyone blowing up a plane because they hate blues, jazz or the sitar; I suspect that music is the purest form of religion.

At the airport, I join the shuffling queue at the security gate, waiting to be scanned for bombs and weapons. When I finally get to the departure lounge, I buy a coffee and prepare for the Ryanair Rumble, the mad charge to board. The flight isn't due to leave for an hour, but a scrum of people are already crowded around the gate, glaring at anyone who looks as if they might be trying to sneak to the front. *Relax, there's a seat for everyone!*

I notice some long-haired guys sitting patiently in the corner. A couple of them are listening to iPods, a few are snoozing, and one is tapping on a laptop. *I recognise him – he's a guitarist.* It's a band on the move. Another rock and roll tour.

Think I'll say hello. . .

25

BEDFORD

Geno Washington
and the Ram Jam Band

FESTIVALS in the UK used to be thin on the ground, mainly because they were a guaranteed way of losing a great deal of money, but these days they seem to be happening all over the place. Apart from the mega–events, there are loads of small festivals. One of the newest is the Rhythm Festival, which is held in a little village called Clapham, just outside Bedford, an hour or so from London. Despite the unpredictability of the British summer weather, festivals are very popular. Glastonbury, for many people, is the highlight of the year, rain or shine. When T in the Park tickets go on sale a year in advance, all 70,000 are instantly snapped up, even though nobody knows who will be playing at it.

The Wickerman Festival in South West Scotland is run by nice people working with a hospitable landowner. In the summer of 2006, let's just say that it is unlikely any of the bands would have attracted much of a crowd if they had been playing anywhere else. Despite this, 23,000 happy campers rolled up and enjoyed a great weekend.

By contrast, the Rhythm Festival had an interesting and varied selection of performers including Donovan, Arlo Guthrie, Nine Below Zero, Wilko Johnson, Roy Harper and Jimmy Page, Desmond Decker and the Aces, John Cooper Clark, the Blues

Band, Roger Chapman, Hugh Cornwall, Ike Turner, Jerry Lee Lewis, and Geno Washington with his Ram Jam Band. Not long ago, almost any of these acts would have packed large venues. Unfortunately, fewer than 3,000 turned up, less than the festival needed to break even.

It had been dogged by bad luck from the start. Jimmy Page had to pull out, Ike Turner called off and Desmond Decker would have loved to come but unfortunately died. Even so, it was a nice festival that deserves to become a regular event. There was a peaceful, relaxed atmosphere, many people had brought their children; it's good to see families enjoying themselves together – some festivals have become the holiday camps of the New Age. The site is a former air force base where Glen Miller was stationed during the war. The main area is like a village cricket field, a bowl-shaped meadow with leafy woods behind the stage, a pleasant spot to listen to music while basking in the hot afternoon sun, and to enjoy the warm colours of the western sky at dusk.

Festivals attract interesting people. Like Marcie, who travelled all the way from San Diego as soon as she discovered that Jimmy Page would be playing. Marcie is Jimmy's soulmate, although he doesn't know it yet. When she was a little girl she was walking in the woods when a giant owl spoke to her. The owl had been taken over by the spirit of an Indian shaman who told her that one day she would meet a man with flowing dark hair from across an ocean who would play music to her. 'He said that when we meet it will be as two burning sticks joining together in a single eternal flame.'

In 1974, Marcie went to see Led Zeppelin at the Forum in Los Angeles and managed to get a seat near the stage. 'When Jimmy smiled at me I knew he was the one. I know that some day we'll be married. Jimmy will never be happy until we are together.'

By offering to work as a volunteer, she has managed to get a backstage pass, and happily cleaned the dressing rooms last night, but doesn't have an assignment today. She spots Roy Harper. He will be playing soon and he looks nervous, twitchy. He must need a big hug, so she throws her arms round him. She has an expensive digital camera, wants a photograph with him. She tells Roy about the shaman. She's disappointed that Jimmy won't be coming. She's travelled all this way and won't get to meet him – something always seems to happen to keep them apart. But it's only a temporary setback. She knows where Jimmy lives, and as soon as the festival is over she will go to London to find him. She's brought a special gift she bought on eBay: a tape of unreleased recordings by Elvis Presley. *Isn't he gonna just love it?*

Backstage, two chefs have the task of feeding the performers. They are stirring a large pot of chilli, keeping it bubbling nicely. It's proper chilli too, with real chocolate in it, just like the Incas used to make it. There's a tasty-looking salsa and vegetable casserole, and plenty of steaming white rice, or, if they prefer, the bands can tuck into a nice salad. At the back of the makeshift kitchen is a deep-fat fryer hot and ready; many musicians can't eat before they go on stage, they're far too jittery. But after they've played their encore they sure could murder a juicy hot dog with chips and a cold Bud.

Out front, fluttering gently in the warm air, are marquees with a choice of woody real ale or frothing draught beer for the thirsty crowd and, a short walk along the festival site, there is plenty of grub on offer from rows of vans and tents. Food at festivals has always been a risky business, but here the catering seems to be excellent. Burgers, made from the caterer's own ex-cows. Vegetarian dishes pretending to be something manly – nut roast, vegetarian meat loaf – but they tasted good. Galettes, adding a touch of Parisian flair. Searing vindaloo and eye-wateringly-hot pakora that I wouldn't dare to try, but delicious Turkish Delight, which I would, and could get fat on very quickly.

At the side is a little funfair with dodgems and a large spinning thing with loads of flashing lights. It's very civilised; there's no sign of anyone wolfing down a curry and six pints and then going on it for a bet. Smiling girls wearing long, flowing dresses are standing behind barrows spread with all sorts of colourful stuff: beads, jade and silver necklaces, dangling earrings, wooden things to wear on your wrist, other wooden things to hang round your neck, more wooden things to stick through your ear lobes, and convenient devices to enhance the pleasures of hash smoking, which appears to have come a long way since those Grateful Dead album covers of the old days.

If you have recently been hovering at the entrance to a tattooist's dark cavern, swithering about joining those who are adorned with body art, there's a lavish array of designs instantly available but which wash off, should you decide not to stay permanently in that nether world. A Hawaiian girl is serving fresh fruit smoothies, but instead of electricity, she uses a stationary bicycle, the back wheel powering a mechanical blender – perhaps something every home will soon need if the bickering in the Middle East isn't resolved. The smoothie was lovely too.

Everyone seemed to be happy as they strolled around the festival site. Feeling that all was well with the world, I wandered backstage and noticed that Marcie had cornered a passing guitar player, telling him how she'd hoped today would be the day she'd finally get to meet Jimmy. Then she notices Mike Read, a well-known DJ and TV show host. She grabs his arm and hands the guitarist her camera. *Click. Can you take it again, please? Just to make sure. Thanks.* The guitar player hurries off and she tells Mike: *I've nearly met Jimmy seven times. A shaman told me. . .* He looks at her warily and edges away.

I went out front to watch Roger Chapman and his band. He used to scare the shit out of me when I was a teenager. If you ever saw him when he played with Family, especially with your consciousness altered by LSD, you'll know what I mean. Family were a brilliant but evil-sounding band, and Roger had the stage presence of Lucifer himself. In the 1980's, at the dawn of the harsh sunlight of the new romantics, he disappeared into the shadows, before fleeing to Bavaria where he apparently recruited many new devotees.

By the time many rock stars reach their 60th year, their voices have been burned away by whisky and cigarettes. They have little to offer but croaky renditions of their glory-day hits, becoming their own tribute acts. But not Roger and his band. They are superb. It is such a treat to see musicians this good. They make it look effortless. The whole set is excellent, but a couple of songs are breathtaking. Occasionally, it's possible to hear perfect musicianship, and the crowd is held as if hypnotised in one of those so-rare moments. Roger has two guitarists, sax, keyboards, drums and bass, and for a spell it sounds as if his voice and the entire band are one instrument. I glance at the people around me, they are staring at the stage, at this man with the soaring, rough voice. He's singing: *No one can sing the blues like Blind Willie McTell.* The crowd is gripped, it's an eerie experience, like being at a crossroads but not daring to move either way. I wonder how many young pop gods will sound anywhere near as good as this in 30 years.

When he finishes playing, Marcie wants to meet him. After a while, he comes out of his Portakabin. She walks up to him and is about to ask for a photograph. Then she looks into his dark eyes. She halts, and backs away. Perhaps not.

John Cooper Clark is on stage. He's a writer with a broad Lancashire accent, he's *from fooking Salford, he is*. He tells jokes and reads poems. He's good, makes the crowd feel as if they are in a packed students' union. He's very funny, is going down a treat, and when he finishes they cheer and clap warmly. I get talking to him backstage – he's instantly likeable. He's been on tour with a punk band and says it's been like *a fooking war every night*. Punchups in the dressing room after every gig, sometimes he tries to calm them, sometimes he just keeps well out t' fooking way. He laughs and shakes his head. He looks very like Ronnie Wood – people often come up to him in the street and ask if he plays with the Rolling Stones. Marcie homes in, camera ready. John bums a cigarette from her. She lights it for him and he looks at it. The smoke smells sweet, like vanilla. *That's different, what's that then?* She's brought them from California, she reckons Jimmy might like them. He politely listens to her story. Judging by his puzzled expression, I don't think there are many giant talking owls in Salford.

Hugh Cornwall is playing. I met him once when I played in a band with Mike Heron a long time ago. The Stranglers were our opening act, although I should mention that it was one of their first gigs. It's slightly disconcerting to hear a middle-aged man singing about walking on beaches looking at the peaches, but I guess his fans want the old Stranglers' songs. He has a drummer and an attractive young bass player called Caroline, who I suspect may become a rock and roll star in the years to come.

Just before Roy Harper goes on, Geno Washington arrives backstage. Climbing out of his manager's gleaming black Audi, he says hi to everyone; he loves to talk and joke. He laughs deeply, his slim body jerking and shaking. *Hell, yeah, I remember Glasgow.*

Used to play the Maryland Club. Crazy nights! There was a band up there called the Dream Po-leece. They became the Average White Band. Great guys, great band. Crazy, crazy nights! He poses with Marcie, yeah, of course she can have a picture. *Sure thang.*

Geno goes to his Portakabin and Marcie looks around to see who else is here. Anyone interesting? She spots a rock photographer laden with Canons and long lenses. She asks him if he has ever photographed Jimmy Page. Just as she reaches the part about the owl, two security guys appear at her side. They speak gently, they are very sorry, but she shouldn't have been given a backstage pass, someone has made a mistake. She is welcome to watch the show, but she must leave the backstage area. Yes, they realise she has a pass, but she must give it back. She sighs, quietly leaves and disappears into the crowd out front.

Every young musician should go out of their way to see Geno Washington – they could learn more in a two-hour gig than in a two-year college course. I've seen him a few times over the years; any time I start to feel jaded, I know it's time to see Geno again. Yeah, you could say I'm a fan. There are very few authentic soul revue shows still on the road. They are expensive to take on tour, and nowadays many soul artistes just use prerecorded backing tracks – they've become travelling karaoke singers. Geno Washington is the real thing.

Geno Washington and the Ram Jam Band play 'covers'. 'Everybody Needs Somebody', 'Can't Turn You Loose', 'Midnight Hour', 'Hold On I'm Coming', all those great songs from Atlantic Records, Stax and Tamla Motown by Wilson Pickett, Otis Redding, and Sam and Dave. Geno makes them sound as if they were written just for him.

Geno first came to Europe with the US Air Force. On leaving, he formed a soul band and quickly became one of the most successful live acts in the UK. He played every club and dance hall in the country, and unless you started queuing very early, it was impossible to get a ticket. Some of the bands that opened for him were also pretty handy: Cream, Jimi Hendrix and Pink Floyd. In 1966, he released a live album that stayed in the charts for 48 weeks – only 'Bridge Over Troubled Water' equalled this. Everyone loved Geno, especially the people who, unlike himself, allegedly made millions from his record sales.

Festival gigs are tricky because the bands can't do proper soundchecks; they play one after the other. Headline acts don't usually allow the crowd to catch a glimpse of them before they go on; they like to make a big entrance. This doesn't bother Geno. He walks on stage with his band, checks his mike, does part of a song to make sure he can hear the monitors, and tells the cheering crowd he'd rather mess about a little and get the sound just right, then he'll come back and play his set.

When everything is sorted, the Ram Jam Band starts the show, playing a couple of instrumentals, the horn section twisting and turning and swinging their saxes in the air. The stage lights are hot and bright, red and blue and green. Everyone starts moving to the pounding beat, it's so damn exciting. Then Geno runs on with a huge grin, and he's singing: *Now you sit, all by yourself. Everybody's dancin', you cain't a-help yourself. You got that feelin', baby, fee-lin'.* He seems to reach out and pull in the whole crowd, even people who clearly have been busy among the trees at the edge of the festival site hurry to get a closer view. He talks to us between songs, like he knows *each and every person here tonight*, his warmth and humour making everyone feel involved, like we are part of the show.

I spot Marcie near the front. Tears were in her eyes when she had her pass taken away, but she's with a guy now and they're dancing together. She's recovered from the car crash last year, when she almost died from head injuries. She's always in pain, but has her medication figured out. She's enjoying having the time and the money to travel wherever she wants – she has just sold her successful insurance business in California. The guy moves a little closer. And she's smiling again.

26
KING TUT'S WAH WAH HUT

The Hedrons

KING Tut's Wah Wah Hut is a Glasgow basement bar with a large room upstairs. From the outside it doesn't look famous, doesn't look like the sort of place a New York magazine would list as one of the world's top 10 must-visit venues. It is near the city centre, in a business district, surrounded by the offices of accountants, lawyers and architects. When a band plays at Tut's, it must not soundcheck before 6pm. Silence. Nobody wants to be tearfully finalising their divorce settlement, or painstakingly drawing plans for a new government building, only to have their stream of thought shattered by a thundering bass drum reverberating through the wall. It's probably only because it has been there so long – I even played it when I was young – that it manages to get an entertainment licence at all.

If a band is going to make the big time, it will have to make it at King Tut's first. The people who go to Tut's have seen them all. This is where Oasis were discovered, where every band wants to play. Anyone can have their chance, from Radiohead, Blur, Travis, Pulp and The Verve who all went on to reach the heights of music superstardom, to the insane but hugely entertaining Friends Outreach Programme, who didn't. Tut's is like a boulder in the middle of a fast-flowing river. It's only one step from there to the other side, but it's a big one.

It cost a staggering amount of money to build the Scottish Parliament building, but it was worth every penny because the nation's new leaders quickly banned smoking in all public places, even in Glasgow pubs where knives were a much higher threat to health. Outside and down a short flight of stairs from street level, there is a huddle of folk in a cloud of smoke puffing frantically, sucking down enough nicotine to keep withdrawal at bay for an hour or so. One thing is for sure; they're not going to miss a moment of the main band tonight. Inside, the four skinny girls who are the members of The Hedrons are working the room, smiling, saying hi to some of the 36,000 friends they've made through myspace.

Like the band, most of them are young – girls in little frayed denim skirts and half-size tee shirts, joking, laughing, drinking, enjoying a good night out. A few of the crowd are older, like Gerard, from London, 43, single, straight, 160cm, average body type, high-school educated, house-painter, likes the *Da Vinci Code*, Fredrick Forsyth, Sven Hassel, Elvis, Bruce Lee, and is on myspace for networking and friends, as it says on his profile listing. He has seen the girls many times, has travelled all over the UK to watch them. In March he will follow them to Austin, Texas, where they are taking part in the annual South by Southwest festival, a music industry showcase that gives hundreds of new bands the opportunity to play in America.

Less than a year earlier, the girls were playing in different groups, rehearsing in one of the many packed studios in Glasgow. They drifted together, and it worked. They are signed to a small record label, have a hard-working management company behind them, and are trucking the length and breadth of the UK, playing bars, building that all-important fan base. It looks like their moment might have come.

The support act, old guys playing 1970's-style riff-and-scream stuff, have finished. It's 10 minutes until show time. Leaving cigarette butts crushed on the cold concrete, the crowd surges into the large, dark room upstairs. Wearing tight jeans and skimpy, low-cut vests, the girls walk onto the stage, check their mikes, and tune their guitars. No roadies, they do it themselves. The crowd is only an outstretched arm from behind the security barrier to the stage. Leaning on the steel barrier is Ian, gazing at Tippi, the front-woman of the band, the star. She is beautiful, and as photogenic as any model. A good photograph can sell a million albums; some pictures of this slim girl from Bellshill, a housing estate east of Glasgow, are every pixel as good as those of the young Sharlene Spiteri or Debbie Harry.

Ian can't take his eyes off her, she's only a touch away, and when she leans over to plug her guitar into the tuner at the front of the stage, he stares at her breasts, takes a deep breath, then wipes his hand across his forehead. Ian is almost 50, but from the moment he first saw Tippi's photograph, nothing could have stopped him seeing her in the flesh. This is the 16th gig he's been to on this tour; and he plans to come to as many more as he can. He works three days a week; the rest of the time he's at the front of every stage Tippi is playing. She notices him – *oh aye, he's here again* – smiles, gives him a nod, friendly, but slightly wary.

Chester will be 60 in a few weeks. He's followed Tippi's career since the day he first saw her on a talent show when she was a teenager. Last week he caught a train to London to see The Hedrons. 'It was a twenty-four-hour trip. I went to the gig, spent the night in the station and travelled back to Glasgow the next morning. It was the sort of thing I used to do when I was young. I love supporting new Scottish bands. I could have stayed in a hotel, but crashing on a bench felt much more rock and roll.'

He's a gentle, softly spoken and likeable guy, a senior manager in an office across the street. 'She is so talented, she really deserves to make it. I've seen her playing sixty-three times.'

The Hedrons play fast, punky sort of pop, the kind of music that students love to leap about to, like musical Red Bull. But when you see Tippi, it's not surprising that so many guys are here to drool; it's strange that she isn't already a star. The band go off for a few minutes, the last few smokers in the sold-out crowd crush in, then The Hedrons run back on stage.

They are terrific.

Tippi is the most exciting front-woman I've seen in Britain for years. She's leaping and jumping, giving it everything, she's got this hard Glaswegian crowd going crazy. She has natural presence and knows how to get the crowd going; there's no way this tough little chick is gonna let anyone here tonight *not* pay attention. This crowd is *hers*. Tippi is the bow-wave of the band, surging forward, carrying them along on a rush of energy. The drummer at her back and the two girls at her side play their stuff, fast and furious, thrusting their hips at the crowd so close in front of them, but they keep an eye on her, ready to move with her any time she turns in their direction.

It's great to see; it's been so long since the UK has produced a really good new rock singer. She belts out the songs, she's not trying to be polite. She's jumping and dancing but not in a choreographed way like Madonna, or strutting like Tina Turner. And she's definitely not like any of those soft-porn singers shimmering their arses on MTV. There is a roughness, an aggression, something about her that draws in everyone; they are staring at her, caught up in the excitement. The bar at the back is open, the staff are alert, but it doesn't look like they'll be pouring many pints while Tippi is on stage.

Ian probably knows he shouldn't be here, he's too old to be among all these young people. But he can't help it, any more than a moth can avoid being drawn to a dazzling light. And someday soon he'll be able to talk about how he was at King Tut's tonight. How he was this close to Tippi before she was famous, how he met her, how he knew what the world would see tomorrow.

Tut's is drenched in sweat. The amps are steaming, bouncing on their flight cases. A string snaps, *who cares? Don't stop, just keep going.* Drumsticks splintering. Last song. Tippi leaps into the crowd. She's singing, screaming the words: *'Be my friend'*. A guy rushes to her, jumping up and down, yelling that he fucking loves her. She dances, she sings, and we all know that soon she won't be able to get this close to a crowd – not without minders to protect her. This is what rock music is all about. This is what pub gigs like King Tut's give to music, what they are for.

27

NEWCASTLE

Darkwater

I NEVER thought I'd manage a band. Managing any band is a 24-hour slog, seven days a week, if you're in it for the right reasons, that is. My son Graham had formed a band called Darkwater with Doog, a friend he'd got to know at Glasgow Concert Hall where they worked as sound engineers. They write great songs together.

Graham had played in other bands, but I'd never managed any of them. I didn't want to interfere and, anyway, he'd never asked me. But when I heard what he and Doog were playing I couldn't sit still, especially when I saw how much of his time was being taken up just getting the band a few gigs and sorting out musicians. As they were painfully discovering, musicians take a lot of organising.

They needed to find a good singer with charisma, not an easy task. They had auditioned a long and depressing queue of people who all talked like seasoned pros, but whose only experience was staggering up to the microphone in a karaoke bar with an overflowing pint glass in their hands. At last the band found a good singer, did a few gigs with her and she was great on stage, and so I hired some guys to shoot a video, which we could show to agents. It looked terrific, but I was a wee bit worried when I discovered the girl was a heavy smoker and enjoyed an extravagantly uninhibited social life. I've played in bands with far too many hard-drinking singers who ended up hoarse after a couple of gigs and so I gently offered to hire a vocal coach who would teach her how to protect her voice. She stormed off in a huff, never to be seen again.

After a year of trying would-be singers and screamers, some of whom started out quite well then revealed disturbing habits involving large amounts of alcohol and drugs mixed with momentous mood swings, Graham and Doog were disheartened. They were on the point of giving up when they asked me to help find someone. About the same time, I was talking to John Wheeler of Hayseed Dixie, who I'd kept in touch with after seeing his band in Wrexham. John mentioned that they would be coming back to the UK to do a tour, all at major venues. We got talking about Graham's band and I offered them as a support group. While we talked, John listened to them on their myspace site. Yeah, he'd love to have them.

I was excited about this. Support tours are gold dust to bands. Everyone wants them and many bands have to pay a lot of money to the headline act for the privilege. Touring with a well-known band is a tremendous step forward for any new band because it puts them in front of big crowds; it's so much better than playing half-empty pub gigs and unsigned band nights. Almost all top bands made the big time after doing support tours. I was very, very excited.

There was only one slight problem.

We didn't have a singer.

Without a singer, we didn't have a band.

And the tour was due to start in only six weeks.

I couldn't possibly turn down this opportunity and launched myself into finding the right singer. The band wanted a girl, someone who was a little bit different, and there had to be someone, somewhere. I advertised in newspapers, stuck notices in all the local music shops and colleges, placed ads on musicians' websites, spent 12-hour sessions trawling through myspace, checking out singers in unsigned UK and European bands, then sending them emails asking if they'd like to audition. I taped posters all over my car and managed to get one pinned up on the staff notice board at the BBC. I hired rehearsal rooms and we tried dozens of people. A few were quite good but most had far higher opinions of themselves than talent. I began getting jittery. What the hell had I got myself into?

After two weeks I was waking up in a cold sweat every night. I couldn't let John Wheeler down, and it would be awful if the band missed this chance. Then I remembered a girl I'd seen on X Factor. Many singers on this show are very good, but they want to be pop stars, a million miles from what Darkwater were looking for. But this girl was different, a small, dark-haired, tattooed punk with a great voice. She could sing. Even though she was completely out of place on the show, like a Hell's Angel in a sea of leggy blonde Britneys, Simon Cowell, Sharon Osbourne and Louis Walsh immediately put her through to the next round. So I contacted X Factor, but there was no chance of them giving me her phone number. And so it was back to random myspace searches, more emails and auditions.

The days raced by, we were quickly running out of time. I reckoned that I'd have to hire a session singer and in desperation I contacted Twinkle in America, even though she was a lot older than the band had in mind. But she had the voice to do the tour, and at least I wouldn't be letting John down. She said she'd love to do it. I slept for the first night in weeks. Then her tour with Dickey Betts added more dates and she was sorry, she couldn't come to the UK and, besides, I'd never be able to get her a work permit in time.

I kept calling singers, and tried out some guys, and one was quite good. There was only one slight problem, he said with a sheepish grin. He was getting married that weekend and going shark diving in South Africa for two weeks. Oh, he was sorry, hadn't he mentioned that already? Sorry. There was a guy who claimed to have a six-octave voice. He had, but he was out of tune on every one, sounding like a newly neutered cat informing the world of its predicament. Another guy appeared in the studio, closed his eyes then started thrashing about and wailing as if possessed. A girl called who sounded very nice and when she told me she'd sung at big festivals including Glastonbury I couldn't get her to the rehearsal room fast enough. At last, someone with experience! When she arrived, she wasn't quite how she'd described herself, she looked old enough to be Doog's mother. She admitted that it had been over 20 years since she'd sung in bands, and would she be able to bring her children on tour? Then a Norwegian girl seemed perfect. She had loads of experience. She loved the band. She loved the music. She wanted to do the tour. Great! Oh, she'd need to take time off in the middle of the tour to sing at a folk music festival in Denmark, but that would be OK, wouldn't it?

I finally narrowed the search down to two girls. One had sung in a chart-topping girl-band and played gigs to as many as 40,000 people, so she was confident and professional on stage. But when she sang with the band she just didn't fit – she had a good voice but it was too disco, too pop. Graham and Doog's songs needed a strong rock voice. The other girl was from Holland, looked terrific and the guys liked her, but her background was mainly in theatre and her voice wasn't quite strong enough. On some songs it was great, but on others it was thin and fragile. I doubted if it would survive a tour playing gigs every night of the week. But it was now less than three weeks to the tour and I was panicking. We had to take one or the other. Time had run out.

Then I thought again of the girl in X *Factor* and began posting hopeful messages on forums linked to the show's website to see if anyone knew who she was. At last, a breakthrough. Someone replied, telling me the girl's name, Lora, and the town near Newcastle she was from. I made a strong coffee, hit the Internet and looked up the phone number of every person in the area then began dialling. I was afraid that most people would think I was a double-glazing salesman or a stalker, but they were very helpful. After only three calls, I was speaking to the girl's uncle. Another call and I had her father's email address. I sent Darkwater tracks to him, with my phone number. Would Lora be interested?

She'd been working a late shift in a bar in the city centre and called me at one in the morning. I was wide-awake anyway. She loved the songs, she'd been looking for a band exactly like Darkwater. I told her I would bring Graham and Doog down next morning to meet her. Six sleepless hours later we jumped in my car and rushed down to Newcastle. When we reached her house Doog plugged his Les Paul into a little amplifier and played one of the songs. She'd stayed up all night learning them and sang it straight off. She was perfect. She agreed to come straight back to Glasgow with us to rehearse. With less than two weeks to the start of the nationwide tour, we finally had our singer.

It was all going wonderfully well, the band were sounding great, They'd been rehearsing every day and Lora had nailed the set. Five days to go to the start of the tour. I told the band to relax, spend time with their girlfriends, rest a little, the tour would be hard work. Then the drummer telephoned and announced he was calling off.

Great. Just bloody great.

Nerves jangling, I called Hugo, the drummer with the Bootleg Beatles. He'd just finished playing a gig with Rod Stewart and was due to start a tour with the Bootlegs in late November but, yes, he'd be happy to help, but wouldn't have any time to rehearse.

I was in a panic. Because Graham and Doog are sound engineers they are very clued up on current technology and so Darkwater's music is quite complex, layered with musical samples and clips that are synched with keyboards. This meant that when they play live, every song has to be played at precisely the right speed, something that is impossible without the drummer using what is known as a 'click track' – essentially an electronic metronome. Top session musicians like Hugo can do this, but few semi-pro drummers can, partly because in the excitement of playing a live gig it takes a lot of discipline not to speed up and, besides, many don't like having to wear headphones to hear the constant clicking with which they must play exactly in time.

I was worried about asking Hugo to come on tour without rehearsal time but it was very good of him to agree to play with the band. Then a drummer who worked as a sound engineer at a big venue in Glasgow telephoned Doog. He'd heard about our drummer walking out at the last minute. He could play to click, and he'd quit his job immediately if we wanted him, even though we couldn't pay him any wages. Four days to go. *Only four days.* I called every rehearsal studio in the west of Scotland, desperately taking any last-minute time or cancelled bookings they had. None of us was getting more than a few hours' sleep, the band were rehearsing every spare moment. Lora had moved into the spare bedroom in my house, and it was fun to see puzzled looks from the neighbours when they saw her black spiky hair, tattoos and lip rings. The keyboard player, who was about to leave his well-paid job as a computer programmer, looked like a ghost through lack of sleep. But they were sounding terrific. When a band sounds right, it's unmistakeable. They were fired up on adrenalin and jumping with excitement. This was it. They were ready to go, they couldn't wait to walk onto the big, bright stage at Dartford for the first gig of the tour. At last I was starting to relax and look forward to the gigs. Then, with one day to go, Lora caught 'flu.

28

UK TOUR

Darkwater

IT always takes longer to drive to London than you plan. The fastest I ever did it was just over five hours in a wee car driven by a maniac, but that was in those glorious days when you could hit the deserted M74 at the old zoo on the edge of Glasgow early on a summer evening and rarely see another vehicle until the traffic lights on Edgware Road, 400 short miles south. Lorries quietly and politely puttered along the inside, and there were no convoys of Spanish super-trucks or Eastern European converted military tractor-trailers battling for control of the middle lane.

Darkwater would be playing the first gig of the Hayseed Dixie tour at the Mick Jagger Centre in Dartford on Sunday and I wanted them there bright and early – one of the unwavering rules about being a support band is that you must always be on time. So we left on Saturday, picking up Lora at her parents' home just outside Newcastle. She was stuffed full of paracetamol and hot lemon drinks and she looked rough, but laughed it off. Like the rest of the band, she was too excited about the tour to let illness bother her.

I just hoped her voice would hold up. The thought of colds, 'flu and throat infections haunts most singers when they are about to go on tour, and the bigger the band gets, the more they worry about it. They pay hefty insurance premiums in case they have to pull out of a gig, but that only covers the costs. Musicians don't like letting down the people who come to see them, it's not like having a Monday-morning hangover, they can't call in sick. If the tour manager holds a mirror in front of their mouth and the glass mists up, they are fit to work. Years ago, I played when I had a slipped disc – some painkillers, whisky and a chair on the stage, no problem. The drummer with the Incredible String Band endured severe diarrhoea during a gig in Holland, and had to buy new breeks next day.

But if the voice goes, the show is off. So much can be wrecked by one little virus. Despite the hard-livin' image some stars like to portray, they take really good care of themselves when they are on tour; no alcohol, definitely no cigarettes; they work out, eat carefully prepared nutritious meals, get plenty of sleep. Rod Stewart always rests his voice every third night. Many stars fly home after their gigs on private jets rather than stay in hotels. Some won't even shake hands.

I had decided to go to the first couple of gigs on the tour, make sure everything was OK, then leave the band to it. I didn't reckon they would want a middle-aged manager hanging around and, besides, I get stressed when having to arrive somewhere at an exact time, especially when I need to fight the sort of traffic that makes driving in the UK such a gut-churner. Exactly how much time do you allow to get anywhere these days? Traffic jams 10 miles long are often caused after the tiniest of vehicle shunts and a couple of neurotics insist on blocking the road while they swap precise insurance details and take meticulous photographs of little dents in the bumpers of their precious 10-year-old Volvos. Or when some moronic caravan driver tries to prevent a harassed truck from overtaking him. We would be driving 4,000 miles around UK motorways in the next few weeks. It would have been very nice to hire a comfortable little tour bus with beds, so we could drive at night and sleep as the miles slipped quietly behind us, but they were far too expensive.

As we left Lora's house, and pulled onto the A1, she opened a case of freshly burned CDs and quickly commandeered the car stereo. Lora likes heavy metal, the blasting, grinding, exploding kind that makes Kiss sound like a Salt Lake City God-rock group, and she had brought all sorts of weird stuff I'd never heard of, wailing bands from bleak Armenian ghettos and whip-cracking sado-masochistic fetish groups from LA's darkest back alleys. It fairly wakes you up.

We'd decided to use my car plus a Transit van for the band's backline – the amplifiers they'd use on stage, drums, keyboards and guitars. Each venue would be providing the PA and lights so we didn't need too much space. Even so, the Transit was crammed; apart from equipment, we also had bags and cases with enough clothes and stuff for the next five weeks – I'd managed to get them onto another tour with an American band in the Czech Republic and Slovakia that would start at the end of the Hayseed tour. And we had cardboard boxes stuffed full of the all-important merchandise we'd had made: stickers, posters, tee shirts, hats and CDs that we could sell at gigs to make some food money.

Most bands could not afford to tour at all without the money they make from selling merch, or swag as some call it. In recent years, however, some venues have cottoned onto this and demand a percentage of the sales. This upsets the Dixie's John Wheeler a lot. 'When they give me a percentage of their bar tab, I'll give 'em a cut of my sales. They make a pile of money on bar sales, but people don't come to drink – they wouldn't be here at all if we weren't playing.' Many gigs, like the Carling Academies, are very helpful and even provide a security guy to stand beside the merchandise point. But some places demand up-front cash payment. 'I'll set a table up in the street outside before I'll pay these people. Some of them want ten per cent. By the time we pay shipping costs and all, we'd be left with nothing. We'd have to pass the cost onto our fans and we ain't gonna do that. We'll set up on the street, even if it's snowin'.

Being on the road with a band has changed very little since I used to tour for a living, except for two things: Travelodges and sat navs. We would be using both every day. In the 1970's, hotels in the UK were very expensive; the headline band could afford them but support bands usually dossed in little guesthouses, often run by grim elderly widows trying to supplement meagre pensions. They were cheap and the owners had clearly spent nothing on routine maintenance in decades. Bathrooms were somewhere down a dank hallway, although there were usually old cracked porcelain sinks in the rooms, which in the middle of the night saved stumbling along the freezing, dark corridor where the landlady's slavering Doberman might be lying in wait. Hot water came from a tiny spluttering gas boiler, and there was rarely enough for more than one guest, usually some fat, chain-smoking salesman in the next room who'd woken everyone at 6am as he stumbled around emitting eruptions of farts and thunderous mucus shifts.

They were cheerless slums harbouring countless little insects behind painted woodchip wallpaper, filthy windows with flaking paintwork and grimy cream-brown plasterwork; and they were damp, always bloody damp, with pink nylon sheets and grey blankets like something an old carthorse might have in its stable. There were two types of mattresses: sagging with broken and jagged metal springs, or rock hard with broken and jagged metal springs, and they all bore worrying stains resembling a map of Australia. No wonder we all drank so much.

There are countless stories of musicians in the 1970's wrecking Holiday Inns and Hiltons, but these are often just tales because by the time we reached that level of accommodation most of us were bloody grateful that at last we had a warm, comfortable bed and clean sheets. Support bands never wrecked guesthouses – although I can think of a few where a bit of rapid destruction would have greatly improved the place.

A new dawn broke in the UK some years ago when Travelodges began to spring up all over the place. Until then hotels thought very highly of themselves and charged per person rather than by the room, presumably to discourage riff-raff. Travelodges sleep as many as you can cram in. Provided you pay, you stay. Each room is clean, cheery and identical: a bathroom, sometimes with soap depending on your luck, a place to hang your leather jacket, a wee alcove to dump your bag, a worktop that you can use to spread out your car keys, the contents of your pockets and to set up your laptop, a thing that is supposed to give you Internet access but that I can never get to work, a little TV, a fawn-coloured plastic kettle and precisely two tea bags. There are no frills, not even a telephone to call reception, which is only staffed part-time anyway. But there is a comfortable double bed, a clean but thin duvet, and a couch that can be unfolded to make two single beds. Book far enough in advance and for only £5 a head you can sleep three road-weary musicians in comfort and warmth, provided you remembered to close the windows and switch on the little electric radiator before you left to go to the gig. And there's plenty of hot water for a shower in the morning – touring bands have never been cleaner or better rested.

Many of these hotels are located at the back of motorway

service stations – nobody selects Travelodge for their accommodation needs in anticipation of a pleasant view of tumbling streams and flower-covered meadows – and even if your room is on the motorway side of the hotel it's amazing how soon you get used to the all-night thunder of traffic. They were originally designed with business travellers in mind, or for families on a tight budget driving to holiday destinations. They are not places to spend time in – you wouldn't hold your wedding reception in one – but simply to grab a night's sleep before heading somewhere else.

Hungry travellers can feast on groaning platters of fried food at Little Chef eateries, which are usually a convenient few steps away. And most rock musicians have modest tastes, happily demolishing all-day Empire Breakfasts – eggs, bacon, sausage, mushrooms, beans, black pudding, tomato and anything else that finds its way onto their heaped plate.

Apart from the cost, there is another reason they appeal to bands. Overnight parking in any city centre is expensive and there is a very high chance of having your equipment stolen from the van if you park in a side street. Bands staying in city hotels used to drag their equipment up to their rooms, not a lot of fun at midnight, then have to lug it all down again next morning. Sometimes they would risk parking on a yellow line outside the hotel, sleep in, and find the van had been towed away in the morning. Travelodges, and the other budget hotel chains, have floodlit car parks right outside their front doors, which are often patrolled all night. And so if you drive into any Travelodge on any motorway in the UK, there's a good chance there will be a bandwagon parked outside. These hotels have made touring much less expensive. I sold my old Gibson guitar on eBay and we were all set.

Satellite navigation also makes life on the road so much easier. A good sat nav can swiftly guide you to the load-in door of any gig, with the exception of only a few cities – Birmingham, Leeds and Gloucester come immediately to mind. In those cities, the wee lady who gives you turn-by-turn instructions in a helpful voice gets a little confused by the split-road and one-way systems the town planners have devised to thoroughly piss off motorists. Leeds had a once-lovely city centre with grand department stores and proud council buildings that conjured up images of plump and prosperous city benefactors wearing pocket watches and black velvet waistcoats, and throngs of happy shoppers ambling along carefree streets, gazing in well-stocked, thoughtfully arranged shop windows. Then it seems like a maniac with a bitter heart seized power and devised a one-way loop system that has ripped the place apart.

Leeds town centre is no longer a haven to stroll in, but an extension of the central reservation on the M62. The poor sat nav couldn't figure it out at all. Gloucester was even more screwed up – its one-way system has strangled the town centre and almost shut off access to the lane where the stage door of the main venue is located. The sat nav lady gave up half a mile from it, with the final apologetic words 'Navigation ends here'. Birmingham also defeated her, as we would discover when we were billeted at the massive Fort Dunlop Travelodge. It is huge, about 12 storeys of vertical concrete and brick, soaring above the industrial estate in which it is located. You can see it for miles from the motorway as you drive past it on your many attempts to find an off-ramp. But, it seems, there is none, and when you reach a certain point in the fast lane, the sat nav lady announces quietly, and a little self-consciously, that as far as she is concerned you have now reached your destination.

We drove into Dartford; at last it was time for the first gig of the tour.

At the side of the big, floodlit stage waiting for the signal to go on, the band paced back and forth, glancing out to the hall, grinning excitedly at each other. None of them had played such a big venue to such a big crowd. This is what they'd been working for all those months, all their lives, really. They'd written all the songs they would be playing, and knew it's always difficult playing to a crowd who had never heard any of their material before. Would they go down well?

I looked at Graham, and remembered how he used to love playing in groups when he was 10, and how excited he'd get before playing school gigs. Over the sound of the background music in the hall, we could hear the hum of 600 people. Waiting. Watching. I glanced at Graham and could see nervousness in his eyes. He looked at me, nodded, then smiled.

It was time.

His time.

By the way...

I may have given the impression that quitting Oxycontin and diazepam was easy. I slightly understated how hard it was. I didn't want to sound like one of those whiners that bleat on about their addictions. Och, you know what we Scots are like. But it took a while.

I'm absolutely not condoning drug use, but highly addictive drugs like oxycodone, temporarily at least, make life bearable for so many people who have to put up with severe and otherwise inescapable pain. And there is no doubt that music can sound greatly enhanced after a pill or two. If a side effect was that I enjoyed listening to bands far more, then I suppose it was a wee bonus.

It always strikes me as amusing when I go, for example, to a Stones gig, and see ultra-conservative people jumping around, shaking their asses to the music. Bankers, politicians, lawyers, accountants, policemen – church-going pillars of the community clearly love them as much as we infidels. It's wonderful. But when Keith wrote those fantastic riffs, was it without the aid of the Devil's candy? Was his blood oxygen-rich and pure as a mountain stream? Somehow I doubt it. I might be completely wrong, but I guess that, as soon as it ceased to be a 9 to 5 job in the Brill building or Tin Pan Alley – in other words, from the Beatles onwards – a huge percentage of rock music was written under the influence of some substance or other. If they did an Olympics-type drug test on all the great rock songs, how many would fail?

Having said that, especially when they are on tour, few professional musicians use addictive drugs, the side effects are far too debilitating. Most musicians who have succeeded in surviving in the most demanding and cut-throat industry imaginable were smart enough to realise early in their careers they needed to have crystal clear minds, at least most of the time.

I would like to thank all the musicians, roadies and managers who were kind enough to let me tag along. It was a joy and a privilege.

write2graham@gmail.com